Markus K. Westner

IS Offshoring

GABLER RESEARCH

EBS Forschung
Schriftenreihe der European Business School (EBS)
International University · Schloss Reichartshausen

Herausgegeben von
Univ.-Prof. Ansgar Richter, PhD

Band 73

Die European Business School (EBS) – gegründet im Jahr 1971 – ist Deutschlands älteste private Wissenschaftliche Hochschule für Betriebswirtschaftslehre im Universitätsrang. Dieser Vorreiterrolle fühlen sich ihre Professoren und Doktoranden in Forschung und Lehre verpflichtet. Mit der Schriftenreihe präsentiert die European Business School (EBS) ausgewählte Ergebnisse ihrer betriebs- und volkswirtschaftlichen Forschung.

Markus K. Westner

IS Offshoring

Essays on Project Suitability and Success

With a foreword by Prof. Dr. Susanne Strahringer

GABLER

RESEARCH

Bibliographic information published by the Deutsche Nationalbibliothek
The Deutsche Nationalbibliothek lists this publication in the Deutsche Nationalbibliografie;
detailed bibliographic data are available in the Internet at http://dnb.d-nb.de.

Dissertation European Business School, International University Schloss Reichartshausen,
Oestrich-Winkel, 2009

D 1540

1st Edition 2009

All rights reserved
© Gabler | GWV Fachverlage GmbH, Wiesbaden 2009

Editorial Office: Claudia Jeske | Britta Göhrisch-Radmacher

Gabler is part of the specialist publishing group Springer Science+Business Media.
www.gabler.de

Umschlaggestaltung: KünkelLopka Medienentwicklung, Heidelberg
Printed on acid-free paper
Printed in Germany

ISBN 978-3-8349-2046-1

Foreword

The industrialization of service industries is a phenomenon which industries such as banking and finance adopted several years ago. Although IT can be considered an enabler in these efforts, the IT industry itself has not yet taken much advantage of industrialization. As this is slowly changing, ideas like global sourcing and global value chains have entered the mindset of top and middle IT management. Although sourcing IT services from near or far away countries in order to profit from labor cost differentials is a topic frequently generating a lot of controversy, it can no longer be ignored as one of several options for staying globally competitive. Even though some businesses promise to refrain from offshoring in order to strengthen local economies, they might not be willing to accept the costs of IT services fully provided domestically. Thus, even businesses which are reluctant when it comes to directly offshoring their own IT services might be indirectly profiting from it as they expect their service providers to stay globally competitive – be it by offshoring or by any other means. With this controversy in mind, it is exceptionally important that offshoring endeavors turn out to be as successful as possible or at least as successful as expected. However, businesses indulging in offshoring do not necessarily report convincing outcomes. Particularly in the case of offshoring from non-English speaking countries, language barriers seem to be significantly impeding offshoring success. One or another of these thoughts made Markus Westner start thinking about the underlying reasons why some businesses manage to be quite successful with offshoring whereas others clearly fail to meet their expectations. His thinking eventually turned into a thoroughly conducted research project which resulted in the thesis at hand. Over a course of two years he studied and explored different aspects of offshore project success and competently summarized his results in three essays on project suitability and success. As a researcher he challenged himself by wanting to conduct both a qualitative-exploratory and a quantitative-confirmatory study and excellently mastered both. Supervising him was a very rewarding experience: to see him progress quickly and to observe his eagerness to raise the bar from essay to essay made my association with his work very rewarding and even made me enjoy the pressure to provide timely feedback. The results he came up with were always interesting to read and are certainly valuable to both researchers as well as practitioners. Both will certainly gain new insights from this thesis and will enjoy reading the three essays as much as I did.

Dresden, August 2009   Susanne Strahringer

Preface

"There is no great achievement that is not the result of patient working and waiting."

- Josiah Gilbert Holland

My deepest gratitude goes to my advisor Susanne Strahringer for her mentoring and support during the last three years. Her commitment to my thesis was invaluable and far beyond what a doctoral student could have expected. She always provided timely, profound, and constructive feedback. This significantly increased the quality of my thesis and of the resulting conference and journal publications. It was a pleasure being granted the opportunity to work with you!

I also thank Frederik Ahlemann for accepting the role as a co-advisor. He provided invaluable comments regarding my publications and the further course of my research. Without him I would probably not have adopted a quantitative-confirmatory research approach in the third essay which – retrospectively – was a very rewarding and positive experience from a personal as well as an academic perspective.

Without naming each individual, I am grateful to the various other supporters of my thesis. I especially appreciated the feedback and comments from academicians under Dr. Strahringer's chairmanship, from my colleagues at Bain & Company, and from numerous anonymous reviewers at conferences and journals.

The editing services of my aunt Joyce Westner in Boston contributed to the thesis' and the publications' quality regarding language and style. My mother-in-law Rita Pohle supported me in transcribing several hundred pages of interview tapes which would otherwise had cost me several months instead of weeks (and presumably my nerves). Thank you both very much!

I thank my wife Anja for her love and unwavering support during all these years. Although he is probably not aware of it, the energy of my two-year old son Samuel and his incredibly good humor was a constant source of motivation and relaxation. Last but not least, I thank my beloved parents, Edeltraud and Konrad, who gifted me with the traits and education that fundamentally enabled me to accomplish this academic endeavor.

Munich, May 2009   Markus K. Westner

Table of Contents

Introduction 1

IS Offshoring: A Systematic Review of the Literature 3

Figures and Tables 7

A Introductions 9

B Conceptualization of IS Offshoring 11

C Methodology 16

D Results 25

E Discussion of Findings and Implications for Future Research 48

F Conclusions 50

Appendix 51

Annotated Bibliography 54

References 62

Offshore Suitability: Criteria for Selecting IS Applications or Projects for Offshoring 67

Figures and Tables 71

A Introductions 72

B Theoretical Frame and Prior Research 75

C Methodology 84

D Data Collection 86

E Analysis 90

F Conclusions 111

Appendix 114

References 134

Determinants of Success in IS Offshoring Projects.. 139

Figures and Tables.. 144

A Introductions... 148

B Theoretical Foundations 151

C Research Model 154

D Methodology.. 161

E Data Collection 171

F Analyses and Results... 174

G Discussion of Results 242

H Conclusions 246

Appendix 249

References 289

Introduction

The thesis at hand consists of three essays. Each of them addresses different aspects related to information systems (IS) projects' suitability for offshore delivery and to success in IS offshoring projects. The first essay is a non-empirical study and contains a review of the existing literature in the field of IS offshoring. Essays 2 and 3 are empirical studies. Essay 2 employs a qualitative-quantitative research approach and identifies criteria for selecting IS projects for offshoring. The third essay follows a quantitative approach and examines determinants of success in IS offshoring projects.

The essays logically build upon each other regarding their research objectives: Essay 1 identifies areas where there is a paucity of research, Essay 2 addresses one of these research areas, and Essay 3 further deepens it. Thus, the thesis – despite being composed of three essays – exhibits a coherent course of research.

Apart from that, the thesis incorporates a combination of research types and methods: Essay 1 is a database-supported literature analysis, Essay 2 is an exploratory-interpretive study primarily using expert interviews with text analysis for results generation, and Essay 3 is a confirmatory study employing a survey design for data gathering and using structural equation modeling for analyzing its research model.

The thesis is not only essay-based with regard to structure but also regarding its actual publication output: by now three publication attempts have been successful. Specifically, at the International Conference on Global Software Engineering (ICGSE) 2007 for Essay 1, the *Journal of Information Technology Management* (JITM) for Essay 2, and the European Conference on Information Systems (ECIS) 2009 for Essay 3.

The following paragraphs describe the main results of the three essays.

The first essay provides a consolidated view of existing academic research in IS offshoring from 1996 to 2006. It identifies relevant research, consolidates and categorizes its results, discusses them, and suggests future research directions. The results show that IS offshoring represents a new research area with most research being published during 2003 to 2006. Non-theory based descriptive research designs predominate. Most studies focus on the questions of *why* to offshore, *how* to offshore, and the *outcome* of IS offshoring. Other aspects such as *what* services to offshore or *which* decision to make are under-researched. The essay suggests that future research could focus on these areas. It states that more empirical-confirmatory research might enrich the IS offshoring body of knowledge by providing findings that are based on more diversified patterns of research designs.

The second essay addresses the paucity of research regarding the aspect *what* services to offshore. Following the notion that the identification of suitable applications or projects is a main initial step in any software development or maintenance related IS offshoring arrangement, the essay identifies evaluation criteria for selecting candidates for offshoring. It analyzes the importance of the criteria and relates them to an organization's offshoring expertise. Based on a literature analysis and interviews with 47 experts from 36 different German companies, the essay identifies several evaluation criteria. The main findings are that in contrast to the literature, *size*, *codification*, and *language* are perceived as important selection criteria by experts. These differences might be due to cultural differences. Additionally, *codification*, *business criticality*, *business specificity*, and *complexity* seem to be less important in the case of organizations with more offshoring expertise.

The third essay incorporates research results of the previous one. Motivated by recent studies indicating that companies engaged in IS offshoring are not fully satisfied with their engagements' performances, the essay examines determinants of IS offshore project success at German companies. It develops a research model based on the implementation process for IS offshoring and empirically tests the model by using structural equation modeling. Specifically, it examines the direct impacts of *offshoring expertise* and *trust in offshore service provider (OSP)* on success as well as their indirect impacts mediated by *project suitability*, *knowledge transfer*, and *liaison quality*. Results show that offshoring expertise plays only a minor role in explaining success and the mediating constructs. Trust in OSP, on the other hand, has a small direct positive impact on success but a medium to large impact on the mediating constructs. Project suitability, knowledge transfer, and liaison quality have a small positive direct impact on success. Essay 3's originality thereby stems from its empirical-confirmatory research approach and its operationalization attempt for offshoring expertise, project suitability, and liaison quality.

IS Offshoring: A Systematic Review of the Literature*

* A shorter version of this paper was presented at the International Conference on Global Software Engineering (ICGSE) 2007: Westner, M., & Strahringer, S. (2007). Current state of IS offshoring research: A descriptive meta-analysis. In J. Mäkiö, S. Betz, & R. Stephan (Eds.), *Offshoring of software development. Methods and tools for risk management* (pp. 7–22). Karlsruhe: Universitätsverlag Karlsruhe.

Abstract: This paper provides a consolidated view of existing academic research in Information Systems (IS) offshoring from 1996 to 2006. It identifies relevant research, consolidates and categorizes its results, discusses them, and suggests future research directions. The results show that IS offshoring represents a new research area with most research being published during 2003 to 2006. Non-theory based descriptive research designs predominate. Most studies focus on the questions of *why* to offshore, *how* to offshore, and the *outcome* of IS offshoring. Other aspects such as *what* services to offshore or *which* decision to make are under-researched. Future research could focus on these areas. More empirical-confirmatory research might enrich the IS offshoring body of knowledge by providing findings that are based on more diversified patterns of research designs.

Keywords: Offshoring, nearshoring, information systems, information technology, literature review, research approaches

Table of Contents

Figures and Tables..7

A Introductions 9
    A.1 Background and Motivation...9
    A.2 Paper Structure 10

B Conceptualization of IS Offshoring..11
    B.1 Definition..11
    B.2 Relation to IS Outsourcing 13
    B.3 History and Current Development...14
        B.3.1 International Perspective...14
        B.3.2 German Perspective 15

C Methodology 16
    C.1 Review Approach Overview 16
    C.2 Literature Retrieval..16
        C.2.1 Literature Source Selection..16
        C.2.2 Literature Item Search..17
    C.3 Literature Item Exclusion..18
    C.4 Literature Categorization Framework 19
        C.4.1 Categorization Framework Overview...19
        C.4.2 Reference Theories..19
        C.4.3 Research Approaches...21
        C.4.4 Research Types 21
        C.4.5 Research Methods..21
        C.4.6 IS Offshoring Stages 22
        C.4.7 Offshored IS Services 23
    C.5 Research Validity 23

D Results..25

D.1   Selection of Relevant Literature 25

D.2   Descriptive Analysis of Relevant Literature 25

    D.2.1   Publication Period 25

    D.2.2   Research Design.. 26

    D.2.3   Research Objectives.. 29

D.3   Findings along IS Offshoring Stages... 29

    D.3.1   Why-Stage... 29

    D.3.2   What-Stage.. 35

    D.3.3   Which-Stage 38

    D.3.4   How-Stage... 38

    D.3.5   Outcome-Stage.. 42

    D.3.6   Meta Studies.. 47

E   Discussion of Findings and Implications for Future Research 48

    E.1   Research Design 48

    E.2   IS offshoring Stages 48

F   Conclusions... 50

Appendix 51

Annotated Bibliography 54

References 62

Figures and Tables

Figure 1-1: Dimensions for IS offshoring 12

Figure 1-2: Illustration of literature review approach 16

Figure 1-3: Dimensions for categorizing literature 19

Figure 1-4: Stage model for IS offshoring (adapted from Dibbern et al., 2004, p. 15) 23

Figure 1-5: Selection of relevant literature 25

Figure 1-6: Publication years of literature items 26

Figure 1-7: Categorization of all literature items regarding research design 27

Figure 1-8: Categorization of empirical literature items regarding research design 28

Figure 1-9: Categorization of non-empirical literature items regarding research design 28

Figure 1-10: Categorization of literature items regarding research objectives 29

Table 1-1: Selected definitions of IS offshoring 11

Table 1-2: Considered IS conferences 17

Table 1-3: Overview of data sources and search parameters 18

Table 1-4: Overview of theoretical foundations (Dibbern et al., 2004, p. 18) 20

Table 1-5: Advantages of IS offshoring 31

Table 1-6: Disadvantages of IS offshoring 34

Table 1-7: Determinants influencing consideration of IS offshoring 35

Table 1-8: Offshored IS services 36

Table 1-9: Criteria and recommendations for evaluating offshoreability 37

Table 1-10: Classification criteria for structuring IS offshoring arrangements 38

Table 1-11: Stages of IS offshoring implementation 39

Table 1-12: Risk control mechanisms for IS offshoring implementation 39

Table 1-13: Observed control modes and arrangement types in IS offshoring 40

Table 1-14: Implementation of knowledge transfer in IS offshoring 40

Table 1-15: Evaluation criteria for IS offshoring implementation decisions 42

Table 1-16: Best practices for IS offshoring implementation 44

Table 1-17: Determinants of success for IS offshoring implementation 46

Table 1-18: Outcome of IS offshoring 46

A Introductions

A.1 Background and Motivation

Information systems (IS) offshoring, the provision of IS services from foreign countries[1], receives growing attention. It appears that the delivery of IS services follows a trend already observed in the manufacturing sector. In this sector, companies economize on labor cost differences and transfer significant parts of their production to countries with lower wage levels. (Henley, 2006; Mithas & Whitaker, 2006; Schaaf, 2004; Scheibe, Mennecke, & Zobel, 2006; Venkatraman, 2004)

IS offshoring's economic benefits seem attractive by offering labor cost differentials up to 80% compared to hourly rates in western countries (Bitkom, 2005; Boes, Schwemmle, & Becker, 2004). Consequently, industry associations, consulting firms and analysts promote IS offshoring as a sourcing option for corporations (Amoribieta, Bhaumik, Kanakamedala, & Parkhe, 2001; BIHK, 2002; Bitkom, 2005; Schaaf & Weber, 2005).

IS researchers and practitioners started to analyze and reflect on IS offshoring's impact on their domain (Hirschheim, Loebbecke, Newman, & Valor, 2005; Mertens, 2005; William, Mayadas, & Vardi, 2006). However, the field of IS offshoring seems not as extensively researched as the related field of IS outsourcing (Dibbern et al., 2004; Smith & McKeen, 2004). This also applies to research in Germany, where only a limited number of academic studies exist (e.g., Dibbern, Winkler, & Heinzl, 2006; Mertens, 2005; Moczadlo, 2002; Wiener, 2006).

The current stream of international and Germany-focused research in IS offshoring particularly lacks a consolidated view of existing research results. The literature review at hand addresses this research deficit. It intends to provide a consolidated view on existing research in IS offshoring. Its main objectives are to identify relevant research contributions regarding IS offshoring, analyze their theoretical foundations and research designs, consolidate and categorize their findings according to IS offshoring stages, and discuss their findings as well as identify implications for future research. The literature review employs an IS managerial and business-oriented point of view and excludes technology-related aspects of offshoring. It partially follows the methodological approach employed by Dibbern et al. (2004) in their literature review for IS outsourcing. Thus, it ensures research continuity by building upon an existing approach and it enables comparability of research findings between studies.

---

[1] For a more detailed definition c.f. Section B.1, p. 11.

A.2 Paper Structure

Section B clarifies the term IS offshoring, points out how it relates to IS outsourcing, and outlines how the IS offshoring phenomenon developed in the past. Section C describes the research methodology applied. It explains the review approach and specifies the selection of literature sources, timeframe, and papers. Section D applies the review approach to the selected literature. It synthesizes its results according to the dimensions why to consider offshoring, what to offshore, which choice to make, how to offshore, and the outcome of offshoring. Section E discusses the findings and outlines possible implications for future research. Section F concludes the paper, shows its contribution to existing research, and its specific limitations.

B Conceptualization of IS Offshoring

B.1 Definition

The term offshoring is not specific to IS. The area of financial economics previously used it to describe locations that serve as tax shelters for international investors (Schaaf, 2004). In the field of IS, offshoring names the phenomenon of shifting IS service provision from one country to another, usually from high-wage countries in the western hemisphere to low-wage countries. Table 1-1 (p. 11) shows selected definitions for the term offshoring from IS/Information Technology (IT) research.

Author(s)	Definition of IS/IT offshoring
Carmel & Agarwal, 2002, p. 65	"The term 'offshore sourcing' includes both offshore outsourcing to a third-party provider as well as offshore insourcing to an internal group within a global corporation."
Chandrasekhar & Ghosh, 2006, p. 92	"Offshoring refers to the relocation of outsourced activities across countries. Once the process of outsourcing a particular activity is generalized across firms, then the shift of the location of the vendor can cause offshoring."
Fish & Seydel, 2006, p. 96	"With this model (aka, offshore) [...] IT work takes place in a country different from that of the outsourcing firm's IT department."
Gopal, Sivaramakrishnan, Krishnan, & Mukhopadhyay, 2003, p. 1671	"Offshore software development [...] occurs when the contracting parties are in different countries and the software is developed in the developer's country, and then shipped to the buyer's organization."
Hirschheim et al., 2005, p. 1003	"Global offshore outsourcing (or simply offshoring) is a relatively new phenomenon [...] offering access to knowledge-worker skills often at reduced costs. IT offshoring refers to the migration of all or part of the development, maintenance and delivery of IT services to a vendor located in a country different from that of the client."
Niederman, Kundu, & Salas, 2006, p. 52	"Offshore outsourcing (offshoring) is the practice of distributing work, particularly in the area of information technology (IT) services and development, to workers outside the national borders of the host country."
Pries-Heje, Baskerville, & Hansen, 2005, p. 6	"Offshore outsourcing, also known as international or global outsourcing, takes place when organizations cross national borders to obtain these commodities."
Rajkumar & Mani, 2001, p. 63	"Offshore development of software occurs when the supplier is from a different country than the company outsourcing its development."
Ramarapu, Parzinger, & Lado, 1997, p. 1	"In its broadest context, foreign or offshore outsourcing is the sharing or transferring of responsibility for some or all IS services to a third-party vendor who operates from a foreign country."
Wiener, 2006, p. 38	"Offshore software development [is] the relocation of software development services to an IT service provider which is located in a foreign country."

Table 1-1: Selected definitions of IS offshoring

The definitions imply four dimensions of IS offshoring. Figure 1-1 illustrates these dimensions. They refer to (a) *location* from where services are provided, (b) transferred *services*, (c) *degree* of transfer, and (d) *organizational* implementation. (Dibbern et al., 2004; Wiener, 2006)

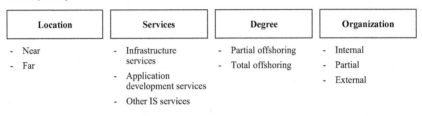

Location	Services	Degree	Organization
- Near - Far	- Infrastructure services - Application development services - Other IS services	- Partial offshoring - Total offshoring	- Internal - Partial - External

Figure 1-1: Dimensions for IS offshoring

(a) All presented definitions agree on the characteristic of location, i.e., that the service-providing country is different from the service-receiving country. Other studies detail this aspect regarding distance. They differentiate between *nearshore* countries that are close and *offshore* countries that are far away. (Erber & Sayed-Ahmed, 2005; Fish & Seydel, 2006; Meyer, 2006; Schaaf, 2004)

(b) Most studies do not specify the transferred IS services. Instead, they use terms such as "IT work" (Fish & Seydel, 2006, p. 96), "development, maintenance and delivery of IT services" (Hirschheim et al., 2005, p. 1003), and "IS services" (Ramarapu et al., 1997, p. 1). Other studies focus on software services and limit their definition to "offshore development of software" (Rajkumar & Mani, 2001, p. 63) or "offshore software development" (Gopal et al., 2003, p. 1671). A categorization consisting of *infrastructure services, application development services*, and *other IS services* incorporates all the above-mentioned services (Fish & Seydel, 2006; Wiener, 2006; William et al., 2006). Infrastructure services refer to hardware infrastructure operation, such as networks, data centers, and servers. They also include software infrastructure operation, such as operating systems or enterprise software, often called application management. Application development services refer to the development of new individual applications, extension, and maintenance of existing ones. Finally, other IS services comprise IS-related services not included in the previous categories, such as user help desk or data entry. (Erickson & Ranganathan, 2006; Schaaf & Weber, 2005)

(c) Only some studies mention the degree of IS offshoring. They distinguish between "migration of all or part" (Hirschheim et al., 2005, p. 1003) or "some or all IS services" (Ramarapu et al., 1997, p. 1). Thus, they actually differentiate between *partial offshoring* on the one hand and *total offshoring* on the other hand.

(d) Regarding the organizational implementation, studies consider external contracting and speak of "vendor/s" (Chandrasekhar & Ghosh, 2006, p. 92; Hirschheim et al., 2005, p. 1003), "third-party vendor" (Ramarapu et al., 1997, p. 1), or "third-party provider" (Carmel & Agarwal, 2002, p. 65). However, internal provision of IS offshore services can also exist, for example, from a company branch in a low-cost country (Carmel & Agarwal, 2002; Mertens, 2005). This implies a distinction among *internal*, *partial*, and *external* offshoring arrangements. An internal arrangement incorporates wholly owned subsidiaries, a partial arrangement is typically a joint venture, and contracting with a third party vendor represents an external arrangement (Dibbern et al., 2004; Scheibe et al., 2006; Wiener, 2006).

The literature review deducts its working definition of IS offshoring from the four IS offshoring dimensions as displayed in Figure 1-1 (p. 12):

> "IS offshoring occurs when the provision of IS services (i.e., infrastructure, application development or other IS services) is partially or totally transferred to a service-providing organization residing in a near or far away country different from that of the service-receiving organization. The service-providing organization can be an internal subsidiary, a partially-owned unit or an external service provider." (Own definition)

B.2 Relation to IS Outsourcing

Table 1-1 (p. 11) shows that several studies perceive IS offshoring as a variation of international IS outsourcing and name it IS offshore outsourcing. This perception does not contradict but rather fits with the previously defined dimensions in Figure 1-1. However, outsourcing usually requires a contracting relationship with an external party (Dibbern et al., 2004). By defining IS offshoring as a variation of IS outsourcing, definitions would limit themselves to external arrangements in the organization dimension.

In terms of this paper's IS offshoring definition, we recognize IS offshore outsourcing not as a variation of IS offshoring but as a combination of both IS offshoring and IS outsourcing, or as Erber & Sayed-Ahmed mention:

> "It is obvious that offshoring can take place either inside a single multinational corporation or through an outsourcing contract with a foreign company. [...] Thus, offshoring and outsourcing are independent options which, if they occur simultaneously, lead to offshore outsourcing [...]." (Erber & Sayed-Ahmed, 2005, p. 102)

B.3 History and Current Development

B.3.1 International Perspective

India, Ireland, and Israel are nations that first provided IS services to customers abroad in absence of a significant domestic market for these services (William et al., 2006). India therefore is a prime example for a developing country that became a noticeable supplier for global IS offshoring services. The country is the leader in the Asian IS offshoring industry (Hirschheim et al., 2005). Illustrating its development simultaneously provides an overview of the IS offshoring industry's history.

The roots of the Indian IS offshoring industry are in the 1970s when Indian IS workers first went to the United States to perform programming tasks (Henley, 2006; William et al., 2006). Building on that experience, IS offshoring companies started to provide their services in the early 1980s (Trampel, 2004). With the economic deregulation in India in the end of the 1980s, the Indian government became aware of this new industry and started to promote and subsidize it (Hawk & McHenry, 2005). From that time on, the Indian IS offshoring sector experienced strong growth (Bhatnagar & Madon, 1997; Hirschheim et al., 2005; Kumar & Willcocks, 1996; Nidumolu, 1993).

Several reasons contributed to the country's strong position in IS offshoring. As a main reason, labor cost differentials in comparison to western countries provided an economic benefit to Indian companies' western clients. Additionally, the "[…] combination of English language skills, large numbers of skilled IS staff, and an excellent technical education system […]" (Hirschheim et al., 2005, p. 1009) served as foundations for the experienced growth. Apart from these factors, better communication technology enabling international cooperation and data exchange, as well as increased software development and project management capabilities, bolstered the country's position in the IS offshoring industry (Bhatnagar & Madon, 1997; Carmel & Agarwal, 2002; Henley, 2006). Finally, the demand for IS services in western countries increased in the late 1990s induced by the Internet Boom as well as the reprogramming efforts required by the millennium change. Indian IS professionals and companies met this demand, thereby further increasing India's popularity as an IS offshoring location (Amoribieta et al., 2001; Bhatnagar & Madon, 1997; Bitkom, 2005; Carmel & Nicholson, 2005). Despite doubts regarding the actual size of the Indian IS offshoring industry, studies agree that the sector is a significant industry in India (Hirschheim et al., 2005). Offshore service providers, such as Wipro, Infosys, or TCS, became multinational corporations with several billion US dollars in revenues (Henley, 2006).

Apart from the development in India, IS offshoring received growing attention by the western public, due to the rising fear of job losses in white-collar professions previously regarded as transfer-safe (Boes & Kämpf, 2006; Erber & Sayed-Ahmed, 2005; William et al., 2006). This fear is not new and already appeared in the 1980s and 1990s (Smith, Mitra, & Narasimhan, 1996). However, the actual effects of IS offshoring on the domestic labor market figures are still unclear and open for discussion (Hirschheim et al., 2005).

B.3.2 German Perspective

IS offshoring research in Germany faces similar challenges regarding reliable statistical data as in the international context (Hirschheim et al., 2005; Schaaf, 2004). Additionally, existing results regarding the phenomenon are rather anecdotal instead of thoroughly researched (Mertens, 2005). Despite this situation, studies seem to agree that IS offshoring is less adopted and developed in Germany than in English-speaking industrial countries such as the United States or the United Kingdom. Reasons cited for this situation are high cultural barriers to cooperation with classical IS offshoring countries in Asia such as India. The German language represents another barrier for collaboration (Schaaf, 2004). Simultaneously, IS offshoring providers mainly focused on clients in English-speaking industrial countries and less on clients in Germany (Ben & Claus, 2005; Bitkom, 2005; Söbbing, 2006). This leaves the German IS offshoring market underdeveloped. IS offshoring companies seem to play a minor role in the German IS services market (Computerwoche, 2006). However, analysts expect strong future market growth and increasing activity of IS offshore service providers in Germany (Schaaf & Weber, 2005).

C Methodology

C.1 Review Approach Overview

The review approach employed consists of four steps. The first step retrieves literature from electronic databases, examines it, and archives all literature items. The second step excludes non-relevant research from further analysis. This exclusion is necessary, since the database-driven search approach might return irrelevant results. Having identified relevant literature items, the third step classifies and tabulates them. The fourth and last step summarizes the research items' findings in verbal as well as in tabular form. It subsequently interprets and discusses the findings. Figure 1-2 illustrates which study sections cover each review step's methodological description and the corresponding results.

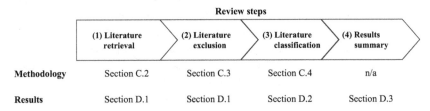

	Review steps			
	(1) Literature retrieval	(2) Literature exclusion	(3) Literature classification	(4) Results summary
Methodology	Section C.2	Section C.3	Section C.4	n/a
Results	Section D.1	Section D.1	Section D.2	Section D.3

Figure 1-2: Illustration of literature review approach

C.2 Literature Retrieval

C.2.1 Literature Source Selection

Journal articles and conference proceedings represent the main channels to share research results in the scientific community. This paper therefore focuses on those two publishing channels to identify relevant knowledge in the field of IS offshoring. The subsequent paragraphs explain the methodology applied for selecting (a) journals and (b) conferences.

(a) Initially, we intended to follow the approach by Dibbern et al. (2004) and search only the most relevant IS journals based on a scientific journal ranking (c.f. Saunders, 2007; Lowry, Romans, & Curtis, 2004). However, a pilot search in the 25 most highly-ranked journals yielded a very low number of results. Therefore, the source selection was adjusted to search in electronic databases for identifying relevant journal articles. The database employed is Ebsco's Business Source Complete. It covers more than 1,200 scholarly business journals. Electronic database search comes with certain limitations, such as availability of journal issues in the database, and record completeness. Nevertheless, we finally opted for a database-driven search because it allows for a wide coverage of literature sources and assures repeatability of the search process by other researchers.

(b) The paper focuses on four renowned IS conferences: Americas Conference on Information Systems (AMCIS), European Conference on Information Systems (ECIS), Hawaii Conference on System Sciences (HICSS), and International Conference on Information Systems (ICIS) (Dibbern et al., 2004, p. 23; Hirschheim et al., 2005, p. 1015; Wiener, 2006, p. 47). AMCIS, HICSS, and ICIS represent important international conferences for IS research. ECIS is a renowned European IS conference. Table 1-2 illustrates the considered conferences and the corresponding data sources for proceedings search and retrieval.

Conference	Data source
Americas Conference on Information Systems (AMCIS)	AIS eLibrary http://aisel.isworld.org/publication.asp?Pub=AMCIS
European Conference on Information Systems (ECIS)	London School of Economics, ECIS proceedings http://is2.lse.ac.uk/asp/aspecis/
Hawaii Conference on System Sciences (HICSS)	IEEE digital library http://csdl2.computer.org/persagen/ DLPublication.jsp?pubtype=p&acronym=hicss
International Conference on Information Systems (ICIS)	AIS eLibrary http://aisel.isworld.org/publication.asp?Pub=icis

Table 1-2: Considered IS conferences

C.2.2 Literature Item Search

The ten years from January 1, 1996 to December 31, 2006 serve as the relevant timeframe for searching literature items from journals and conferences.[2] Article titles, abstracts, subject terms, and assigned keywords represent the relevant search fields for journal articles. For conference papers, their paper titles are searched.

The corresponding query string is "offshor* OR off-shor* OR nearshor* OR near-shor* OR (global AND outsourc*) OR (international* AND outsourc*)". The wildcard symbol "*" reduces the terms to their principal forms (so-called stemming, c.f. Ferber, 2003). It ensures that the search also covers term variations such as offshor*ing*, offshore, and offshor*ed*. The search term "global AND outsourc*" and "international* AND outsourc*" identifies literature items that address the aspect of offshore outsourcing but do not explicitly use the keyword offshoring (e.g., Apte, Sobol, Hanaoka, Shimada, Saarinen, & Salmela et al., 1997).

Using the keywords above yields more than 900 search results with low relevancy, for example, research regarding manufacturing offshoring or the oil drilling industry. Therefore, we use a database subject filter to focus on content-relevant research. The subject filter for journals is "'Information Technology' OR 'Strategic Information System' OR 'Management

---

[2] Except for ECIS where proceedings of the 2006 conference were not yet available.

Information Systems'". The search excludes journal articles shorter than five pages.
Additionally, the database filter "Scholarly (peer-reviewed) journals" ensures a minimum
quality in research results. Table 1-3 shows the data sources and corresponding search
parameters.

	Journals	Conferences
Data sources	Ebsco's Business Source Complete	AIS eLibrary (AMCIS, ICIS)
		IEEE digital library (HICSS)
		LSE ECIS proceedings (ECIS)
Time frame	Jan. 1, 1996 to Dec. 31, 2006	1996 to 2006 (AMCIS, ICIS, HICSS)
		1996 to 2005 (ECIS)
Search fields (ebsco field identifier in brackets)	Title (TI)	Title
	Keywords (KW)	
	Abstract (AB)	
	Subject terms (SU)	
Keywords (OR-connected)	offshore* OR off-shor*	offshore* OR off-shor*
	nearshor* OR near-shor*	nearshor* OR near-shor*
	global AND outsourc*	global AND outsourc*
	international* AND outsourc*	international* AND outsourc*
Filters (ebsco field identifier in brackets)	Only scholarly (peer-reviewed) journals	No filter
	Subjects (DE) "Information Technology", "Strategic Information System", "Management Information Systems"	
	More than four pages	

Table 1-3: Overview of data sources and search parameters

C.3 Literature Item Exclusion

The literature review at hand excludes non-relevant research to assure that it only contains
content-relevant literature. Research is non-relevant when it has a non-IS context or does not
have an IS managerial or business-oriented research focus, such as studies on manufacturing
offshoring or on IS education. Additionally, the analysis excludes conference papers that
resulted in a journal article and conference papers with no original content such as
announcements for discussion boards or research agendas and proposals.

C.4 Literature Categorization Framework

C.4.1 Categorization Framework Overview

This paper partially builds upon the literature categorization framework employed by Dibbern et al. (2004). Relevant dimensions for categorizing the identified research items are (a) the *reference theories* the items build upon, (b) their *research approaches*, (c) their *research types*, (d) their employed *research methods* in terms of data gathering and data analysis, (e) the specific *IS offshoring stage(s)* they address, and (f) the *IS services* they focus on. Figure 1-3 illustrates these dimensions. The following sections explain them in detail.

Reference theory	Research approach	Research type	Research method	IS offshoring stage	IS service

- Strategic theories
  - Resource theories
  - Strategic management theories
- Economic theories
  - Agency theory
  - Transaction cost theory
- Social/Organizational theories
  - Social exchange theory
  - Power and politics theory
  - Relationship theory
- Other
	- Empirical
	- Non-empirical
		- Confirmatory
		- Exploratory-interpretive
		- Descriptive
		- Formulative
			- Data gathering
			  - Survey
			  - Interview
			  - Case study
			  - Other
			- Data analysis
			  - 1st generation statistics
			  - 2nd generation statistics
			  - Interpretation
			  - Other
				- Why
				- What
				- Which
				- How
				- Outcome
					- Infrastructure
					- Application development
					- Other

Figure 1-3: Dimensions for categorizing literature

All literature items are classified along these dimensions. Sometimes a piece of research covers more than one aspect of a dimension. In this case it is correspondingly classified in more than one category. As the results show (c.f. Section D.2., p. 25), this multi-classification does not happen often and primarily occurs in the dimensions IS offshoring stage and IS service.

C.4.2 Reference Theories

Reference theories act as a theoretical foundation for researchers to formulate their research hypotheses and explanation constructs. One can distinguish between *strategic, economic,* and *social/organizational theories.* "Strategic theories focus on how firms develop and implement strategies [...] Economic theories focus on the coordination and governance of economic agents regarding their transactions with one another [and] Social/organizational theories [...] concentrate on the relationships that exist between individuals, groups, and organizations"

20

Methodology

(Dibbern et al., 2004, p. 17). In their literature review, Dibbern et al. (2004) tabulated the most relevant theoretical foundations, described their basic assumptions, main variables and listed the corresponding key authors. Table 1-4 shows their findings (for a more detailed description c.f. Dibbern et al., 2004, pp. 17–20).

Theory	Level of analysis	Basic assumptions	Main variables	Key authors
Strategic theories				
Resource theories	Organizational	A firm is a collection of resources, and resources are central to a firm's strategy	Internal resources, resources in the task environment	Barney, 1991; Penrose, 1959; Pfeffer & Salancik, 1978; Thompson, 1967
Strategic management theories	Organizational	Firms have long-term goals, and they plan and allocate resources to achieve these goals	Strategic advantage, strategies, choice of individuals	Chandler, 1962; Miles & Snow, 1978; Porter, 1985; Quinn, 1980
Economic theories				
Agency theory	Organizational	Asymmetry of information, differences in perceptions of risk, uncertainty	Agent costs, optimal contractual relationships	Jensen & Meckling, 1976
Transaction cost theory	Transaction	Limited rationality, opportunism	Transaction costs, production costs	Coase, 1937; Williamson, 1981; Williamson, 1985
Social/organizational theories				
Social exchange theory	Individual, organizational	Participation in exchange occurs with the assumption of rewards and obligation to return rewards	Exchange of activities, benefits/costs, reciprocity, balance, cohesion, and power in exchanges	Blau, 1964; Emerson, 1972; Homans, 1961
Power and Politics theories	Individual, organizational	Power, idiosyncratic interests, and politics play major roles in organizational decision-making	Different degrees of power, organizational politics	Pfeffer, 1981; Pfeffer, 1982; Marcus, 1983
Relationship theories	Organizational	Parties in the relationship assume that the outcome of a relationship is greater than that achieved by individual parties separately	Cooperation, interactions, social and economic exchanges	Klepper, 1995; Kern, 1997

Table 1-4: Overview of theoretical foundations (Dibbern et al., 2004, p. 18)

C.4.3 Research Approaches

Research approaches represent the general ways to conduct research. One can distinguish between (a) *empirical* and (b) *non-empirical* research approaches. Empirical research intends to generate knowledge by analyzing data resulting from observation. Non-empirical research, however, is more abstract in nature and relies on analytical reasoning. (Dibbern et al., 2004)

C.4.4 Research Types

Following previous studies regarding IS meta-research (Boudreau, Gefen, & Straub, 2001; Dibbern et al., 2004; Vessey, Ramesh, & Glass, 2002), this literature review differentiates (a) *confirmatory*, (b) *exploratory-interpretive*, (c) *descriptive*, and (d) *formulative* types of research.

(a) Confirmatory research attempts to test a priori specified relationships through structured scientific instruments of data gathering and analysis (Dibbern et al., 2004). (b) In contrast to that, exploratory-interpretive allows methods and data to define the nature of relationships. It specifies these relationships only in the most general form. Furthermore, it intends to examine a research area by accessing participants' perceptions of the phenomenon (Boudreau et al., 2001; Orlikowski & Baroudi, 1991). (c) Descriptive research is usually not theoretically grounded and does not try to interpret a phenomenon. It rather presents what the researchers believe to be objective, factual observations (Orlikowski & Baroudi, 1991). Finally, (d) formulative research's primary objective is to construct a model or something other than a model such as an algorithm, a taxonomy, guidelines, concepts, or frameworks (Vessey et al., 2002).

Confirmatory and exploratory-interpretive research usually involves empirical approaches. Descriptive research occurs with empirical and non-empirical research approaches. Formulative research, however, primarily tends to employ non-empirical approaches.

C.4.5 Research Methods

Research methods are "more narrowly focused techniques and procedures for conducting research" (Dibbern et al., 2004, p. 20). They address the issues of *data gathering* and *data analysis.*

Data gathering research methods are (a) *surveys*, (b) *interviews*, (c) *case studies*, or (d) *other types* of data gathering. Interviews and case studies are, of course, not mutually exclusive. Case studies often also use interviews for data gathering. If this applied, we coded case study since it represents the primary data gathering method. Interview as a separate method, however, is still adequate, because some research relies on interviews in terms of a phenomenological study (Creswell, 1994, p. 13) but does not conduct a case study.

Data analysis research methods refer to quantitative statistical methods, including (a) *first generation statistics* such as descriptive statistics or simple multiple regression analysis, (b) *second generation statistics* such as structural equation modeling (Boudreau et al., 2001), qualitative non-statistical (c) *interpretation* (Creswell, 1994), or (d) *other forms* of data analysis.

C.4.6 IS Offshoring Stages

Reference theories, research approaches and research methods cover the methodological aspects of research. However, the content perspective is of equal importance. The following stage model for IS offshoring addresses this perspective.

IS offshoring represents a decision regarding the production or procurement of services within an organization, followed by its implementation. Therefore, it seems appropriate to follow Dibbern et al. (2004) and use their adapted version of Simon's decision making model (Simon, 1960). They distinguish among five decision dimensions to categorize research items: (a) *why* to consider offshoring, (b) *what* to offshore, (c) *which* decision to make, (d) *how* to offshore, and finally (e) *outcome* of offshoring. Stages (a), (b), and (c) cover the actual decision-making. Stages (d) and (e) address the implementation. Figure 1-4 illustrates the sequence of the five stages in the context of IS offshoring.

(a) Why to consider offshoring examines the determinants that lead to the consideration of offshoring as a sourcing option. Research at this stage tries to understand potential advantages and disadvantage or risks and benefits associated with IS offshoring.

(b) What to offshore looks at the aspects of the areas and functions, for example, IS department activities or applications, that are offshoreable but also addresses the structure of the offshoring arrangement, for example, regarding the degree of offshoring in terms of IS budget.

(c) Which choice to make refers to the decision whether to offshore or not. It examines the procedures, guidelines, and stakeholders involved to evaluate the available options and make the decision.

(d) How to offshore looks at the implementation of the offshoring decision, e.g., on setting up an offshore unit or selecting an offshore service provider, structuring the arrangement and managing it. Research at this stage solely focuses on the structure or conceptualization of the implementation but not on the outcome or its quality.

(e) Outcome of offshoring addresses the result of the implementation of offshoring relating to experiences such as best practices, types of success, and the various determinants for success of the offshoring decision (Dibbern et al., 2004).

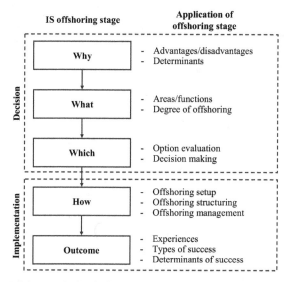

Figure 1-4: Stage model for IS offshoring (adapted from Dibbern et al., 2004, p. 15)

C.4.7 Offshored IS Services

Regarding offshored services and activities, the literature review follows its own definition of IS offshoring (c.f. Section B.1, p. 11) and distinguishes (a) *infrastructure* services, (b) *application development* services, and (c) *other* IS services.

(a) Infrastructure services refer to the operation of hardware infrastructure, such as networks, data centers and servers, but also to the operation of infrastructure software, such as operating systems or enterprise software, often also called application management. (b) Application development services refer to development of new applications, extension, and maintenance of existing ones. (c) Other IS services comprise IS-related services not included in the previous categories, such as user help desk, or data entry.

C.5 Research Validity

The database-driven literature search represents a critical aspect for this research's validity. An unfortunate selection of search keywords, subjects, search fields, or the underlying database can unfavorably bias search results. Therefore it is an imperative to assess the search approach's validity regarding employed (a) databases, (b) search keywords, (c) subject terms, and (d) search fields.

(a) We compared database search results of Business Source Complete to those of Academic Search Premier, Computer Source, and the ProQuest database. The results confirmed that Business Source Complete does not ignore relevant articles.

(b) Initial research showed that studies use the term offshoring in varying ways, for example, with a hyphen (off-shoring) or without (offshoring). To avoid potential biases resulting from search keywords, we incorporated "wildcards" into the search term and wrote the search term in a hyphenated and non-hyphenated form (c.f. Section C.2.2, p. 17).

(c) Subjects acted as a filter to initially exclude research from non-IS domains. They were thoroughly deducted from the database's subject thesaurus. This deduction was double-checked by comparing search results without subject filters to search results with one or more of the filters in place. The results supported the selection of the previously described subjects (c.f. Table 1-3, p. 18).

(d) We compared the amount and content-relevancy of search results when using different search fields to select the search fields. A search in titles, abstracts, keywords, and subject terms, but not in the articles' full texts, yielded the most useful results.

D Results

D.1 Selection of Relevant Literature

The databases were searched in March 2007. The search resulted in a total of 66 journal articles with more than four pages published between January 1, 1996, and December 31, 2006. Additionally, the search identified 38 conference contributions. This resulted in a total of 104 literature items in-scope for the literature review.

We examined these items, archived them, and analyzed their relevancy regarding IS offshoring research (for exclusion criteria c.f. Section C.3, p. 18). 45 journal articles and 23 conference contributions are considered non-relevant. As a result, 21 journal articles and 15 conference papers remain, thus totaling relevant 36 literature items. Figure 1-5 illustrates the selection of relevant literature. The annotated bibliography (c.f. p. 54) contains all relevant literature items.

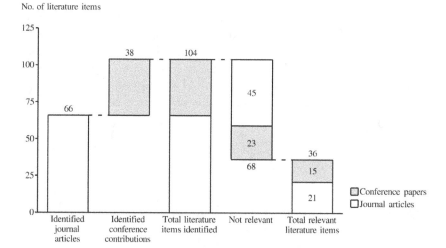

Figure 1-5: Selection of relevant literature

D.2 Descriptive Analysis of Relevant Literature

D.2.1 Publication Period

Figure 1-6 illustrates the publication years of the relevant literature items. Most research was published in the four years from 2003 to 2006 with the majority of 18 items in 2006. It seems that research in IS offshoring barely existed before 2003 and increased from that time on. This marks a difference from the research situation in IS outsourcing where a significant amount of publications exists starting from as early as 1992 (Dibbern et al., 2004).

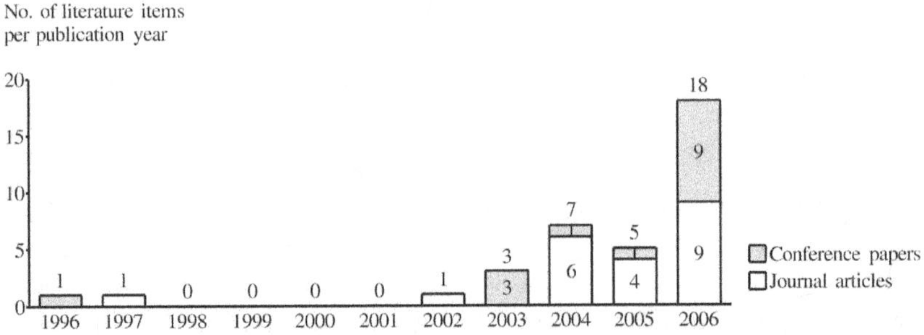

No. of literature items
per publication year

Figure 1-6: Publication years of literature items

D.2.2   Research Design

Most of the literature items do not draw on theoretical foundations to conduct their research (23 items). If they apply a theoretical foundation, transaction cost economics dominates (5 items), followed by resource theories (2 items). More empirical (20 items) than non-empirical (16 items) research exists. Descriptive research dominates the literature (19 items), specifying either no data gathering methods at all (16 items) or applying case study approaches (11 items). Correspondingly, studies use either no data analysis methods (16 items) or apply interpretation (15 items). Figure 1-7 illustrates the categorization of all literature items regarding research design.

Categorization of relevant literature items
(No. of items)

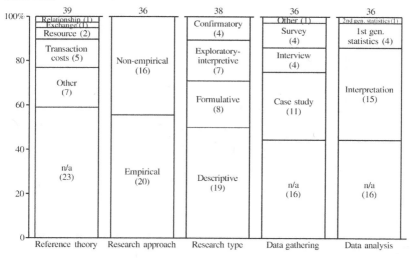

Note: Multiple allocations within one category possible

Figure 1-7: Categorization of all literature items regarding research design

A detailed categorization by differentiating empirical and non-empirical papers sheds further light into the design patterns within IS offshoring research. As Figure 1-8 illustrates, empirical papers are predominantly descriptive (8 items) or exploratory-interpretive (7 items) but less confirmatory (4 items). They use case studies (11 items), interviews (4 items), or surveys (4 items) as data gathering methods. Regarding data analysis methods they rely on interpretation (15 items) or descriptive first generation statistics (4 items).

Categorization of empirical literature items
(No. of items)

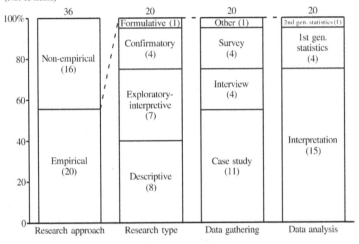

Note: Multiple allocations within one category possible

Figure 1-8: Categorization of empirical literature items regarding research design

Non-empirical empirical research is either descriptive (11 items) or formulative (7 items). It does not apply any data gathering or data analysis techniques. Figure 1-9 illustrates these results.

Categorization of non-empirical literature items
(No. of items)

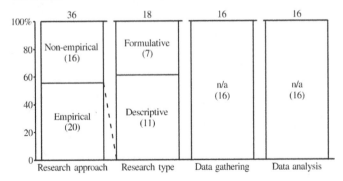

Note: Multiple allocations within one category possible

Figure 1-9: Categorization of non-empirical literature items regarding research design

D.2.3 Research Objectives

As Figure 1-10 illustrates, most literature items address the why-stage (17 items), outcome-stage (14 items), and how-stage (12 items) of IS offshoring. The what-stage is less frequently researched (7 items). No literature item examines the which-stage, thus leaving this stage un-researched in terms of the literature review. Most items do not explicitly state which offshored IS services are the focus of their research (19 items). However, if they specify a specific service, application development dominates (17 items).

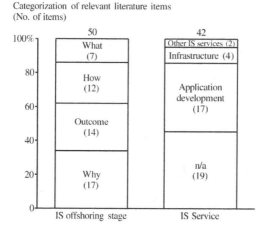

Figure 1-10: Categorization of literature items regarding research objectives

D.3 Findings along IS Offshoring Stages

D.3.1 Why-Stage

Literature items at the why-stage focus on advantages and disadvantages of IS offshoring or they examine the determinants that influence the consideration of IS offshoring as a sourcing option.

D.3.1.1 Advantages of IS Offshoring

The most frequently found advantage of IS offshoring seem to be (a) cost advantages incurred by companies engaging in IS offshoring. These cost advantages mainly result from labor cost differentials between the onshore and the offshore location. (b) Efficiency is another frequently mentioned advantage. It refers to reduced development or production efforts

enabled by round-the-clock development because of time zone differences. A better
utilization of internal resources and productivity enhancement also contribute to the perceived
increase in efficiency. A rise in (c) quality due to better process control and processes of
higher quality and reliability represents an additional advantage of IS offshoring. This quality
increase is supposed to be a result of the offshore vendor's accumulated expertise in providing
IS services. Companies also see advantages related to (d) strategy. They can focus on their
core competencies and processes by offshoring non-strategic activities that would otherwise
tie up managerial resources. In addition, IS offshoring can facilitate access to markets in
developing countries by utilizing an existing relationship with an offshore vendor or a self-
owned offshore facility in these countries. Finally, the aspect of (e) resources represents a
benefit. By entering IS offshoring engagements, companies try to get access to larger pools of
IS professionals, thereby solving a supposed shortage of IS professionals. Table 1-5 illustrates
the advantages of IS offshoring as found in the literature.

Focus	Cited advantages	Studies	Empirical
(a) Cost	Significant cost reductions	Apte et al., 1997	Yes
	Labor cost differences, economies of scale	Chua & Pan, 2006	Yes
	Lower costs	Dhar & Balakrishnan, 2006	Yes
	Cost efficiency	Khan, Currie, & Weerakkody, 2003	Yes
	Costs	Sayeed, 2006	Yes
	Labor cost reductions	Smith & McKeen, 2004	Yes
	Labor cost savings	Delmonte & McCarthy, 2003	No
	Labor and maintenance cost cuts, change of fixed costs to variable costs	Erber & Sayed-Ahmed, 2005	No
	Cost savings	Gonzalez, Gasco, & Llopis, 2006; Kliem, 2004	No
	Cost reductions, "pay-as-you-go" IT	Kakumanu & Portanova, 2006	No
	Operating cost reductions	Pfannenstein & Tsai, 2004	No
	Lower development costs, tax incentives	Tafti, 2005	No

(table continues)

Focus	Cited advantages	Studies	Empirical
(b) Efficiency	Reduced cycle time	Apte et al., 1997	Yes
	Optimal allocation and utilization of internal resources, reduced time to market	Dhar & Balakrishnan, 2006	Yes
	Round-the-clock service	Khan et al., 2003	Yes
	Efficiency and documentation	Sayeed, 2006	Yes
	Productivity enhancement	Delmonte & McCarthy, 2003	No
	Reduced IT development time, reduced timeframe of production processes	Erber & Sayed-Ahmed, 2005	No
	Increased flexibility and speed	Gonzalez et al., 2006	No
	Around-the-clock development	Kakumanu & Portanova, 2006	No
	Improved flexibility, reduced time to complete work, 24/7 operating hours	Pfannenstein & Tsai, 2004	No
(c) Quality	Better control over processes	Chua & Pan, 2006	Yes
	Predictable outcome, higher quality and reliability, higher degree of success	Dhar & Balakrishnan, 2006	Yes
	Assurance of quality development	Khan et al., 2003	Yes
	Quality increase	Erber & Sayed-Ahmed, 2005	No
	More quality	Gonzalez et al., 2006	No
	Quality, value, process advantages	Pfannenstein & Tsai, 2004	No
	Higher quality	Tafti, 2005	No
(d) Strategy	Improved access to global market	Apte et al., 1997	Yes
	Improved flexibility to respond to the changing demand and business environment	Dhar & Balakrishnan, 2006	Yes
	Simplicity and ability to remain focused on core competencies, competitive advantage	Khan et al., 2003	Yes
	Ability to focus on core competency	Sayeed, 2006	Yes
	Ability to focus on value-added activities	Erber & Sayed-Ahmed, 2005	Yes
	Ability to focus on core business	Kakumanu & Portanova, 2006	No
	Entering new markets	Gonzalez et al., 2006	No
(e) Resources	Access to a larger pool of IS professionals	Apte et al., 1997	Yes
	Solution to shortage of resources	Chua & Pan, 2006	Yes
	Solution to the IT skills shortage	Khan et al., 2003	Yes
	Skilled IS resources	Kakumanu & Portanova, 2006	No
	Solution to shortage of IT talents	Tafti, 2005	No

Table 1-5: Advantages of IS offshoring

D.3.1.2   Disadvantages of IS Offshoring

Additionally incurred (a) costs are an often cited disadvantage of IS offshoring. These additional costs arise, for example, from relationship preparation activities, contract negotiation and fulfillment costs, or knowledge transfer efforts. Difficulties arising from different (b) cultures between client and offshore service provider are a second disadvantage. Problems in language and communication result from these cultural difficulties. (c) Geopolitical risks encompassing governmental rules, regulatory differences or legal and political uncertainty in general are also frequently mentioned. Another area are issues related to (d) control in terms of giving up control to the vendor or threats of adverse behavior. A corresponding issue is the problem of (e) intellectual property security where a foreign offshore service provider might get access to a company's proprietary knowledge and exploit it for its own advantage. Problems related to (f) collaboration address aspects of project management and actual implementation of offshoring ventures, such as definition of detailed specifications or clashes due to working in different time zones. Poor (g) technology or infrastructure in the offshoring country can degrade the service delivery in an offshore sourcing arrangement. Other disadvantages refer to potentially lower (h) quality, a negative perception of the company engaging in offshoring by (i) society, and negative motivational effects on the offshoring client's own (j) human resources. Table 1-6 provides an overview of the perceived disadvantages associated with IS offshoring.

Focus	Cited disadvantages	Studies	Empirical
(a) Cost	Scope, cost, and time estimate efforts, knowledge transfer efforts, performance measurement efforts	Dhar & Balakrishnan, 2006	Yes
	Unexpected costs, hidden costs	Khan et al., 2003	Yes
	Transaction costs	Smith & McKeen, 2004	Yes
	Switching costs, supplier search costs	Erber & Sayed-Ahmed, 2005	No
	Hidden costs	Gonzalez et al., 2006; Tafti, 2005	No
	Contract negotiation and fulfillment costs	Kakumanu & Portanova, 2006	No
	Financial risks	Kliem, 2004	No
	Vendor selection, legal/contract, and work transition costs	Pfannenstein & Tsai, 2004	No

(table continues)

Focus	Cited disadvantages	Studies	Empirical
(b) Culture	Difficulty in verbal communications, differences in culture	Apte et al., 1997	Yes
	Cultural and communication barriers	Benamati & Rajkumar, 2002	Yes
	Cross culture, people	Dhar & Balakrishnan, 2006	Yes
	Cultural differences	Smith & McKeen, 2004	Yes
	Problems of national nature	Gonzalez et al., 2006	No
	Language and cultural barriers	Kakumanu & Portanova, 2006	No
	Language barriers, cultural differences	Delmonte & McCarthy, 2003	No
(c) Geopolitical	Unclear governmental rules and regulations	Apte et al., 1997	Yes
	Regulatory differences	Benamati & Rajkumar, 2002	Yes
	Geopolitical risks	Khan et al., 2003	Yes
	Legal and political uncertainties	Smith & McKeen, 2004	Yes
	Country-specific risks	Erber & Sayed-Ahmed, 2005	No
	Legal risks	Kliem, 2004	No
	Political risks	Delmonte & McCarthy, 2003	No
(d) Control	Giving up control to vendor	Benamati & Rajkumar, 2002	Yes
	Threat of opportunism	Khan et al., 2003	Yes
	Reduced control	Smith & McKeen, 2004	Yes
	Managerial & behavioral risk	Kliem, 2004	No
	Outsourcing contract itself, decision process, outsourcing scope	Tafti, 2005	No
(e) Intellectual property security	Intellectual property rights violations	Apte et al., 1997	Yes
	Trust and security concerns	Khan et al., 2003	Yes
	Intellectual property rights issues	Sayeed, 2006	Yes
	Intellectual property security	Erber & Sayed-Ahmed, 2005	No
	Security of intellectual property and equipment, loss of knowledge	Kakumanu & Portanova, 2006	No
	Privacy and security, loss of IT expertise	Tafti, 2005	No

(table continues)

Focus	Cited disadvantages	Studies	Empirical
(f) Collaboration	Time differences in working hours	Apte et al., 1997	Yes
	Requirement for detailed specifications	Khan et al., 2003	Yes
	Different time zones	Gonzalez et al., 2006	No
	Communication failures	Delmonte & McCarthy, 2003	No
(g) Technology/ infrastructure	Difficulties in data communication	Apte et al., 1997	Yes
	Technical incompatibilities	Benamati & Rajkumar, 2002	Yes
	Poor infrastructure in offshore countries	Gonzalez et al., 2006	No
	Technical risks	Kliem, 2004	No
(h) Quality	Deficient quality	Gonzalez et al., 2006	No
	Lack of expertise by the offshore vendor	Kakumanu & Portanova, 2006	No
	Diminished technical returns	Tafti, 2005	No
(i) Society	Negative publicity	Sayeed, 2006	Yes
	Social justice and public perception	Smith & McKeen, 2004	Yes
	Negative public perception in response to offshoring	Kakumanu & Portanova, 2006	No
(j) Human Resources	Organizational commitment, job satisfaction, motivation, psychological contracts, job involvement, increased turnover intention	Brooks, 2006	No
	Layoffs of experts and experienced IS managers	Kakumanu & Portanova, 2006	No

Table 1-6: Disadvantages of IS offshoring

D.3.1.3   Determinants Influencing Consideration of IS Offshoring

Only few studies examine the determinants that influence the consideration for offshoring as a sourcing option (c.f. Table 1-7). Perceived risk and experience of prior outsourcing arrangements seem to influence the decision for or against offshoring, but not the external environment (Benamati & Rajkumar, 2002).

Furthermore, an empirical study in the U.S. shows that the stronger a company's IT infrastructure and its business process knowledge, the higher the likelihood that it engages in IS-driven business process outsourcing (BPO) offshoring. The same applies if a firm pursues a cost cutting strategy and has an IT department with a strong innovation focus (Whitaker, Mithas, & Krishnan, 2005).

Cited determinants	Type of influence	Study	Empirical
Perceived risk of outsourcing	Influence given, but direction not specified	Benamati & Rajkumar, 2002	Yes
Prior outsourcing relationships	Influence given, but direction not specified	Benamati & Rajkumar, 2002	Yes
External environment	No influence	Benamati & Rajkumar, 2002	Yes
Firm has strong IT infrastructure	Increased likelihood for BPO offshoring	Whitaker et al., 2005	Yes
Firm has strong business process knowledge	Increased likelihood for BPO offshoring	Whitaker et al., 2005	Yes
Firm pursues cost cutting strategy and has strong IT department with focus on innovation	Increased likelihood for BPO offshoring	Whitaker et al., 2005	Yes

Table 1-7: Determinants influencing consideration of IS offshoring

D.3.2 What-Stage

Research at the what-stage examines what IS services are offshored, describes the criteria for evaluating offshoreability of services, projects or applications, or develops classification criteria for structuring IS offshoring arrangements.

D.3.2.1 Offshored IS Services

The most commonly offshored services are application services, especially (a) application maintenance and (b) application development. Apart from that, some studies mention offshoring of (c) other IS services such as support operation, call center, problem or change management, security management, and training and education. Table 1-8 illustrates offshored IS services.

Focus	Cited services	Studies	Empirical
(a) Application maintenance	Software maintenance	Apte et al., 1997	Yes
	Maintenance work	Chua & Pan, 2006	Yes
	Application maintenance	Fish & Seydel, 2006	Yes
	Legacy application maintenance	Sayeed, 2006	Yes
	Application maintenance	Murthy, 2004	No
(b) Application development	Software development, integrated system development	Apte et al., 1997	Yes
	Development work	Chua & Pan, 2006	Yes
	Application development	Fish & Seydel, 2006	Yes
(c) Other IS services	Support operation, disaster recovery, training and education	Apte et al., 1997	Yes
	Call center, problem management, change management, security management	Chua & Pan, 2006	Yes

Table 1-8: Offshored IS services

D.3.2.2 Criteria for Evaluating Suitability for Offshoring

Several criteria contribute to a service's, application's or project's suitability for offshoring. As Table 1-9 shows, one criterion is (a) proximity. It means that services that require no physical presence or have a low need for customer interaction are more amenable to offshore delivery. The same applies to applications with low (b) criticality to business operations. Offshoring seems unsuitable when there is only limited (c) impact, for example, when teams are so small that cost savings from offshoring would not be material. Offshoreability seems to be high for services with high (d) information intensity. Information intensity of an activity is defined as the amount of time spent on dealing with information in an activity in comparison to the total time spent on that activity. Thus, it relates activities' intangible value creation to their total tangible and intangible value creation (Apte et al., 1997; Apte & Mason, 1995). Finally, offshoring is suitable for projects with high (e) modularity and scale or applications with limited (f) specificity in terms of intellectual property or company-specific customization.

Focus	Cited evaluation criteria	Offshoreability	Studies	Empirical
(a) Proximity	Physical presence required for task	Not offshoreable	Chua & Pan, 2006	Yes
	Low customer contact need, low physical presence need	Offshoreable	Apte et al., 1997	Yes
(b) Criticality	Critical applications (too risky)	Not offshoreable	Chua & Pan, 2006	Yes
(c) Impact	Teams where cost saving is not material (not cost effective)	Not offshoreable	Chua & Pan, 2006	Yes
(d) Information intensity	High information intensity	Offshoreable	Apte et al., 1997	Yes
(e) Modularity	High modularity and scale of the projects	Offshoreable	Sayeed, 2006	Yes
(f) Specificity	Applications with low intellectual property and limited customization	Offshoreable	Murthy, 2004	No

Table 1-9: Criteria and recommendations for evaluating offshoreability

D.3.2.3 Classification Criteria for Structuring IS Offshoring Arrangements

Only a study by Gonzalez et al. (2006) examines potential classification criteria for structuring IS offshoring arrangements. As Table 1-10 shows, the study argues that there are five dimensions for an IS offshoring taxonomy. These are the (a) customer and the customer's industry sector. (b) Property relationships between offshore service provider and client, e.g., whether it is a third party contract, a joint venture, or whether the client is establishing a self-owned subsidiary. Additional dimensions are based on whether an (c) agent is involved in the offshoring relationships, what (d) service type is being contracted (e.g., body-shopping paid per hour vs. contracting of whole activities), and the (e) proximity between offshore service provider and customer (i.e., near- vs. offshoring).

Focus	Cited classification criteria	Study	Empirical
(a) Customer	Customer's industry sector	Gonzalez et al., 2006	No
(b) Property	Property relationship (contracting out, joint venture or own subsidiary)	Gonzalez et al., 2006	No
(c) Agent	Presence or absence of an agent in the relationship	Gonzalez et al., 2006	No
(d) Service type	Service contracted (body-shopping vs. contracting)	Gonzalez et al., 2006	No
(e) Proximity	Greater or lesser proximity between customer and provider (near- vs. offshoring)	Gonzalez et al., 2006	No

Table 1-10: Classification criteria for structuring IS offshoring arrangements

D.3.3 Which-Stage

In terms of this literature review, no study covers this stage. Research at the which-stage would address the conceptual decision procedures and guidelines regarding IS offshoring. It could, for example, examine who makes the decision or whether it is an informal or formal one.

Research examining the decision process exists, but it explores the implementation of the decision (c.f. Section D.3.4.5, p. 41) and therefore fits into the how-stage.

D.3.4 How-Stage

Research at the how-stage examines the implementation of IS offshoring. It analyzes aspects of the implementation process, risk management, questions of governance and control, knowledge transfer, and the actual sourcing decision, location and vendor selection.

D.3.4.1 Overall IS Offshoring Implementation Process

Two studies address the different stages within the IS offshoring implementation process. As Table 1-11 illustrates, the first stage is (a) initiation comprising the actual decision to offshore as the preferred sourcing option. Subsequently, (b) vendor selection takes place. IT contains an initial evaluation, a thorough analysis after the request for proposal process, and the final vendor selection. Having decided on a vendor, the (c) transition of the service delivery from the client to the vendor happens. During this phase, offshore vendor employees "learn about the environments, architectures, systems, applications, and processes of the business [...] [and] work in parallel with the corporate personnel" (Murray & Crandall, 2006, p. 9). After the transition, (d) delivery of the transferred services takes place and the contract needs to be managed. In the case of a temporary delivery contract, an (e) assessment regarding the project's outcomes and lessons learned finalizes the client-vendor relationship.

Focus	Cited construct	Studies	Empirical
(a) Initiation	Offshore decision	Murray & Crandall, 2006	No
(b) Vendor selection	Vendor selection	Erber & Sayed-Ahmed, 2005	No
	Initial vendor evaluation	Murray & Crandall, 2006	No
	Request for proposal process	Murray & Crandall, 2006	No
	Final vendor selection	Murray & Crandall, 2006	No
	Vendor contract	Murray & Crandall, 2006	No
(c) Transition	Transition period	Erber & Sayed-Ahmed, 2005	No
	Vendor development/project monitoring and business management	Murray & Crandall, 2006	No
	Test phase	Murray & Crandall, 2006	No
(d) Delivery	Managing contract	Erber & Sayed-Ahmed, 2005	No
	Managing change	Murray & Crandall, 2006	No
(e) Finalization	Assessment	Murray & Crandall, 2006	No

Table 1-11: Stages of IS offshoring implementation

D.3.4.2   Risk Control

Kliem (2004) descriptively examines potential risks in IS offshoring implementation. The study proposes three different control mechanisms for managing risks that might arise during implementation. These are (a) preventive controls that attempt to mitigate the impact of a risk or avoid it before it can have an impact at all. (b) Detective controls are relevant during implementation and try to identify risks in order to preclude future impact. Correspondingly, (c) corrective controls determine the impact of a risk and the establishment of measures to prevent future impact. Table 1-12 illustrates these three risk control mechanisms.

Focus	Cited construct	Studies	Empirical
(a) Preventive controls	Impact mitigation of a risk or stopping it before having an impact	Kliem, 2004	No
(b) Detective controls	Risk identification and preclusion of future impact under similar conditions	Kliem, 2004	No
(c) Corrective controls	Impact determination of a risk and establishing measures to preclude future impacts	Kliem, 2004	No

Table 1-12: Risk control mechanisms for IS offshoring implementation

D.3.4.3   Governance and Control

Balaji, Ahuja, & Ranganathan (2006) examine how knowledge transfer requirements and the clients' capabilities in offshore IS development influence the sourcing arrangement between client and vendor. The study also analyzes the types of control modes the client uses to control the vendor. As Table 1-13 shows, the study observes that the higher the complexity inherent in the offshore project, the more resources the clients usually invest into the project. These resources result in a portfolio of control modes being exercised. Likewise, clients seem to seek a partner relationship if they have a strong IS development capability, in order to acquire new knowledge and routines from the vendor.

Cited project situation	Cited observed control mode	Studies	Empirical
Low knowledge transfer requirements	Formal controls and pure-offshore models predominate	Balaji et al., 2006	Yes
High knowledge transfer requirements	Portfolio of control modes and hybrid models are preferred	Balaji et al., 2006	Yes
Low client offshore IS development capability	One-off relationships favored	Balaji et al., 2006	Yes
High client offshore IS development capability	Partner relationships preferred	Balaji et al., 2006	Yes

Table 1-13: Observed control modes and arrangement types in IS offshoring

D.3.4.4   Knowledge Transfer

Chua & Pan (2006) differentiate three dimensions of knowledge transfer in IS offshoring. As Table 1-14 shows, the first dimension is (a) direction. Knowledge can either be pushed from the onshore to the offshore team or the offshore team can pull the knowledge on request from the onshore teams. Regarding (b) location, knowledge transfer can either take place in the offshore location, i.e., client personnel travel to the vendor site; or in the onshore location, i.e., vendor personnel absorb knowledge at the client's domestic site. Finally, "rich" face-to-face channels such as personal interaction are (c) mechanisms used for transferring knowledge.

Focus	Cited construct	Studies	Empirical
(a) Direction	Knowledge transfer pushed from onshore to the offshore team	Chua & Pan, 2006	Yes
	Knowledge transfer pulled by one offshore team from each onshore team	Chua & Pan, 2006	Yes
(b) Location	Transfer predominantly in the offshore location	Chua & Pan, 2006	Yes
	Transfer predominantly in the onshore location	Chua & Pan, 2006	Yes
(c) Mechanisms	"Rich" face-to-face channels and mechanisms	Chua & Pan, 2006	Yes

Table 1-14: Implementation of knowledge transfer in IS offshoring

D.3.4.5 Sourcing, Location and Vendor Decision

Regarding the general (a) sourcing decision, i.e., when to offshore or not, Pu Li & Kishore (2006) employ transaction cost economics to construct a framework. The study argues that offshore outsourcing is preferable when asset specificity is low. In that case the benefits from labor cost advantages outweigh additional governance cost incurred from the contracting relationship. As part of the (b) location decision, five evaluation criteria seem to dominate. These criteria focus on a location's infrastructure, the country's specific risk, its government's policy, the available human capital in terms of IT professionals, and the costs for service provisioning, usually labor and communication costs. The decision on a specific (c) vendor focuses on the vendor's delivery capabilities, its domain expertise in terms of the client's business and processes, the vendor's collaboration expertise, and its local presence regarding on-, near-, and offshore locations. Table 1-15 illustrates these evaluation criteria.

Focus	Cited evaluation criteria		Studies	Empirical
(a) Sourcing	Asset specificity		Pu Li & Kishore, 2006	No
(b) Location	Infrastructure		Graf & Mudambi, 2005; Li, Wang, & Yang, 2006	No
	Country risk		Graf & Mudambi, 2005; Li et al., 2006	No
	Government policy		Graf & Mudambi, 2005; Li et al., 2006	No
	Human capital		Graf & Mudambi, 2005; Li et al., 2006	No
	Cost		Li et al., 2006	No
(c) Vendor	Delivery capabilities	Delivery competence	Feeny, Lacity, & Willcocks, 2005	Yes
		Transformation competence	Feeny et al., 2005	Yes
		Maturity of process & methodology	Sakaguchi & Raghavan, 2003	Yes
		Cost	Sakaguchi & Raghavan, 2003	Yes
		Quality of resources	Sakaguchi & Raghavan, 2003	Yes
		Speed of delivery	Sakaguchi & Raghavan, 2003	Yes
		Project management	Sakaguchi & Raghavan, 2003	Yes
		Certification	Sakaguchi & Raghavan, 2003	Yes
		Full-outsourcing capabilities	Sakaguchi & Raghavan, 2003	Yes
		Multivendor capabilities	Sakaguchi & Raghavan, 2003	Yes
		Technical capabilities	Sakaguchi & Raghavan, 2003	Yes
		Technical expertise of the vendor	Sayeed, 2006	Yes

(table continues)

Focus	Cited evaluation criteria	Studies	Empirical
Domain expertise	Business process expertise	Sakaguchi & Raghavan, 2003	Yes
	Vendor expertise relevant to client's business	Sayeed, 2006	Yes
Collaboration expertise	Relationship competence	Feeny et al., 2005	Yes
	Collaboration experience of the vendor	Sayeed, 2006	Yes
Location	Presence in the U.S.	Sakaguchi & Raghavan, 2003	Yes
	Near-shore capabilities	Sakaguchi & Raghavan, 2003	Yes
	Political climate	Sakaguchi & Raghavan, 2003	Yes

Table 1-15: Evaluation criteria for IS offshoring implementation decisions

D.3.5 Outcome-Stage

Research at the outcome-stage focuses on best practices for IS offshoring implementation, determinants for success, and other effects resulting from IS offshoring.

D.3.5.1 Best Practices for IS Offshoring

Best practices for IS offshoring provide experiences for (a) preparation of the offshoring engagement, (b) collaboration between the offshore service provider and the client, and the actual (c) delivery of the offshored service. Within these categories, the described individual best practices are rather heterogeneous as Table 1-16 shows.

Regarding (a) preparation, studies emphasize different aspects such as the need for definitive project specifications, careful selection of the offshore service provider and the delivery location, thorough preparation of the delivery infrastructure, an informed choice for a specific service delivery contract, and the client's self-preparation in terms of inter-cultural collaboration skills and process expertise.

Best practices in (b) collaboration emphasize the importance of empowerment and escalation mechanisms between client and service provider, the benefit of informal communication, the advantage of having a dedicated person for coordination issues, and the importance of stakeholder buy-in to facilitate the implementation and adoption of IS offshoring.

Only one study provides best practices for the actual service (c) delivery. These recommend that several pilot projects should be used to escalate an organization's learning curve regarding IS offshoring, that a supplier portfolio is beneficial because it helps to lower delivery risks, that projects should be divided into segments to protect intellectual property but also that clients should improve their own capability maturity model (CMM) capabilities. Clients should try to educate their vendors in terms of required business-specific knowledge in order to increase delivery quality and lower development costs. Knowledge transfer can be facilitated by the personal on-shore presence of supplier staff. Finally, defined metrics help to monitor delivery performance and vendor controlling.

Focus	Cited construct	Studies	Empirical
(a) Preparation	Specify projects more definitively	Benamati & Rajkumar, 2002	Yes
	Consider vendors' project management and development processes more carefully	Benamati & Rajkumar, 2002	Yes
	Select an offshore outsourcing destination based on business objectives	Rottman & Lacity, 2006	Yes
	Use offshore supplier competition to lower domestic supplier rates	Rottman & Lacity, 2006	Yes
	Ready the infrastructure	Rottman & Lacity, 2006	Yes
	Understand how different contracts give suppliers different incentives	Rottman & Lacity, 2006	Yes
	Elevate the organization's CMM certification to close the process gap between the organization and its supplier	Rottman & Lacity, 2006	Yes
	Address telecommunication infrastructure	Rao, 2004	No
	Address legal and security issues	Rao, 2004	No
	Address time zone differences	Rao, 2004	No
	Address cultural differences	Rao, 2004	No
	Address language barriers	Rao, 2004	No
(b) Collaboration	Empower employees and escalate issues	Dhar & Balakrishnan, 2006	Yes
	Hold informal communication sessions	Dhar & Balakrishnan, 2006	Yes
	Establish stakeholder buy-in	Dhar & Balakrishnan, 2006	Yes
	Place a coordinating person at each other's site to improve collaboration between client and vendor	Kumar & Willcocks, 1996	Yes
	Allow business users to share in the benefits of offshoring to motivate adoption	Rottman & Lacity, 2006	Yes
	Factor the use of an on-site engagement manager into the staffing models and ratios	Rottman & Lacity, 2006	Yes

(table continues)

Focus	Cited construct	Studies	Empirical
(c) Delivery	Escalate the learning curve with a program of pilot projects	Rottman & Lacity, 2006	Yes
	Diversify the supplier portfolio to minimize risk and maximize competition	Rottman & Lacity, 2006	Yes
	Break projects into segments to protect intellectual property	Rottman & Lacity, 2006	Yes
	Bring in a CMM expert with no domain expertise to flush out ambiguities in requirements	Rottman & Lacity, 2006	Yes
	Negotiate "Flexible CMM"	Rottman & Lacity, 2006	Yes
	Give offshore suppliers domain-specific training to protect quality and lower development costs	Rottman & Lacity, 2006	Yes
	Overlap onshore presence to facilitate supplier-to-supplier knowledge transfer	Rottman & Lacity, 2006	Yes
	Create balanced score-card metrics	Rottman & Lacity, 2006	Yes

Table 1-16: Best practices for IS offshoring implementation

D.3.5.2 Determinants of Success

Similar to best practices, determinants of IS offshoring success focus on the dimensions of (a) preparation, (b) collaboration, and (c) delivery. Additionally, they address the aspect of (d) expertise on the client as well as the vendor side. Table 1-17 illustrates the categories and the corresponding research findings.

Determinants of success in the dimension of (a) preparation are the right selection of what to offshore and what to keep in-house, the right selection of the offshore service provider, thorough planning and preparation of the offshoring endeavor, as well as the right selection of the staff involved on the client and vendor side.

Factors influencing success in the dimension of (b) collaboration are a joint understanding of goals, culture, processes, responsibility, and trust between client and vendor. Furthermore, the main factors are commitment of top management to the offshore delivery, and buy-in of the business process owners. Finally, management of cross-cultural issues, but also of HR-related training needs and processes are important.

Regarding (c) delivery, studies emphasize the importance of organizational skills such as IS systemic thinking, a global IS resource management, as well as IS change and vendor management. Additionally, efficient project governance and team management are determinants of success. Finally, effective knowledge transfer and clearly defined delivery processes contribute to the success of IS offshoring implementation.

Determinants of success in the dimension of (d) expertise are a mature management team and mature operational processes. In line with these, another study emphasizes the importance of the transition management team's and the operation team's capabilities for IS offshoring success.

Focus	Cited construct	Studies	Empirical
(a) Preparation	Deciding what to outsource and what to keep in-house	Dhar & Balakrishnan, 2006	Yes
	Selecting the right vendor	Dhar & Balakrishnan, 2006	Yes
	Client project planning and control capability	Erickson & Ranganathan, 2006	Yes
	Limited process complexity	Ganesh & Moitra, 2004	Yes
	Proper transition planning	Ganesh & Moitra, 2004	Yes
	Reliable infrastructure	Ganesh & Moitra, 2004	Yes
	Clarity of objectives	Delmonte & McCarthy, 2003	No
	Level of preparation	Delmonte & McCarthy, 2003	No
	Right choice of the outsourced project	Krishna, Sahay, & Walsham, 2004	No
	Right choice of staff and incentives	Krishna et al., 2004	No
(b) Collaboration	Shared goals	Bhat, Gupta, & Murthy, 2006	Yes
	Shared culture	Bhat et al., 2006	Yes
	Shared processes	Bhat et al., 2006	Yes
	Shared responsibility	Bhat et al., 2006	Yes
	Trust	Bhat et al., 2006	Yes
	Top management commitment	Ganesh & Moitra, 2004	Yes
	Buy-in of business process owner	Ganesh & Moitra, 2004	Yes
	Joint definition of contract structure	Ganesh & Moitra, 2004	Yes
	Working relationships between client and vendor if the contract can not be specified in detail	Kumar & Willcocks, 1996	Yes
	Trust (consensus, commitment, cultural com-patibility)	Holmstroem, O'Conchuir, Agerfalk, & Fitzgerald, 2006	Yes
	Management of cross-cultural relationship	Krishna et al., 2004	No
	Management of training needs and processes	Krishna et al., 2004	No

(table continues)

Focus	Cited construct	Studies	Empirical
(c) Delivery	IS systemic thinking	Balaji & Ranganathan, 2006	Yes
	Global IS resource management	Balaji & Ranganathan, 2006	Yes
	IS change management	Balaji & Ranganathan, 2006	Yes
	IS vendor management	Balaji & Ranganathan, 2006	Yes
	Project governance	Erickson & Ranganathan, 2006	Yes
	Team management	Erickson & Ranganathan, 2006	Yes
	Effectiveness of knowledge transfer	Ganesh & Moitra, 2004	Yes
	Clearly defined software processes to facilitate communication and coordination	Holmstroem et al., 2006	Yes
(d) Expertise	Capability of the transition management team	Ganesh & Moitra, 2004	Yes
	Capability of the operations team	Ganesh & Moitra, 2004	Yes
	Maturity of the management team	Delmonte & McCarthy, 2003	No
	Maturity of the organization's processes	Delmonte & McCarthy, 2003	No

Table 1-17: Determinants of success for IS offshoring implementation

D.3.5.3   Other Effects

Whitaker, Krishnan, & Fornell (2006) examine the effects of offshoring for firms and consumers. The study finds that business process and IT offshoring positively influence the perceived value and quality of a company's services by its customer. In the end this increased customer appreciation leads to higher customer satisfaction. Table 1-18 illustrates the findings.

Proposed effect of offshoring	Supported	Study	Empirical
Higher perceived value	Yes	Whitaker et al., 2006	Yes
Higher perceived quality	Yes	Whitaker et al., 2006	Yes
Higher customer satisfaction	Yes	Whitaker et al., 2006	Yes

Table 1-18: Outcome of IS offshoring

D.3.6 Meta Studies

Niederman et al. (2006) contribute the only meta-study regarding IS offshoring. The study attempts to assemble "the relevant theoretical and empirical bases for developing a research agenda for offshoring" (Niederman et al., 2006, p. 55). It examines IT offshoring on the individual, the organizational and the national or regional dimension and suggests researching the relationships between these dimensions.

E Discussion of Findings and Implications for Future Research

E.1 Research Design

Certain research design patterns dominate current IS offshoring research: most studies do not draw upon any reference theory and use a descriptive research type. They are purely conceptual or use case studies as data gathering approaches, and apply interpretation as data analysis methods. Noticeably, this research situation marks a contrast to research in IS outsourcing where a significant body of knowledge already exists and research tends to be more theory-driven and confirmatory (Behrens, 2007; Dibbern et al., 2004).

A potential explanation for this observation is that the IS offshoring phenomenon itself is a rather new area of knowledge and consequently less researched. The fact that most research was published between 2003 and 2006 supports this perception. Therefore, the research community might currently be at the stage of establishing an initial understanding of the phenomenon, its constituting variables, and underlying theories. Such a research situation would explain the dominance of non-theory guided, descriptive and conceptual research because this research design is most suitable in settings where "variables are largely unknown, and the researcher wants to focus on the context that may shape the understanding of the phenomenon being studied" (Creswell, 1994, p. 10).

However, this situation exhibits some drawbacks. First of all, the domination of one research design pattern provides a one-sided research view on the IS offshoring phenomenon. Furthermore, if research is empirical, sample sizes are often low. If research is non-empirical, findings are often conceptual and not theory-backed. This undermines the generalizability of results and limits the comparability between different studies.

A greater variety in research designs could enrich the body of knowledge in IS offshoring research. In particular, more confirmatory, empirical research that uses theory-derived hypotheses and research frameworks could provide a better understanding of the phenomenon. Such empirical research would add most value if it built upon greater sample sizes, used statistical methods beyond descriptive statistics, and clearly stated its methodological approaches.

E.2 IS offshoring Stages

The content of research in IS offshoring mainly examines the why- and outcome-stages. Research regarding the stages how to offshore and what to offshore is less frequent and there is no research addressing the which-stage. Perhaps this is because research questions at the why- and outcome-stage, namely advantages and disadvantages or best practices and determinants of success, are more interesting and represent easier starting points for conducting descriptive-conceptual research.

In line with that, research results are often listings of aspects regarding the IS offshoring phenomenon. This particularly applies to the why-stage with its advantages and disadvantages of IS offshoring, and the outcome-stage with its best practices and determinants of success. In particular, research at the outcome-stage often enumerates heterogeneous items that can barely be summarized or aggregated as for example Section D.3.5 (p. 42) showed.

Although the stages what, which, and how are currently under-researched, they represent critical aspects of IS offshoring. These stages directly affect most of the described best practices and determinants of success. They influence, for example, the selection of the right projects, informed decision making regarding vendors, or efficient collaboration and delivery.

Interesting research questions at the what-stage are what services, activities or projects are currently offshored, what are the criteria to identify these services and to what degree are they offshored. Research at the which-stage could focus on the question of which individuals are involved in the offshoring decision, what other stakeholders influence the decision and how the decision process itself is structured. Finally, research questions at the how-stage could further examine how locations and vendors are actually selected, how transaction costs can be projected or how knowledge transfer and transition could be best structured.

Apart from that, empirical tests of the already described best practices and determinants of success could provide a deeper understanding at the stages why and outcome. This would move the existing findings beyond descriptive listings towards an empirically tested body of knowledge which other researchers could build upon.

F Conclusions

The literature review at hand attempted to provide a consolidated view of existing research in IS offshoring. It argues that IS offshoring is a rather new area of academic research. As a result, most research is descriptive and conceptual in nature and focuses on the aspects of why to offshore and the outcome of offshoring.

Limitations of this study clearly come from its database-driven search approach. Despite thorough validity checks, it is possible that the search approach missed relevant research. Better results might arise from searching more databases and conferences. Another limitation is that the IS offshoring phenomenon is less researched. Often only a single paper addresses a specific aspect of the IS offshoring phenomenon. That makes a critical comparison or consolidation of research results difficult, and restricts their heuristic value in terms of this literature review. Therefore, repeating the literature review at a later date and comparing the results might provide additional insights.

Clear research opportunities for research design and research focus exist. Regarding research design, more confirmatory, empirical research with clearly stated methodologies – especially at the why- and outcome-stages – would be preferable. Regarding research focus, more studies addressing the stages what, which, and how would deepen the understanding of the IS offshoring phenomenon especially because these stages represent critical dimensions of IS offshoring.

Appendix

Literature Categorization

Study Author	Year	Res. theories	Strategic mgmt.	Agency	Transaction cost	Exchange	Power-politic	Relationship	Other (Theory)	n/a (Theory)
		Strategic		Economic		Social/ Organizational			Oth.	n/a
Apte, U. M. et al.	1997									X
Balaji, S.; Ranganathan, C.	2006	X								
Balaji, S.;Ahuja, M.K.;Ranganathan, C.	2006								X	
Benamati, J., & Rajkumar, T.	2002								X	
Bhat, J. M., Gupta, M., & Murthy, S. N.	2006									X
Brooks, N.	2006									X
Chua, A.-L.; Pan, S.	2006									X
Delmonte, A.J.; McCarthy, R.V.	2003									X
Dhar, S., & Balakrishnan, B.	2006				X					
Erber, G., & Sayed-Ahmed, A.	2005									X
Erickson, J.M.;Ranganathan, C.	2006	X							X	
Feeny, D., Lacity, M., & Willcocks, L. P.	2005									X
Fish, K. E., & Seydel, J.	2006									X
Ganesh, Jai; Moitra, Deependra	2004									X
Gonzalez, R., Gasco, J., & Llopis, J.	2006									X
Graf, M., & Mudambi, S. M.	2005									X
Holmstroem, H. et al.	2006					X				
Kakumanu, P., & Portanova, A.	2006									X
Khan, N.; Currie, W.L.; Weerakkody, V.	2003									X
Kliem, R.	2004									X
Krishna, S., Sahay, S., & Walsham, G.	2004									X
Kumar, K; Willcocks, L.	1996				X			X	X	
Li, H.; Wang, J.; Yang, D.	2006								X	
Murray, M. J., & Crandall, R. E.	2006									X
Murthy, S.	2004									X
Niederman, F., Kundu, S., & Salas, S.	2006								X	
Pfannenstein, L. L., & Tsai, R. J.	2004									X
Pu Li, J.; Kishore, R.	2006				X					
Rao, M. T.	2004									X
Rottman, J. W., & Lacity, M. C.	2006									X
Sakaguchi, Toru; Raghavan, Vijay	2003									X
Sayeed, L.	2006				X					
Smith, H. A., & McKeen, J. D.	2004									X
Tafti, M. H. A.	2005									X
Whitaker, J. W.; Krishnan, M.S.; Fornell, C.	2006								X	
Whitaker, J.W.; Mithas, S.; Krishnan, M.S.	2005				X					
Total		2	0	0	5	1	0	1	7	23

Approach		Research type				Data gathering					Data analysis				
Empirical	Non-empirical	Confirmatory	Exploratory-interpretive	Descriptive	Formulative	Survey	Interview	Case study	Other	n/a (Data gathering)	1st generation statistics (e.g. Regression)	2nd generation statistics (e.g. SEM)	Interpretation	Other	n/a (Data analysis)
X				X		X					X				
X			X					X					X		
X			X					X					X		
X		X							X				X		
X				X				X					X		
	X				X					X					X
X				X				X					X		
	X			X						X					X
X		X						X					X		
	X			X						X					X
X			X					X					X		
X				X				X					X		
X				X		X					X				
X			X					X					X		
	X			X	X					X					X
	X				X					X					X
X			X					X					X		
	X			X						X					X
X				X				X					X		
	X			X	X					X					X
	X			X						X					X
X			X					X					X		
	X				X					X					X
	X			X						X					X
	X			X						X					X
	X				X					X					X
	X			X						X					X
	X				X					X					X
	X			X						X					X
X				X			X						X		
X					X	X						X			
X			X				X						X		
X				X			X						X		
	X			X						X					X
X		X					X				X				
X		X				X					X				
20	16	4	7	19	8	4	4	11	1	16	4	1	15	0	16

	Offshoring stage					Service covered			
Why	What	Which	How	Outcome		Infrastructure	Application development	Other IS services	n/a (Service)
X	X					X	X	X	
				X			X		
			X				X		
X				X			X		
				X			X		
X									X
X	X		X			X	X		
X				X			X		
X				X					X
X			X						X
				X			X		
			X						X
	X					X	X	X	
				X					X
X	X								X
			X						X
				X			X		
X							X		
X									X
X			X				X		
				X			X		
				X			X		
			X						X
			X				X		
	X					X	X		
X	X		X	X			X		
X									X
			X						X
				X					X
				X					X
			X						X
X	X		X						X
X									X
X									X
				X					X
X									X
17	7	0	12	14		4	17	2	19

Annotated Bibliography

Source	Annotations
Apte et al., 1997	A survey of 149 companies in the USA, Japan, and Finland regarding their domestic and global outsourcing practices. Based on 48 responses the study shows that 11.3% (Finland), 12.8% (Finland), and 16.7% (USA) of the companies conduct global outsourcing. **Why** Companies in the three countries perceive similar advantages and disadvantages of global outsourcing. A main advantage is significant cost reduction. Other advantages of global outsourcing are "improved access to a much larger pool of highly skilled professionals", "reduced cycle time", and "improved access to global markets" (Apte et al., 1997, p. 297). The most important perceived disadvantages are difficulties in verbal and data communications. Additionally, U.S. companies "rated the uncertainty surrounding governmental rules and regulations as the most important obstacle to global outsourcing" (Apte et al., 1997, p. 297). **What** The authors state that "the development and maintenance of software are the most frequently outsourcing [*sic*] functions, particularly in Japan and Finland" (Apte et al., 1997, p. 295). The corresponding number for the USA are lower where "support operation", "disaster recovery", and "training and education" (Apte et al., 1997, p. 295) are more frequently globally outsourced. The authors explain this difference with potential statistical biases in the company responses. Tasks seem more suitable for offshoring if they require low customer contact need, low physical presence need, and have high information intensity, e.g., programming.
Balaji et al., 2006	Based on four case studies, the authors examine how knowledge transfer requirements and clients' offshore IS development capabilities influence the choice of the offshore model, control modes and the relationships in offshored application development projects. **How** They suggest "that formal controls and pure-offshore models predominate in projects involving low knowledge transfer requirements, while a portfolio of control modes and hybrid models are preferred in projects involving high knowledge transfer requirements. Partner relationships are preferred in projects having high client ISD capability, while one-off relationships are favored in low ISD capability projects" (Balaji et al., 2006, p. 1).
Balaji & Ranganathan, 2006	Drawing on resource theories and based on pilot case studies, the authors examine the key capabilities required for a successful offshore IS sourcing endeavor. **Outcome** The authors suggest that IS systemic thinking, IS vendor management, global IS resource management and IS change management are critical for effective IS offshoring of application development.

Source	Annotations
Benamati & Rajkumar, 2002	The authors conduct ten interviews with executives at seven international firms and derive a model that explains what influences the decision about on- and offshore outsourcing of application development.

Why

The study looks for "support for the assertion that perception of risk influences the decision to outsource". The most common concern mentioned is "giving up control" (Benamati & Rajkumar, 2002, p. 40). Interview partners stated that offshore outsourcing heightened the risk of outsourcing and introduced new ones such as "cultural and communication barriers, technical incompatibilities, and regulatory differences" which must be compensated through "substantially reduced costs" (Benamati & Rajkumar, 2002, p. 40). External factors seemed to have little effect on the decision to outsource. However, prior relationships seemed to influence the decision to outsource. Interview partners preferred "onshore over offshore simply based on more experience and comfort with those types of relationships" (Benamati & Rajkumar, 2002, p. 40).

Outcome

Interviewees in this study stated that "more attention must be paid to minimize additional risk or to justify it through substantially reduced cost", e.g., by providing "more definitive project specifications with offshore application development" (Benamati & Rajkumar, 2002, p. 40).

Bhat et al., 2006	Based on several cases at an Indian IT-services firm, the authors describe success factors and best practices for the requirements engineering phase in offshore application development projects.

Outcome

They suggest a close alignment between vendor and client where "shared goals", "shared culture", "shared processes", "shared responsibility" and mutual "trust" (Bhat et al., 2006, p. 42) are key success factors. These factors must be addressed in three dimensions which are "people", "processes", and "technology" (Bhat et al., 2006, p. 43).

Brooks, 2006	The study formulates a conceptual framework to analyze the potential effects of IT outsourcing and offshoring on individual employees.

Why

Considering two dimensions, "environmental challenges" and "employee challenges", (Brooks, 2006, pp. 48–49) the authors argue that total offshoring comes with high environmental challenges and leads to high employee challenges. This might negatively impact employees' perceptions of occupational stress, perceived job security, organizational commitment, job satisfaction, motivation, psychological contracts, job involvement, and turnover intention.

Source	Annotations
Chua & Pan, 2006	The authors conduct two in-depth case studies at the technology departments of a multinational bank to examine knowledge transfer in IS offshoring.

Why
Cost saving through cost arbitrage and economies of scale, as well as shortage of resources and better control over processes are the main objectives for offshoring.

What
All development and maintenance work was in-scope for offshoring except for critical applications, teams where cost savings from offshoring would not have been material and tasks that required physical presence. Additionally, call center operations, problem and change management as well as security management was in-scope for offshoring.

How
They focus on the knowledge transfer and find varying modes of transferring knowledge. Knowledge was either pushed by the onshore team or pulled by the offshore team. The knowledge transfer happened either in the offshore or in the onshore location. It took between one to twelve months and rich face-to-face channels and mechanisms had been used.

| Delmonte & McCarthy, 2003 | Based on desk research, the authors describe risks, benefits and critical success factors for offshore application development. |

Why
The main benefits are labor cost savings and an enhanced productivity due to an offshore partner's experience. Risks include communication failures, language barriers, cultural differences, and political risks.

Outcome
Four critical success factors may be indicators for an organization's likelihood to succeed in offshore software development. These are maturity of the management team, the organization's processes, clarity of objectives, and level of preparation. Based on desk research case studies, they evaluate their findings.

| Dhar & Balakrishnan, 2006 | Guided by transaction cost economics, the authors examine in two in-depth case studies the objectives, the associated major risk factors, and best practices for global IS outsourcing. |

Why
Lower costs, optimal allocation and utilization of internal resources, flexibility to respond to demand changes, predictable outcome, higher degree of success, and higher quality and reliability are the key benefits of global IT outsourcing. The important risk factors are knowledge transfer, performance measurement, and formulating scope, cost, and time estimates.

Outcome
"Selecting the right vendor and deciding what to outsource and what to keep in-house" (Dhar & Balakrishnan, 2006, p. 59) are the most important challenges to global IT outsourcing, followed by setting up a governance model, and ongoing vendor management. Best practices to address these challenges include empowerment and escalation, holding informal communication sessions, and establishing stakeholder buy-in.

Source	Annotations
Erber & Sayed-Ahmed, 2005	The authors conceptually describe the phenomenon of offshore outsourcing. **Why** They mention lower labor costs, reduced IT development time, lower maintenance costs, and a reduced timeframe of production processes as main advantages of IS offshore outsourcing. In addition, quality might increase, fixed costs can be changed to variable costs, and enterprises can focus on their value-added core activities. The article perceives country-specific risks, intellectual property security, switching costs, and supplier search costs as the main disadvantages of IS offshore outsourcing. **How** Mention a three phase model in offshore projects. These three phases are (1) selecting a vendor, (2) the transition period "when knowledge is transferred from onshore workers to members of the outsourcing team" (Erber & Sayed-Ahmed, 2005, p. 104), and (3) managing the contract, i.e., the actual offshore relationship.
Erickson & Ranganathan, 2006	Based on case studies, the authors examine the impact of project management capabilities on the effectiveness of offshore outsourcing of application development. **Outcome** They describe key project management sub-capabilities that clients need to possess in order to effectively offshore application development. These are project planning and control, project governance, and team management.
Feeny et al., 2005	Based on past research, the authors describe three potentially important areas for evaluating on- and offshore BPO suppliers' competencies. **How** These are delivery competency, transformation competency and relationship competency. Within these three areas they suggest twelve critical supplier capabilities to be evaluated.
Fish & Seydel, 2006	A survey of 181 upper level IT professionals in the USA regarding what functions they are currently outsourcing and what their future plans are. The authors include offshore outsourcing but do not present the results differentiated by on- and offshore outsourcing. **What** The results show that currently applications development and applications maintenance is most commonly outsourced. Interviewees plan to increase outsourcing of applications development, applications maintenance and personal computer maintenance in the future.
Ganesh & Moitra, 2004	The authors perform case studies at Indian offshore providers and examine what factors determine a successful transition management for offshore business process outsourcing. **Outcome** They find that limited process complexity, top management commitment, buy-in of the business process owner, proper transition planning, joint definition of contract structure, capability of the transition management team, capability of the operations team, effectiveness of knowledge transfer, a reliable infrastructure, and low transition cost are the key determinants of an effective transition management.

Source	Annotations
Gonzalez et al., 2006	In their literature-based descriptive analysis, the authors examine the phenomenon of IS offshore outsourcing.

Why
Advantages are cost savings, technical feasibility in terms of communication, increased flexibility and speed regarding time to market, more quality, entering new markets, and – from a macro-economic perspective – more efficient markets. Disadvantages are hidden costs, poor infrastructure in offshore countries, different time zones, deficiencies in quality, problems of national nature, and – from a macro-economic perspective – more unemployment in western countries.

What
They propose a classification taxonomy for offshore outsourcing relationships. They suggest five classifying dimensions. These are the customer's sector, property relationships, presence or absence of an agent in the relationship, type of service contracted, and greater or lesser proximity between customer and provider.

| Graf & Mudambi, 2005 | The authors formulate a model to decide on offshore locations for IT-enabled business processes, thereby drawing up a framework for examining international production. |

How
They argue that infrastructure, country risk, government policy and human capital influence a location's attractiveness to investors. This influence is moderated by firm-specific factors such as outsourcing objectives and experience as well as situation-specific factors such as the nature of the business process and customer expectations.

| Holmstroem et al., 2006 | The study draws on exchange theory and employs a case study approach to examine the elements of a successful offshoring relationship. |

Outcome
These elements are primarily about trust, expressed by attributes such as consensus, commitment, and cultural compatibility, but also include clearly defined software processes to facilitate communication and coordination.

| Kakumanu & Portanova, 2006 | The authors conceptually describe the benefits and risks in offshore outsourcing. |

Why
The reasons for offshoring are cost effective labor, a shortage of skilled labor, cost reduction, focusing on core business, changing fixed IS costs to variable costs, and around-the-clock development. Typical downsides mentioned are security of intellectual property and equipment, lack of knowledge by the offshore vendor, language and cultural barriers, losing knowledge, contract negotiation and fulfillment costs, layoffs of experts and experienced IS managers as well as negative public perception in response to offshoring.

| Khan et al., 2003 | The authors explore in case studies the benefits and risks of offshore IT outsourcing |

Why
The benefits are a solution to the IT skills shortage, cost efficiency, competitive advantage, simplicity round the clock service, assurance of quality development, and allowing the company to remain focused on core competencies. Risks are the threat of opportunism, unexpected costs, trust and security concerns, hidden costs, geopolitical risk, and the requirement for detailed specification. They argue that the type of offshored products and services can be distinguished according to the dimensions "value added" and "risk", whereas services with high added value are associated with higher risk.

Source	Annotations
Kliem, 2004	The author conceptually describes a framework of risks associated with IS offshore development projects. **Why** The main risks are financial, technical, managerial, behavioral and legal. **How** The author proposes a framework of three control types for controlling risks in offshore IS development projects. These are (1) preventive controls to mitigate risk before it has an impact, (2) detective controls to reveal any risk and preclude future impact under similar conditions, and (3) corrective controls to determine the impact of a risk and preclude future impact.
Krishna et al., 2004	The authors describe critical success factors in managing cross-cultural issues in global software outsourcing. **Outcome** The authors state that the right choice of outsourced project minimizes the difficulties of cross-cultural factors. Furthermore, "management of the cross-cultural relationship" seems important as well as the "choice of staff and incentives" and "training needs and processes" (Krishna et al., 2004, pp. 64–65).
Kumar & Willcocks, 1996	Examining how offshore outsourcing fits with the theory and practice of IT outsourcing, the authors apply findings from IT outsourcing research to longitudinal case studies and conclude that the findings are supported by the cases. **Outcome** The main findings are that close working relationships between client and vendor are essential for successful offshore work if the contract can not be specified in detail. In addition, they find that onsite offshoring incurs costs that reduce the cost advantages of using offshore personnel significantly, and that collaboration between client and vendor can be improved by placing a coordinating person at each other's site.
Li et al., 2006	The study formulates a decision-aid model to support the selection of an offshore outsourcing location. **How** Dimensions considered are infrastructure, country risk, government policy, and the value of human capital and cost.
Murray & Crandall, 2006	Drawing upon the system development lifecycle, the authors describe the lifecycle phases of a typical information systems offshore outsourcing project. **How** These phases are (1) the decision to offshore, (2) initial vendor evaluation, (3) request for proposal process, (4) final vendor selection, (5) vendor contract, (6) vendor development/project monitoring and business management, (7) the test phase, (8) managing change, and (9) assessment.
Murthy, 2004	The author conceptually examines the impact of IS offshoring on IT firms. **What** He states that shorter development cycles, requirements volatility, and the need for constant developer-user interaction makes off-shore outsourcing challenging. The author mentions "that the type of product or service is critical in addressing the decision to outsource" (Murthy, 2004, p. 543). He argues that application maintenance is best suited for offshoring. Furthermore, the higher the intellectual (or proprietary) content, the higher the risk when outsourcing.

Source	Annotations
Niederman et al., 2006	The authors present a multi-level theoretical framework and research agenda for IT software development offshoring. **Why, What, How, Outcome** They argue that the phenomenon is worthy of investigation as an offshoring domain and suggest researching IS offshoring on the individual, organizational, and national level. The authors suggest areas for future research.
Pfannenstein & Tsai, 2004	The authors conceptually describe the status and effect of offshore IT outsourcing on the American IT industry thereby identifying advantages and disadvantages of IS offshoring. **Why** Advantages are reduced operating costs, improved flexibility, 24/7 operating hours, and reduced time to complete work. Typical disadvantages are new up-front costs regarding vendor selection, legal/contract issues, and the cost of work transition to the offshore vendor.
Pu Li & Kishore, 2006	The authors draw on transaction cost economics to formulate a framework for firms' decisions and choices about offshore outsourcing, domestic outsourcing and internal procurement. **How** They propose that offshore outsourcing is preferable when asset specificity is low. Asset specificity thereby includes specificity of sites, physical assets, human assets, business processes, and domain knowledge. Firms start favoring domestic outsourcing as asset specificity increases. Finally, firms would rather produce the work internally when asset specificity becomes very high.
Rao, 2004	The study conceptually describes factors that influence effective management of offshore IT sourcing relationships. **Outcome** These factors are related to telecommunications infrastructure, legal and security issues, time zone differences and the friction of distance, cultural issues, and language issues. The author subsequently postulates a set of best practices to address these factors.
Rottman & Lacity, 2006	The authors describe best practices that they believe will help organizations to use offshore labor more effectively. **Outcome** They emphasize the importance of detailed management of the offshoring relationship and describe 15 best practices for implementing offshoring.
Sakaguchi & Raghavan, 2003	The authors formulate an instrument to assess offshore vendor capabilities for an outsourced IS project. The instrument could be used in structural equation models. The authors make the constructs measurable and assess their reliability with a pilot sample using factor analysis. **How** Constructs include maturity of process and methodology, cost, quality of resources, speed of delivery, project management, business process expertise, certification, full-outsourcing capabilities, presence in the U.S., multivendor capabilities, near-shore capabilities, political climate, and technical capability.

Source	Annotations
Sayeed, 2006	Guided by transaction cost economics, the authors conduct interviews of executives at fifteen large to medium size companies to investigate the decision process leading to offshoring IT projects. **Why** Influencing factors are the client's core competency, the offshore vendor's local presence, virtual team management, employee turnover rate, negative publicity in the popular media, modularity of projects, and internal efficiencies achieved as a result of offshore sourcing. **What** Maintenance of legacy applications is a main offshore sourcing candidate. Additionally, modularity and scale of the projects are key characteristics for evaluating offshore viability. **How** Technical expertise of the vendor, vendor expertise relevant to the client's business, and collaboration experience of the vendor represent the main characteristics of reliable offshore partners.
Smith & McKeen, 2004	Based on a focus group of senior IT managers from different companies, the authors research the evolution of sourcing and how sourcing strategies are shifting. They look at emerging sourcing models and particularly at offshore/nearshore outsourcing. **Why** With respect to IS offshoring, the authors identify cost reduction as the main advantage. Transaction costs, reduced control, legal and political uncertainty, cultural differences, as well as social justice and public perception are the main risks associated with IT offshoring.
Tafti, 2005	The study describes risks associated with offshore IT outsourcing. **Why** As offshoring benefits, he mentions lower development costs, meeting the shortage of IT talent, higher quality, and foreign tax incentives. Associated risks in his framework are the outsourcing contract itself, privacy and security, the decision process, the outsourcing scope, diminished technical returns, hidden costs, and a loss of IT expertise.
Whitaker et al., 2005	Guided by transaction cost economics, the authors surveyed 244 publicly traded firms in the U.S. and examined what determines the adoption of onshore and offshore BPO. **Why** The find a positive association between a strong IT infrastructure and an increased likelihood of on- and offshore BPO. They also find evidence that business process knowledge is also associated with an increased likelihood of both onshore BPO and offshore BPO. Furthermore they discover that firms pursuing a cost cutting strategy and which have strong IT departments focusing on innovation have an increased likelihood of offshore BPO.
Whitaker et al., 2006	The authors analyze secondary data of 68 firms and business units from 1997 to 2004 to study the relationship between offshoring and customer satisfaction. **Outcome** They examine to what extent offshoring is associated with an increase in both perceived value and perceived quality. Based on secondary data, they test their model and find a positive relationship between offshoring and perceived value, perceived quality, and customer satisfaction.

62 References

References

Amoribieta, I., Bhaumik, K., Kanakamedala, K., & Parkhe, A. D. (2001). Programmers abroad: A primer on offshore software development. *McKinsey Quarterly*, (2), 128–139.

Apte, U. M., & Mason, R. O. (1995). Global disaggregation of information-intensive services. *Management Science, 41*(7), 1250–1262.

Apte, U. M., Sobol, M. G., Hanaoka, S., Shimada, T., Saarinen, T., & Salmela, T., et al. (1997). IS outsourcing practices in the USA, Japan, and Finland: A comparative study. *Journal of Information Technology, 12*(4), 289–304.

Balaji, S., Ahuja, M. K., & Ranganathan, C. (2006). Offshore software projects: Assessing the effect of knowledge transfer requirements and ISD capability. In *Proceedings of the 39th Annual Hawaii International Conference on System Sciences* (pp. 1–10). Hawaii.

Balaji, S., & Ranganathan, C. (2006). Exploring the key capabilities for offshore IS sourcing. In W. Haseman, D. W. Straub, & S. Klein (Eds.), *Proceedings of the 27th International Conference on Information Systems* (pp. 543–552). Milwaukee, WI.

Barney, J. (1991). Firm resources and sustained competitive advantage. *Journal of Management, 17*(1), 99–120.

Behrens, S. (2007). *Information systems outsourcing: Five essays on governance and success.* Aachen: Shaker.

Ben, E. R., & Claus, R. (2005). Offshoring in der deutschen IT Branche. *Informatik Spektrum, 28*(1), 34–39.

Benamati, J., & Rajkumar, T. (2002). The application development outsourcing decision: An application of the technology acceptance model. *Journal of Computer Information Systems*, (Summer), 35–43.

Bhat, J. M., Gupta, M., & Murthy, S. N. (2006). Overcoming requirements engineering challenges: Lessons from offshore outsourcing. *IEEE Software, 23*(5), 38–44.

Bhatnagar, S. C., & Madon, S. (1997). The Indian software industry: moving towards maturity. *Journal of Information Technology, 12*(4), 277–288.

BIHK (2002). *Offshore IT für den Mittelstand: Leitfaden zur Schaffung und Sicherung von Arbeitsplätzen durch offshore IT-Entwicklung im Rahmen der Internationalisierung des Mittelstandes in Bayern.* Retrieved March 07, 2007, from http://www.software-offensive-bayern.de/pdf/OffshoreIT.pdf.

Bitkom (2005). *Leitfaden Offshoring.* Retrieved March 07, 2007, from http://www.bitkom.org/files/documents/BITKOM_Leitfaden_Offshoring_31.01.2005.pdf.

Blau, P. (1964). *Exchange and power in social life.* New York: Wiley.

Boes, A., & Kämpf, T. (2006). Offshoring und die Notwendigkeit nachhaltiger Internationalisierungs-strategien. *Informatik Spektrum, 29*(4), 274–280.

Boes, A., Schwemmle, M., & Becker, E. (2004). *Herausforderung Offshoring: Internationalisierung und Auslagerung von IT-Dienstleistungen.* Düsseldorf: Hans-Böckler-Stiftung.

Boudreau, M.-C., Gefen, D., & Straub, D. W. (2001). Validation in information systems research: A state-of-the-art assessment. *MIS Quarterly, 25*(1), 1–16.

Brooks, N. (2006). Understanding IT outsourcing and its potential effects on IT workers and their environment. *Journal of Computer Information Systems, 46*(4), 46–53.

Carmel, E., & Agarwal, R. (2002). The maturation of offshore sourcing of information technology work. *MIS Quarterly Executive, 1*(2), 65–78.

Carmel, E., & Nicholson, B. (2005). Small firms and offshore software outsourcing: High transaction costs and their mitigation. *Journal of Global Information Management, 13*(3), 33–54.

Chandler, A. (1962). *Strategy and structure*. Cambridge MA: MIT Press.

Chandrasekhar, C., & Ghosh, J. (2006). IT-driven offshoring: The exaggerated "development opportunity". *Human Systems Management, 25*(2), 91–101.

Chua, A.-L., & Pan, S. (2006). Knowledge transfer in offshore insourcing. In W. Haseman, D. W. Straub, & S. Klein (Eds.), *Proceedings of the 27th International Conference on Information Systems* (pp. 1039–1054). Milwaukee, WI.

Coase, R. (1937). The nature of the firm. *Economica, 4*(November), 386–405.

Computerwoche (2006, January 06). Inder verlieren den Anschluss. *Computerwoche*,

Creswell, J. W. (1994). *Research design: Qualitative and quantitative approaches*. Thousand Oaks, CA: Sage.

Delmonte, A. J., & McCarthy, R. V. (2003). Offshore software development: Is the benefit worth the risk. In A. Hevner, P. Cheney, D. Galletta, & J. Ross (Eds.), *Proceedings of the 9th Americas Conference on Information Systems* (pp. 1607–1613). Tampa, FL.

Dhar, S., & Balakrishnan, B. (2006). Risks, benefits, and challenges in global IT outsourcing: Perspectives and practices. *Journal of Global Information Management, 14*(3), 39–69.

Dibbern, J., Goles, T., Hirschheim, R., & Jayatilaka, B. (2004). Information systems outsourcing: A survey and analysis of the literature. *The Data Base for Advances in Information Systems, 35*(4), 6–102.

Dibbern, J., Winkler, J., & Heinzl, A. (2006). *Offshoring of application services in the banking industry: A transaction cost analysis*, from Universität Mannheim: http://wifo1.bwl.uni-mannheim.de/fileadmin/files/publications/Working_Paper_16-2006.pdf.

Emerson, R. (1972). Exchange theory, part I: A psychological basis for social exchange and exchange theory, part II: Exchange relations and network structures. In J. Berger, M. Zelditch & B. Anderson (Eds.), *Sociological theories in progress*. New York: Houghton Mifflin.

Erber, G., & Sayed-Ahmed, A. (2005). Offshore outsourcing: A global shift in the present IT industry. *Intereconomics, 40*(2), 100–112.

Erickson, J. M., & Ranganathan, C. (2006). Project management capabilities: Key to application development offshore outsourcing. In *Proceedings of the 39th Annual Hawaii International Conference on System Sciences* (pp. 199–208). Hawaii.

Feeny, D., Lacity, M. C., & Willcocks, L. (2005). Taking the measure of outsourcing providers. *Sloan Management Review, 46*(3), 41–48.

Ferber, R. (2003). *Reduktion von Wörtern auf ihre Grundformen*. Retrieved March 02, 2007, from http://www.information-retrieval.de/irb/ir.part_1.chapter_3.section_2.subdiv1_1.html.

Fish, K. E., & Seydel, J. (2006). Where IT outsourcing is and where it is going: A study across functions and department sizes. *Journal of Computer Information Systems, 46*(3), 96–103.

Ganesh, J., & Moitra, D. (2004). An empirical examination of the determinants of successful transition management in offshore business process outsourcing. In *Proceedings of the 10th Americas Conference on Information Systems* (pp. 3493–3500). New York.

Gonzalez, R., Gasco, J., & Llopis, J. (2006). Information systems offshore outsourcing: A descriptive analysis. *Industrial Management & Data Systems, 106*(9), 1233–1248.

Gopal, A., Sivaramakrishnan, K., Krishnan, M., & Mukhopadhyay, T. (2003). Contracts in offshore software development: An empirical analysis. *Management Science, 49*(12), 1671–1683.

Graf, M., & Mudambi, S. M. (2005). The outsourcing of IT-enabled business processes: A conceptual model of the location decision. *Journal of International Management, 11*(2), 253–268.

Hawk, S., & McHenry, W. (2005). The maturation of the Russian offshore software industry. *Information Technology for Development, 11*(1), 31–57.

Henley, J. (2006). Outsourcing the provision of software and IT-enabled services to India. *International Studies of Management & Organization, 36*(4), 111–131.

Hirschheim, R., Loebbecke, C., Newman, M., & Valor, J. (2005). Offshoring and its implications for the information systems discipline. In D. Avison, D. Galletta, & J. I. DeGross (Eds.), *Proceedings of the 26th International Conference on Information Systems* (pp. 1003–1018). Las Vegas, NV.

Holmstroem, H., O'Conchuir, E., Agerfalk, P., & Fitzgerald, B. (2006). The irish bridge: A case study of the dual role in offshore sourcing relationships. In W. Haseman, D. W. Straub, & S. Klein (Eds.), *Proceedings of the 27th International Conference on Information Systems* (pp. 513–526). Milwaukee, WI.

Homans, G. (1961). *Social behavior: Its elementary forms.* New York: Harcourt Brace Jovanovich.

Jensen, M., & Meckling, W. (1976). Theory of the firm: Managerial behavior, agency costs and ownership structure. *Journal of Financial Economics, 3,* 305–360.

Kakumanu, P., & Portanova, A. (2006). Outsourcing: Its benefits, drawbacks and other related issues. *Journal of American Academy of Business, 9*(2), 1–7.

Kern, T. (1997). The gestalt of an information technology outsourcing relationship: An exploratory analysis. In *Proceedings of the 18th International Conference on Information Systems* (pp. n/a). Atlanta, GA.

Khan, N., Currie, W. L., & Weerakkody, V. (2003). Offshore information systems outsourcing: Strategies and scenarios. In Ciborra C.U., Mercurio R., de Marco M., Martinez M., & Carignani A. (Eds.), *Proceedings of the 11th European Conference on Information Systems* (pp. n/a). Naples, Italy.

Klepper, R. (1995). The management of partnering development in I/S outsourcing. *Journal of Information Technology, 10,* 249–258.

Kliem, R. (2004). Managing the risks of offshore IT development projects. *Information Systems Management, 21*(3), 22–27.

Krishna, S., Sahay, S., & Walsham, G. (2004). Managing cross-cultural issues In global software outsourcing. *Communications of the ACM, 47*(4), 62–66.

Kumar, K., & Willcocks, L. (1996). Offshore outsourcing: A country too far? In J. D. Coelho, J. Tawfik, W. König, H. Krcmar, R. O'Callaghan, & M. Sääksjarvi (Eds.), *Proceedings of the 4th European Conference on Information Systems* (pp. 1309–1325). Lisbon, Portugal.

Li, H., Wang, J., & Yang, D. (2006). Where to outsource: Using a hybrid multi-criteria decision aid method for selecting an offshore outsourcing location. In I. Garcia & R. Trejo (Eds.), *Proceedings of the 12th Americas Conference on Information Systems* (pp. 3131–3139).

Lowry, P. B., Romans, D., & Curtis, A. (2004). Global journal prestige and supporting disciplines: A scientometric study of information systems journals. *Journal of the Association for Information Systems, 5*(2), 29–77.

Marcus, M. (1983). Power, politics, and MIS implementation. *Communications of the Association for Computing Machinery, 26*(6), 430–444.

Mertens, P. (2005). *Die (Aus-)Wanderung der Softwareproduktion: Eine Zwischenbilanz.* Erlangen: Univ. Erlangen-Nürnberg Inst. für Informatik.

Meyer, T. (2006). *Nearshoring to Central and Eastern Europe: Offshoring to new shores.* Retrieved November 06, 2006, from http://www.dbresearch.de/PROD/DBR_INTERNET_DE-PROD/PROD0000000000201757.pdf.

Miles, R., & Snow, C. (1978). *Organizational strategy, structure and process.* New York: McGraw-Hill.

Mithas, S., & Whitaker, J. W. (2006). Effect of information intensity and physical presence need on the global disaggregation of services: Theory and empirical evidence. *SSRN eLibrary.* Retrieved December 06, 2006, from http://ssrn.com/paper=891519.

Moczadlo, R. (2002). *Chancen und Risiken des Offshore-Development: Empirische Analyse der Erfahrungen deutscher Unternehmen.* Retrieved November 07, 2006, from http://www.competence-site.de/offshore.nsf/8FB68EAB823EF285C1256D72005BBCD1/$File/studie_offshore_prof_moczadlo.pdf.

Murray, M. J., & Crandall, R. E. (2006). IT offshore outsourcing requires a project management approach. *SAM Advanced Management Journal, 71*(1), 4–12.

Murthy, S. (2004). The impact of global IT outsourcing on IT providers. *Communications of the AIS, 2004*(14), 543–557.

Nidumolu, S. G. S. (1993). Computing in India: An Asian elephant learning to dance. *Communications of the Association for Computing Machinery, 36*(June), 15–22.

Niederman, F., Kundu, S. K., & Salas, S. (2006). IT software development offshoring: A multi-level theoretical framework and research agenda. *Journal of Global Information Management, 14*(2), 52–74.

Orlikowski, W. J., & Baroudi, J. J. (1991). Studying information technology in organizations: Research approaches and assumptions. *Information Systems Research, 2*(1), 1–28.

Penrose, E. (1959). *The theory of the growth of the firm.* New York: Blackwell.

Pfannenstein, L. L., & Tsai, R. J. (2004). Offshore outsourcing: Current and future effects on american IT industry. *Information Systems Management, 21*(4), 72–80.

Pfeffer, J. (1981). *Power in organizations.* Marshfield, MA: Pitman.

Pfeffer, J. (1982). *Organizations and organization.* Boston, MA: Pitman.

Pfeffer, J., & Salancik, G. (1978). *The external control of organizations: A resource dependence perspective.* New York: Harper & Row.

Porter, M. (1985). *Competitive advantage: Creating and sustaining superior performance.* New York, London: Free Press.

Pries-Heje, J., Baskerville, R., & Hansen, G. I. (2005). Strategy models for enabling offshore outsourcing: Russian short-cycle-time software development. *Information Technology for Development, 11*(1), 5–30.

Pu Li, J., & Kishore, R. (2006). Offshore or not?: An transaction cost economics analysis. In I. Garcia & R. Trejo (Eds.), *Proceedings of the 12th Americas Conference on Information Systems* (pp. 3140–3147).

Quinn, J. (1980). *Strategies for change: Logical incrementalism.* Homewood, IL: Richard D. Irwin.

Rajkumar, T., & Mani, R. (2001). Offshore software development: The view from Indian suppliers. *Information Systems Management, 18*(2), 63–73.

Ramarapu, N., Parzinger, M. J., & Lado, A. A. (1997). Issues in foreign outsourcing. *Information Systems Management, 14*(2), 27–31.

Rao, M. T. (2004). Key issues for global IT sourcing: Country and individual factors. *Information Systems Management, 21*(3), 16–21.

Rottman, J. W., & Lacity, M. C. (2006). Proven practices for effectively offshoring IT work. *Sloan Management Review, 47*(3), 56–63.

Sakaguchi, T., & Raghavan, V. (2003). Metrics of vendor capabilities in offshore outsourcing of information technology functions: Measurement and analysis. In A. Hevner, P. Cheney, D. Galletta, & J. Ross (Eds.), *Proceedings of the 9th Americas Conference on Information Systems* (pp. 1644–1652). Tampa, FL.

Saunders, C. (2007). *MIS journal rankings.* Retrieved February 20, 2007, from http://www.isworld.org/csaunders/rankings.htm.

Sayeed, L. (2006). A qualitative investigation of IS offshore sourcing. In I. Garcia & R. Trejo (Eds.), *Proceedings of the 12th Americas Conference on Information Systems* (pp. 3199–3206).

Schaaf, J. (2004). *Offshoring: Globalisierungswelle erfasst Dienstleistungen.* Retrieved November 06, 2006, from http://www.dbresearch.de/PROD/DBR_INTERNET_DE-PROD/PROD0000000000178654.pdf.

Schaaf, J., & Weber, J. (2005). *Offshoring report 2005: Ready for take-off.* Retrieved November 06, 2006, from http://www.dbresearch.de/PROD/DBR_INTERNET_DE-PROD/PROD0000000000188986.pdf.

Scheibe, K. P., Mennecke, B. E., & Zobel, C. W. (2006). Creating offshore-ready IT professionals: A global perspective and strong collaborative skills are needed. *Journal of Labor Research, 27*(3), 275–290.

Simon, H. (1960). *The new science of management decision.* New York: Harper.

Smith, H. A., & McKeen, J. D. (2004). Developments in practice XIV: IT sourcing - how far can you go? *Communications of AIS, 2004*(13), 508–520.

Smith, M. A., Mitra, S., & Narasimhan, S. (1996). Offshore outsourcing of software development and maintenance: A framework for issues. *Information & Management, 31*(3), 165–175.

Söbbing, T. (2006). *Handbuch IT-Outsourcing: Recht, Strategie, Prozesse, IT, Steuern, samt Business Process* (3. Auflage). Heidelberg: C.F. Müller.

Tafti, M. H. A. (2005). Risks factors associated with offshore IT outsourcing. *Industrial Management & Data Systems, 105*(5), 549–560.

Thompson, R. (1967). *Organizations in action.* New York: McGraw-Hill.

Trampel, J. (2004). *Offshoring oder Nearshoring von IT-Dienstleistungen?: Eine transaktionskostentheoretische Analyse* (Nr. 39). Münster: IfG.

Venkatraman, N. (2004). Offshoring without guilt. *Sloan Management Review, 45*(3), 14–16.

Vessey, I., Ramesh, V., & Glass, R. L. (2002). Research in information systems: An empirical study of diversity in the discipline and its journals. *Journal of Management Information Systems, 19*(2), 129–174.

Whitaker, J. W., Krishnan, M., & Fornell, C. (2006). Does offshoring impact customer satisfaction? In I. Garcia & R. Trejo (Eds.), *Proceedings of the 12th Americas Conference on Information Systems* (pp. 3248–3256).

Whitaker, J. W., Mithas, S., & Krishnan, M. (2005). Antecedents of onshore and offshore business process outsourcing. In D. Avison, D. Galletta, & J. I. DeGross (Eds.), *Proceedings of the 26th International Conference on Information Systems* (pp. 85–96). Las Vegas, NV.

Wiener, M. (2006). *Critical success factors of offshore software development projects: The perspective of German-speaking companies.* Wiesbaden: Dt. Univ.-Verl.

William, A., Mayadas, F., & Vardi, M. Y. (2006). *Globalization and offshoring of software: A report of the ACM job migration task force.* Retrieved December 12, 2006, from Association for Computing Machinery: http://www.acm.org/globalizationreport.

Williamson, O. E. (1981). The economics of organization: The transaction cost approach. *American Journal of Sociology, 87*(3), 548–577.

Williamson, O. E. (1985). *The economic institutions of capitalism.* New York: Free Press.

Offshore Suitability: Criteria for Selecting IS Applications or Projects for Offshoring[*]

[*] A shorter version of this paper has been published in the Journal of Information Technology Management (JITM): Westner, M., & Strahringer, S. (2008). Evaluation criteria for selecting offshoring candidates: An analysis of practices in German businesses. *Journal of Information Technology Management, 19*(4), 16–34

Abstract: The identification of suitable applications or projects is a main initial step
in any software development or maintenance related IS offshoring arrangement. This paper identifies evaluation criteria for selecting candidates
for offshoring, analyzes the importance of the criteria, and relates them to
an organization's offshoring expertise. Based on a literature analysis and
interviews with 47 experts from 36 different German companies, we identified several evaluation criteria. The main findings are that in contrast to the
literature, *size*, *codification*, and *language* are perceived as important selection criteria by experts. These differences might be due to cultural differences. Additionally, *codification, business criticality, business specificity*,
and *complexity* seem to be less important in the case of organizations with
offshoring expertise.

Keywords: Offshoring, nearshoring, what to offshore, information systems, information
technology

Table of Contents

Figures and Tables.. 71

A   Introductions 72

    A.1 Background and Motivation... 72

    A.2 Research Questions 73

    A.3 Research Focus... 73

    A.4 Paper Structure 74

B   Theoretical Frame and Prior Research... 75

    B.1 Theory-Derived Selection Criteria 75

        B.1.1   Transaction Cost Economics... 75

        B.1.2   Resource-Based View 76

        B.1.3   Knowledge-Based View.. 77

        B.1.4   Cultural Aspects.. 77

    B.2 Prior Research on Selection Criteria 78

    B.3 IS Offshoring Expertise Frameworks.. 80

        B.3.1   Framework #1: Carmel & Agarwal (2002).. 81

        B.3.2   Framework #2: Gannon & Wilson (2007) 81

        B.3.3   Framework #3: Mirani (2006)... 82

        B.3.4   Framework #4: Rajkumar & Mani (2001) 82

        B.3.5   Framework Selection 83

C   Methodology 84

    C.1 Research Approach.. 84

    C.2 Research Design 84

D   Data Collection 86

    D.1 Expert Interviews and Case Samples 86

    D.2 Survey.. 88

E   Analysis... 90

E.1   Expert Panel.. 90

E.2   Selection Criteria 92

    E.2.1   Size... 93

    E.2.2   Codification.. 94

    E.2.3   Language 94

    E.2.4   Business Criticality 95

    E.2.5   Technology Availability... 95

    E.2.6   Business Specificity 96

    E.2.7   Complexity... 96

    E.2.8   Interaction 97

    E.2.9   Modularity.. 97

    E.2.10   Process Formalization 98

    E.2.11   Other Criteria 98

E.3   Comparison with Prior Research on Selection Criteria................................ 98

E.4   Comparison with Theoretical Views.. 100

E.5   Criteria Contribution to Offshoring Success 102

E.6   Criteria Importance in Relation to Offshoring Expertise 104

F   Conclusions.. 111

F.1   Main Contributions.. 111

F.2   Limitations... 112

F.3   Opportunities for Future Research 113

Appendix 114

References 134

Figures and Tables

Figure 2-1: Citation frequency of selection criteria (based on literature analysis, ordered
    by citation frequency) 80

Figure 2-2: Process of identifying experts and conducting interviews 87

Figure 2-3: Experts' positions, their offshoring expertise, and countries of expertise 91

Figure 2-4: Industry sectors of experts and of their companies 91

Figure 2-5: Citation frequency of selection criteria (based on expert interviews, ordered
    by citation frequency) 93

Figure 2-6: Comparison of selection criteria's citation frequencies between literature
    analysis and expert interviews 99

Figure 2-7: Perceived case success related to suitability of selection criteria...................... 103

Figure 2-8: Perceived criteria importance in relation to different offshoring expertise
    levels (all experts) 105

Figure 2-9: Perceived criteria importance in relation to different offshoring expertise
    levels (experts differentiated by levels of expertise)... 107

Table 2-1: Criteria for selecting application or project candidates for offshoring (based on
    literature analysis, alphabetical order) 79

Table 2-2: Overview offshoring expertise frameworks (alphabetical order) 83

Table 2-3: Applied two-stage research approach 84

Table 2-4: Operationalization of organization's offshoring expertise for survey 89

Table 2-5: Mapping of most frequently cited criteria to theoretical views 102

Table 2-6: Mann-Whitney test for criteria importance scores in relation to offshoring
    expertise 108

A Introductions

A.1 Background and Motivation

Information system (IS) offshoring describes the transfer of IS services to a service-providing entity in a near or far away country. This entity can be an internal subsidiary, a partially-owned unit, or an external service provider. The services themselves are partially or totally transferred. (Carmel & Agarwal, 2002; Hirschheim, Loebbecke, Newman, & Valor, 2005; Jahns, Hartmann, & Bals, 2006/7; Mirani, 2006; Niederman, Kundu, & Salas, 2006; Rajku-mar & Mani, 2001)

Labor cost differentials are the main reason contributing to IS offshoring's attractiveness from an economic perspective. Especially labor-intensive services, such as application development or maintenance, offer cost saving potentials when they are offshored (Apte, Sobol, Hanaoka, Shimada, Saarinen, & Salmela et al., 1997; Carmel & Agarwal, 2002; Erber & Sayed-Ahmed, 2005; Schaaf & Weber, 2005; William, Mayadas, & Vardi, 2006). Consequently, industry as-sociations, consulting firms and analysts perceive IS offshoring as a viable sourcing option for businesses (Amoribieta, Bhaumik, Kanakamedala, & Parkhe, 2001; Bitkom, 2005; Schaaf & Weber, 2005).

Current research in IS offshoring primarily focuses on the questions of *why* to offshore, i.e., the risks and benefits associated with IS offshoring, *how* to offshore, i.e., the structure or con-ceptualization of the offshoring implementation, and the *outcome* of IS offshoring, i.e., best practices, types of success, and the various determinants for success. Other aspects such as *what* to offshore, i.e., the applications and projects that are offshored, or *which* decision to make, i.e., the procedures, guidelines and stakeholders involved to evaluate the available op-tions, seem less researched. (Dibbern, Goles, Hirschheim, & Jayatilaka, 2004; Westner, 2007)

One of the first activities before engaging in an offshore sourcing arrangement is to identify applications and projects that might be in-scope for offshore delivery. Once identified, these offshoring candidates then represent the core objects in the subsequent implementation of IS offshoring. Accordingly, research and practice suggest that identifying suitable application or project candidates is a main step in pursuing an IS offshoring endeavor. Therefore, the aspect *what* to offshore represents a central facet of the IS offshoring phenomenon. (Aron & Singh, 2005; Bruhn, 2004; Chua & Pan, 2006; Dibbern, Winkler, & Heinzl, 2006; Kumar & Palvia, 2002; Mirani, 2007)

Nevertheless, existing research in IS offshoring only partially examines what applications and projects are offshored. There are studies that suggest appropriate selection criteria but they are often based on a low number of empirical observations and are conceptual in nature (Westner, 2007). Additionally, the selection criteria presented are often static and do not take into account increasing offshoring expertise which an offshore-consuming organization gradually accumulates. This deficit has already been observed in the literature (Ben & Claus, 2005; Hirschheim et al., 2005; Jahns et al., 2006/7; Kumar & Palvia, 2002; Mirani, 2006).

To the best of our knowledge, there seems to be a paucity of research that examines criteria for selecting applications or projects for offshoring based on a sound theoretical- and empirically-grounded view in relation to an organization's offshoring expertise. There is a particular lack of research for organizations in countries where English is not the native language.

A.2 Research Questions

Considering this research situation, the study at hand intends to examine the following research questions:

1. What are the evaluation criteria for selecting application or project candidates for offshoring?

2. How important are these criteria in relation to each other and for application or project success?

3. Does criteria importance change in relation to an organization's offshoring expertise, and if so, how?

The answers to these research questions are relevant to research as well as management practice. For research, our paper addresses the research deficit regarding the aspect *what* to offshore. It also adds to existing research because of its empirical foundation.

For management practice, our paper gives indications on how to evaluate and select application or project candidates before further proceeding with the offshoring process. This may, for example, be useful for the screening of companies' application or project portfolios in order to determine candidates that may serve as pilots for an IS offshoring arrangement or later on in order to extend the arrangement's scope.

A.3 Research Focus

We employ a managerial point of view for approaching our research objectives. In doing so, we focus our research along three dimensions *IS service*, *region*, and *arrangement*:

IS service: we focus on application development and maintenance as well as the projects arising therefrom. Application development covers the development of new applications but also reengineering or recoding of existing applications. Application maintenance is understood in a development-near fashion subsuming, for example, the functional extension of existing applications such as programming new modules. (Amoribieta et al., 2001; Apte et al., 1997; Fish & Seydel, 2006; Wiener, 2006; William et al., 2006)

Region: we focus on enterprises in Germany. First, the amount of research focusing on German businesses' IS offshoring practices is limited. Second, Germany seems to be a follower country regarding the adoption of IS offshoring due to language and cultural barriers. (Dibbern et al., 2006; Mertens, 2005; Moczadlo, 2002; Wiener, 2006; ZEW, 2007)

Arrangement: we focus on the offshore consuming side in an offshore arrangement, referred to as the *client organization*. This is usually a corporate IT department. We do not focus on offshore service-providing (OSP) organizations.

A.4 Paper Structure

Section B.1 employs different theoretical views to derive criteria for selecting applications or projects for offshoring. Subsequently, the literature analysis in Section B.2 identifies selection criteria on which previous studies elaborated. Section B.3 then illustrates four different frameworks that can be used to describe and operationalize an organization's level of offshore expertise. Section C outlines our applied research approach and research design. Section D describes the data collection procedures we performed. Finally, Section E shows the results of our analysis and interprets the findings. It provides descriptive data on our expert sample (Section E.1), describes the most frequently cited selection criteria in detail (Section E.2), and compares these findings to the results from the literature analysis (Section E.3) and our initial expectations drawn from the theoretical views (Section E.4). Section E.5 focuses more specifically on how criteria contribute to offshoring success by examining case samples. Subsequently, Section E.6 analyzes the survey results with respect to changes in the importance of various criteria in relation to an organization's offshoring expertise. Finally, Section F concludes the paper, shows its specific limitations, and suggests areas for future research.

B Theoretical Frame and Prior Research

B.1 Theory-Derived Selection Criteria

B.1.1 Transaction Cost Economics

Mainly shaped by Coase (1937), and Williamson (1985) transaction cost economics (TCE) argues "that making use of the market is costly and that economic efficiency can be achieved through comparative analysis of production costs and transaction costs" (Dibbern et al., 2004, p. 19). An organization's success depends on the efficient management of the occurring transactions. TCE assumes limited rationality and opportunistic behavior between two contracting parties. The type of governance for the entered contract thereby depends on the transaction's characteristics which influence its corresponding production and transaction costs. Three factors influence production and transaction costs: asset specificity, uncertainty, and frequency. (Apte, 1992; Dibbern et al., 2006; Kumar & Palvia, 2002)

TCE helps to examine make-or-buy decisions within organizations and has therefore been widely used in IS outsourcing research (Carmel & Nicholson, 2005; Dibbern et al., 2004). Regarding IS offshoring, it can particularly be applied to offshoring arrangements with external partners, i.e., so-called offshore outsourcing.

Offshoring as a sourcing arrangement potentially offers lower production cost. However, high transaction costs due to high asset specificity, high uncertainty and high frequency might offset this cost advantage.

Asset specificity can be high due to technical resource specificity (for example when the involved applications are unique and custom-built for the organization), human resource specificity (for example when the involved staff is organization-specifically trained), or technical procedure specificity (for example when the technical procedures and processes are unique to the organization). (Kim & Chung, 2003; Dibbern et al., 2006)

Uncertainty is influenced by technological uncertainty (for example when it is difficult to specify requirements), measurement uncertainty (for example when it is hard to evaluate and monitor the quality of the delivered services), and demand uncertainty (for example fluctuations in demand and requirements during the contract). (Apte, 1992; Kim & Chung, 2003)

Frequency increases transaction costs only when contracts are re-entered or re-negotiated every time. However, in IS outsourcing individual transactions are usually performed in the context of a frame contract, thus frequency seems not be an important factor driving transaction costs (Apte, 1992; Kim & Chung, 2003) and we therefore excluded it from further analysis.

Applied to the offshoring of applications or projects, the question is how asset specificity and uncertainty impact transaction costs and thus influence whether applications or projects are offshored. Asset specificity is expected to be low for applications or projects which involve general business knowledge, common technology, or which are highly standardized with respect to the corresponding development and maintenance processes. These applications and projects might therefore have lower transaction costs and could be initially offshored. Regarding uncertainty, less complex application or projects with high stability and a high degree of codification, in terms of documentation and specification, decrease transaction costs and are anticipated to be offshored first.

However, during the course of an offshore sourcing arrangement, the perceived degree of asset specificity and uncertainty might change depending on the accumulated expertise. Therefore, organizations with longer lasting sourcing arrangements might offshore applications and projects which were initially considered unsuitable due to high asset specificity and high uncertainty.

B.1.2   Resource-Based View

Mainly shaped by Barney (1991), and Penrose (1959) the resource-based view (RBV) argues that firms are collections of resources and capabilities. Short-term competitive advantage and long-term superior performance result from the heterogeneity and immobility of these resources between different firms. (Dibbern et al., 2004; Wade & Hulland, 2004)

Resources, in terms of IS, can be processes as well as assets, e.g., technical IS skills, managerial IS skills, or technology such as applications or an application portfolio. Resources contribute to a firm's competitive advantage if they are valuable, rare, and the firm can exploit them appropriately. Simultaneously, they also have to be imperfectly imitable, non-substitutable, and imperfectly mobile. (Barney, 1991; Mata, Fuerst, & Barney, 1995; Wade & Hulland, 2004)

The RBV can be applied to internal IS offshoring as well as external offshoring to the effect that the offshored resources, i.e., applications or projects, should not threaten a firm's competitive position. This indicates that non-strategic applications, with no valuable intellectual property, and which are uncritical for business operations could be offshored at the beginning of an offshore arrangement.

Similar to TCE, the assessment and evaluation should be dynamic, i.e., a resource's perceived strategic importance or business criticality might change over time. Reasons might be a more trustful sourcing relationship or a higher confidence in service delivery by the offshore service-providing organization.

B.1.3   Knowledge-Based View

Formed by Polanyi (1983), and Nonaka & Takeuchi (1995) the knowledge based view (KBV) states that organizations possess knowledge and that this knowledge needs to be managed properly to be successful. Two types of knowledge can be distinguished. Knowledge that can be articulated and exchanged in formal ways, such as documents or specifications, is referred to as explicit knowledge. Opposed to that, there is tacit knowledge which is difficult to articulate and to share because it is embedded in actions, routines, commitment, and involvement in a specific organizational context. Thus, transfer or diffusion of tacit knowledge requires higher effort and is more costly in comparison to explicit knowledge. (Chua & Pan, 2006; Dibbern et al., 2004; Maskell, Pedersen, Petersen, & Dick-Nielsen, 2007)

With respect to IS, software development and maintenance activities represent knowledge-intensive work. As a product of this work, software applications can be perceived as knowledge assets. Knowledge pertinent to applications can either be explicit, such as software documentation, technical specification, or standardized development processes, but it can also be tacit, such as practices like norms of communication or non-specified processes and activities. (Chua & Pan, 2006; Nicholson & Sahay, 2004)

In an offshore sourcing arrangement, knowledge inherent to an application but also knowledge concerning the affected business and IS development processes need to be transferred. Since tacit knowledge is harder to transfer in terms of time and effort, we can anticipate that initially, applications and projects with a high share of explicit knowledge are offshored. These might, for example, be applications with a high degree of documentation or specification, a low level of business-specificity in terms of proprietary industry knowledge required for developing or maintaining the application, and structured IS development activities.

However, since successful knowledge transfer also depends on the absorptive capacity of the knowledge receiving entity – in this case the offshore service-providing entity – more tacit knowledge is disseminated among the two parties during the offshore sourcing arrangement. Thus, it might become possible to offshore applications and projects with a higher degree of tacit knowledge.

B.1.4   Cultural Aspects

The offshore provision of IS services happens in an international context. Therefore, cultural aspects are pertinent to IS offshoring. One of the most important constructs that can be used to grasp and describe differences between members of different nations is the concept by Hofstede (1980). He differentiates among nations' characteristics in four dimensions: individualism, power distance, uncertainty avoidance, and masculinity. These dimensions have to be considered when collaborating in an intercultural environment.

Accordingly, several studies have highlighted the impact of cultural aspects on IS offshoring arrangements and perceive it as a major issue that requires management attention, for example, regarding communication styles, language and time differences, or criticism behavior. (Gurung & Prater, 2006; Heeks, Krishna, Nicholsen, & Sahay, 2001; Winkler, Dibbern, & Heinzl, 2006)

This might indicate that initially applications and projects are selected for offshoring where potential issues arising from cultural differences can be minimized. This can only be achieved if there is little need for interaction and communication, which would be the case for applications or projects with low complexity, low end-user interaction requirements, and high stability in runtime or requirements. Additionally, if the operating language of an application or project is English, the potential language gap between native German-speaking staff, most of whom are proficient in English, and English-speaking offshore staff is narrowed.

During the course of an offshore arrangement, the mutual cultural competence of both offshoring parties might increase. Thus, more complex, less stable applications and projects with higher interaction needs can be offshored once both partners accumulate greater offshoring expertise.

B.2 Prior Research on Selection Criteria

Initially, we conducted a database-driven literature search (on databases ProQuest, Ebsco's Business Search Premier, AIS and IEEE digital libraries, and conference proceedings) to identify research in IS offshoring that examines criteria for selecting applications or projects for offshoring. We analyzed the resulting studies and manually coded the criteria. We then performed a meaningful aggregation of the individual results according to common criteria.

In total, we identified 36 relevant studies addressing the aspect of offshore application or project selection criteria. Twenty-seven or 75% of these studies are of an academic nature, the remaining 9 or 25% are practitioner contributions. Regarding their research approach, 26 or 72% are non-empirical, the other 10 or 28% employ an empirical research approach. This supports our perception of a considerable research gap in empirically grounded research (c.f. Section A.1, p. 72).

As a final result of our literature analysis, we identified 17 common selection criteria across all studies. Interestingly, no study considered an organization's offshoring expertise and how it might impact criteria importance. Table 2-1 provides an overview on these criteria (first column), describes them (second column), and indicates their impact of applications' or projects' suitability for offshore delivery as perceived by these studies (third column).

Criteria	Description	Perceived suitability for offshoring high, if...
Business criticality	Importance for fulfilling daily business operations	...business criticality low
Business specificity	Inherent internal business process knowledge, proprietary industry knowledge or high customization	...business specificity low
Codification	Degree of documentation or specification	...codification high
Complexity	Scope, number and size of interfaces, number of users and sites involved or characteristics of inputs and outputs	...complexity low
Cost level	Cost budget in comparison to other applications	...cost level high
Intellectual property	Inherent intellectual property	...intellectual property low
Interaction	Required personal contact with customer during development and maintenance	...interaction requirements low
Labor intensity	Labor effort in relation to total effort	...labor intensity high
Lifespan	Expected remaining lifespan of application or project	...remaining lifespan long enough to justify transition costs
Modularity	Separability of applications or projects	...modularity high
Process formalization	Development or maintenance activities' degree of specification and structure	...process formalization high
Proximity	Required proximity during development and maintenance, e.g., due to reliance on local knowledge or activities that can only be performed locally	...proximity requirements low
Regulation	Exposure to external regulatory constraints	...regulation low
Size	Scope and duration	...minimum size and duration achieved
Stability	Application stability, stability of requirements	...stability high
Strategic importance	Importance in terms of helping to implement a company's core competency and differentiate itself in the marketplace	...strategic importance low
Technology availability	Technology and the availability of knowledgeable resources in the marketplace	...technology availability high

**Table 2-1: Criteria for selecting application or project candidates for offshoring
(based on literature analysis, alphabetical order)**

Analyzing the citation frequency of all 17 criteria, it is noticeable that only seven criteria are cited more frequently than the citation frequency mean of 21% (or 7.5 citations). These are, in order of citation frequency, *interaction, business criticality, complexity, business specificity, size, stability,* and *strategic importance.* Especially *interaction,* describing the degree of required personal contact during development and maintenance, is cited by 17 or 47% of all analyzed studies. Figure 2-1 illustrates these results. Each bar represents one criterion as mentioned in Table 2-1. The bar heights show the corresponding citation frequencies in percentage points. Criteria that are mentioned more frequently than the citation frequency mean of 21% are highlighted in gray. The Appendix (p. 114) lists in detail which studies mention which criterion.

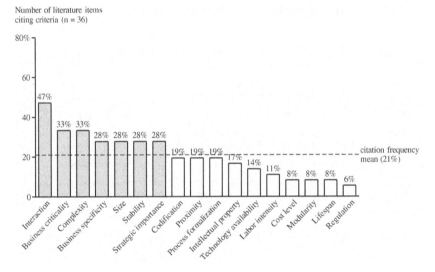

Figure 2-1: Citation frequency of selection criteria
(based on literature analysis, ordered by citation frequency)

B.3 IS Offshoring Expertise Frameworks

Section B.1 (p. 75) highlighted the dynamic aspect of the selection criteria's importance in relation to an organization's offshoring expertise. To understand the construct offshoring expertise, the following subsections provide an overview of frameworks that conceptualize organizations' expertise with IS offshoring. In alphabetical order by author, we describe the frameworks and briefly evaluate their applicability to our study's research objective.

B.3.1 Framework #1: Carmel & Agarwal (2002)

Carmel & Agarwal (2002) analyze the sourcing behavior of offshore-consuming organizations. Based on 13 case studies at companies in the U.S., the authors identify four stages of maturation depending on the consumer's offshoring expertise.

Companies in the first stage are referred to as *Offshore Bystanders*. They perform only domestic sourcing. The second stage are so-called *Offshore Experimenters*. These organizations perform offshoring for cost reduction reasons on an ad hoc, single project basis. They do not coordinate or manage their offshore suppliers and have no coherent offshore sourcing strategy. This situation changes at stage three, *Proactive Cost Focus*. At this stage, offshore sourcing becomes a viable, acceptable strategy. Cost reduction is still the main purpose for offshoring but an additional objective is to free capacity for the IS department so that it can focus on more interesting and higher value-added tasks. Typically offshored tasks at stage three are characterized as non-core and structured, such as system maintenance, quality assurance, software testing, or application ports. Finally, *Proactive Strategic Focus* represents stage four. At this stage, offshore consumers perceive offshore sourcing as an important and attractive strategy for achieving strategic objectives such as developing new products or accessing new markets. Offshore consumers at this stage engage in strong partnerships with selected offshore suppliers.

Carmel & Agarwals' framework has a strong empirical foundation in comparison to the other ones described below. The framework concentrates on the offshore consumer perspective, which fits better with the research objective of our paper. However, the authors stay on a macro level and describe the offshored services' characteristics only in an abstract way. Finally, their focus on the U.S. limits the transferability of findings to other cultural settings.

B.3.2 Framework #2: Gannon & Wilson (2007)

Gannon & Wilson (2007) propose a preliminary maturity framework for offshore IS suppliers based on desk research. The authors differentiate four maturity stages depending on suppliers' offshoring expertise and their delivery capabilities.

Suppliers in the first stage are so-called *Domestic Suppliers* with domestic sourcing only and no offshore capability. Suppliers in the second stage are *Tactical Offshore Suppliers* that have started to experiment with offshoring. They have an ad hoc experience in offshore development and a small or internally-focused offshore capability. *Niche Offshore Suppliers* represent the third stage. They have established onshore and offshore capabilities but are still focused on a special industry or geographic region. Finally, stage four represents *Multi-Shore Suppliers* with large onshore and offshore capabilities and a broad coverage of industries and regions.

The suggested framework is well embedded in existing research. However, it is conceptual with no empirical evidence. Furthermore, in the context of this study, the framework only focuses on the offshore supplier side and does not address specific application or project selection criteria.

B.3.3   Framework #3: Mirani (2006)

Mirani (2006) presents an evolutionary framework for consumer-supplier relationships in the context of offshore application development. He supports his framework by a case study and distinguishes three stages depending on the relationship's age.

The first relationship stage is called *Contracts*. At this stage, offshoring is primarily conducted for cost reduction and therefore transaction-oriented, price-based contracts dominate. Typically, small applications of low complexity with complete specification and structured development processes are offshored. *Networks* represent the second maturity stage. At this stage the consumer puts more trust in the supplier and switches to a loose, informal and network-like relationship. The offshored applications become gradually more complex. The third and last stage is named *Hierarchies*. Applications become even more complex and business critical. For that reason the offshore consumer changes to a more hierarchical and command-based relationship by partial or full ownership of the supplier organization.

The study's originality stems from its focus on the consumer-supplier relationship itself instead of focusing on only one of the parties. Nevertheless, the framework is based on merely one case, which limits its generalizability beyond that specific context. Additionally, it is also questionable whether consumers are always willing and able to establish an ownership stake in their supplier (c.f. Carmel & Agarwal, 2002). Finally, the author does not analyze application or project selection criteria in detail.

B.3.4   Framework #4: Rajkumar & Mani (2001)

Rajkumar & Mani (2001) concentrate on IS offshore suppliers' relationships with the service consumers in the context of software development. They identify four stages of relationship growth based on the relationship age.

The first stage is called *Initiate*, which represents the entry level for offshore consumers. Small, pilot projects being offshored characterize this stage. The projects have a high onshore and onsite share and are usually obtained through a formal bidding process. The second stage is described as *Confidence Building Projects*. Projects at this stage exhibit a significant mix of offshore with onshore development. The project size increases simultaneously. The third stage is named *Large Projects*. The supplier now implements large projects with an even higher share of offshore development capacity. Finally, at the fourth stage *Virtual Software Arm*, the supplier is recognized as a key partner in fulfilling the client's application development needs.

Although the authors claim their own practical experience, their framework is conceptual and not based on empirical evidence. As opposed to this paper's approach, the authors do not focus on the offshore consumer but on the supplier's skills and delivery capabilities. Furthermore, they do not elaborate on selection criteria, but rather emphasize business model aspects.

B.3.5 Framework Selection

We selected Carmel & Agarwal's framework to capture and operationalize the construct offshoring expertise for the purposes of our study. We based our selection on two criteria (c.f. Table 2-2). The first evaluation criterion refers to the frameworks' research foci and their alignment with our research objective (second column). Only Carmel & Agarwal's framework focuses on offshore consuming organizations and is thus more applicable to our study's research objective. The second evaluation criterion refers to the empirical foundation of the proposed frameworks (third column). Again, Carmel & Agarwal's framework with its underlying 13 cases shows the highest degree of empirical support and we therefore selected it as the most applicable to our study's research objective.

Expertise framework	Research focus	Empirical evidence
Carmel & Agarwal, 2002	Client	13 cases (U.S.)
Gannon & Wilson, 2007	Supplier	None
Mirani, 2006	Client-supplier	1 case (U.S.)
Rajkumar & Mani, 2001	Supplier	None

Table 2-2: Overview offshoring expertise frameworks (alphabetical order)

C   Methodology

C.1 Research Approach

The study at hand is empirical and pursues an exploratory-interpretive research approach, with offshored applications or projects as the unit of analysis. An exploratory-interpretive approach is suitable because it allows methods and data to define the nature of a phenomenon's relationships. It specifies these relationships only in the most general form. Furthermore, it intends to examine a research area by accessing participants' perceptions of the phenomenon (Boudreau, Gefen, & Straub, 2001; Orlikowski & Baroudi, 1991).

Within this setting, our research approach is of a qualitative and quantitative nature (Creswell, 1994). It is qualitative because we performed expert interviews and sampled several case studies which we analyzed using structured content analysis to identify selection criteria and their respective importance (Mayring, 2002). However, it is also quantitative because we sent a brief survey to all interviewed experts and analyzed the results statistically. This quantitative analysis examines whether the perceived criteria importance changes in relation to an organization's offshoring expertise.

C.2 Research Design

We separated our research into two phases. Research phase one, addressing research questions one and two (c.f. Section A.2, p. 73), was conducted from October 2007 to March 2008. Research phase two, addressing research question three, was conducted from May to July 2008. Table 2-3 illustrates the two phases of our research approach (first and second column), the time period when they were conducted (first row), the research questions they addressed (second row), the data collection methods applied (third row), the analysis procedures we carried out (fourth row), and the sections covering the research phases (fifth row). The following paragraphs describe each research phase in detail.

	Research phase 1	Research phase 2
Time period:	October 2007 – March 2008	May 2008 – July 2008
Addressed research questions:	Questions 1 and 2	Question 3
Data collection methods:	Literature search Expert interview	Survey
Data analysis methods:	Literature analysis Structured content analysis	Statistical analysis
Covered in sections:	D.1 (p. 86) E.1 to E.5 (pp. 90-102)	D.2 (p. 88) E.6 (p. 96)

Table 2-3: Applied two-stage research approach

In research phase one, we first performed a database-driven literature analysis in order to gain an initial understanding of evaluation criteria that can be used to select applications or projects for offshoring (c.f. Section B.2, p. 78). Based on this preliminary understanding we interviewed experts at different German corporations.

In the interviews, we inquired on an abstract level about potential evaluation criteria for selecting applications or projects for offshoring. Afterwards we let the experts describe one or more brief real-live cases of offshored applications or projects from their professional experience. In these concise cases, the experts illustrated the usage of evaluation criteria and whether the undertaking was perceived as successful.

In this way we collected a series of small case studies with offshored applications or projects being the unit of analysis via the expert interviews. The nature of our research question, and its implied multiple case-study approach, results in a rather large number of cases which increase the empirical foundation of our research. Insights arising from just one case or a limited number of cases have a higher likelihood of bias and of applying only to these specific cases or very similar ones. In contrast to that, similar converging conclusions that evolve from multiple independent cases imply similar causes and have a higher explanatory power and generalizability. Furthermore, a case study research design fits into our exploratory-interpretive research type with an empirical component. Case studies are most suitable to explore and understand a phenomenon where research and theory are at a formative stage. (Benbasat, Goldstein, & Mead, 1987; Creswell, 1994; Yin, 1996)

We wanted to avoid biasing the experts' statements. Therefore, we did not distribute or mention the results of the literature analysis to them and used pre-formulated questions during the interviews. All interviews and sampled cases were tape-recorded, transcribed and anonymized afterwards. The interview transcripts consist of 156,000 words and we analyzed them hermeneutically using the software NVivo 8. Interview results were contrasted against findings from literature.

In research phase two we distributed the results from phase one's content analysis to the interviewed experts and clarified any questions raised by them. Then, we invited the experts to participate in an online survey. In this survey we listed the most frequently cited evaluation criteria from the interviews and asked the experts to assign a score (7-point likert-scale) to each criterion based on its perceived importance for selecting suitable application or project candidates for offshoring. By doing so we wanted to quantify and thereby add more insight to the previous qualitative findings. Afterwards we tested for statistically significant differences between assigned scores for organizations with no to low offshoring expertise and assigned scores for organizations with medium to high offshoring expertise. Since data was not normally distributed, we used the non-parametric Mann-Whitney test as implemented by statistic software package SPSS 12.

D Data Collection

D.1 Expert Interviews and Case Samples

We focused on Germany's Top 100 companies (ranked by revenue), Top 20 banks (ranked by balance sheet total), Top 20 insurance companies (ranked by insurance premiums) and Top 20 IT firms (ranked by revenue) to find potential interview partners. We used publicly available ranking lists to identify these firms. The rankings were published by the newspaper Süddeutsche Zeitung and the consulting company Lünendonk. The Appendix contains the rankings used for our study (c.f. pp. 115-120). Using these company names as keywords we conducted a search on Germany's most popular business social network XING (www.xing.com, over five million members as stated by the company) to identify experts. We further refined the search by using the search term "offshor* OR nearshor* OR off-shor* OR near-shor*" in XING's "I offer" search-field. "*" ensures that also variations of the term are found such as offshoring or offshore.

The search was conducted from November 26-30, 2007. Figure 2-2 illustrates how many experts we contacted and how many interviews we could actually conduct. Our search yielded 246 experts (first bar). We contacted them using the XING-mail-function with a standard cover letter (c.f. Appendix, p. 121). One hundred eighty-seven people did not respond (second bar). Fifteen rejected our interview request (third bar). During the interview phase (November 30, 2007 to February 5, 2008) we interviewed 44 experts (fourth bar) who referred us to seven additional experts (fifth bar) not previously identified via XING. In the end, we conducted 51 interviews (sixth bar) of which 47 had content that was relevant (seventh and eighth bar), i.e., complied with our research focus regarding IS service, region, and arrangement. Thus, we achieved a 19% response rate based on our initial search result of 246 experts.

No. of experts/interviews

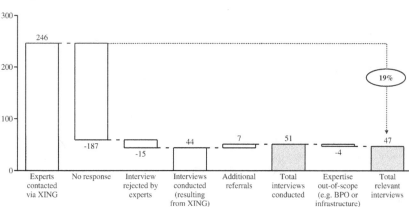

Figure 2-2: Process of identifying experts and conducting interviews

We carried out all interviews via telephone in German. The interviews lasted on average 45 minutes. They consisted of three sections, which were approximately a five minute introduction, a 30 minute question part, and a final 10 minute feedback part. The interviews were semi-structured with open questions. We opted for semi-structured interviews with open questions for two reasons. First, this method enhances comparability of results between different interviews because the questions themselves are always identical and avoids potential biases from different formulations of questions. Second, open-ended interviews do not restrict the interview partners' responses. By allowing new patterns and insights to emerge spontaneously, this method elicits richer and more insightful answers. A test-run of the questions before the actual interviews showed that the questions were understandable and unambiguous.

The interview's beginning served to introduce us to the interview partner and illustrate the purpose of our research. In the question part, we inquired about the expert's years of personal expertise in IS offshoring. We then asked for evaluation criteria when selecting applications or projects for offshoring. This question was positioned on an abstract level and not related to a specific real-life case or example experienced by the expert.

Afterwards we let the experts describe one or more brief cases from their current or past professional experience. During these case descriptions we noted whether the specific application or project was perceived to be successful, and what evaluation criteria were applied. In the feedback part of the interview, we provided the experts with preliminary results from the interviews. The Appendix (p. 123) contains the interview guideline. The guideline is in German as we conducted all interviews in German.

D.2 Survey

Thirty-five or 74% of the participating 47 experts completed the survey by June 2008 (nine did not respond and three showed no interest in participation). The 35 actual respondents had managerial positions, personal offshoring expertise, and industry sectors comparable to those in our original sample (c.f. Figure 2-3, p. 91). The Appendix (p. 122) graphically illustrates the characteristics of all interviewed experts in comparison to the subset of experts who answered the survey.

In the survey we asked the experts to put themselves in the position of an external third party which consults an organization on how to apply evaluation criteria to the selection of applications or projects for offshoring. For each criterion from phase one's interview round with above average citation frequency, the experts were requested to assign a score representing a criterion's perceived importance for identifying suitable candidates for offshoring delivery. The score was based on a 7-point likert-scale with value 1 ("unimportant") to value 7 ("very important").

The survey thereby consisted of two questions. The first question assumed an organization with no to low offshoring expertise. The second question assumed an organization with medium to high offshoring expertise. The levels of offshoring expertise were derived and operationalized based on the existing taxonomy proposed by Carmel & Agarwal (2002). However, to limit the survey's complexity and thus increase the experts' willingness to complete it, we combined Carmel & Agarwal's initially suggested four phases to two expertise levels. By doing so, we could decrease the amount of rating items from 40 to 20 and increase discriminatory power between the two levels. Our *no to low* expertise level corresponded to Carmel & Agarwal's *Offshore Bystander* and *Offshore Experimenter*. Our *medium to high* expertise level corresponded to Carmel & Agarwal's *Proactive Cost Focus* and *Proactive Strategic Focus*. Table 2-4 shows Carmel & Agarwal's maturity stages (first column), how we related them to our applied two expertise levels (second column), and how we operationalized these expertise levels in the survey (third column). The operationalization is in German since we wanted to be sure that experts understood the expertise levels correctly and that there were no misunderstandings due to language issues.

Maturity stage (c.f. Carmel & Agarwal, 2002)	Expertise level as applied in survey	Operationalization (as used in the survey, thus in German)
(1) Offshore Bystander (2) Offshore Experimenter	No to low	„Wenig" Erfahrung würde auf ein Unternehmen zutreffen, das einen Ad-hoc Ansatz für das IT Offshoring verfolgt, in dem es wenig Koordination und Wissensaustausch zu IT Offshoring zwischen Abteilungen und noch keine kohärente IT Offshoring Sourcing Strategie bzw. Richtlinie gibt. Kostenreduktion wäre in einem solchen Unternehmen der Haupttreiber für IT Offshoring.
(3) Proactive Cost Focus (4) Proactive Strategic Focus	Medium to high	„Mittlere" Erfahrung würde auf eine Organisation zutreffen, in der es schon erste organisatorische Strukturen gibt, um die IT Offshore-Aktivitäten zu managen und bspw. Anreize etabliert sind, damit IT Offshoring genutzt wird. Neben der Kostenreduktion ist ein weiterer Treiber für IT Offshoring, dass sich die IT Abteilung auf höherwertigere Aufgaben konzentrieren kann. „Viel" Erfahrung würde auf eine Organisation zutreffen, in der IT Offshoring integraler Bestandteil der Sourcing-Strategie ist, Kernaktivitäten der Firma offgeshored werden und eine strategische Partnerschaft mit Off-/Nearshore Service Providern besteht.

Table 2-4: Operationalization of organization's offshoring expertise for survey

A test run of the survey showed that all experts unambiguously understood our questions. However, the group of experts with less personal offshoring expertise (i.e., one to three years of expertise) seemed to experience difficulties with rating the importance of criteria when assuming an organization with medium to high offshoring expertise. That was because of the inherent structural expertise gap (it is difficult to put oneself in the position of an organization with a high expertise level when one's personal expertise level is low). We took account of this issue and later analyzed the survey scores segmented by experts' personal offshoring expertise (c.f. Section E.6, p. 104). The complete survey with its two parts can be found in the Appendix (pp. 126-129).

E Analysis

E.1 Expert Panel

As a result of our mailings, we conducted relevant interviews with 47 experts (c.f. Section D.1, p. 86). Thirty-eight or 81% of these experts hold managerial positions (i.e., managers, senior managers, or executives) in the companies they work for. Senior managers (19 or 40%) form the largest group among the experts, followed by managers (16 or 34%), employees (9 or 19%), and executives (3 or 6%).

Twenty-six or 55% of the experts have one to three years of personal expertise in the field of IS offshoring, 12 or 28% four to five years expertise, 8 or 17% more than five years of expertise, and 1 expert or 2% did not state his expertise in terms of years.

We also asked for the country or countries in which they have gathered their expertise (multiple answers were possible). Twenty-eight experts mention India as the country where they have accumulated their IS offshoring expertise. Other countries mentioned were the Czech Republic (4 experts), Armenia, Hungary, Malaysia, the Philippines, Poland, Romania, and Russia (each with 2 experts) as well as Latvia, Moldavia, Slovakia, and Ukraine (each with 1 expert).

Figure 2-3 illustrates the positions the interviewed experts hold (first column), their offshoring expertise in number of years (second column), and the countries with which they gathered their IS offshoring expertise (third and fourth column). The bars in the figure are scaled to 100% to illustrate the relative distribution of the expert sample's characteristics. The Appendix (p. 124) contains a disguised list showing all interviewed experts and the companies they work for.

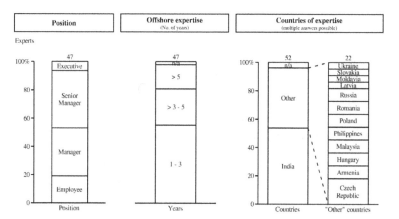

Figure 2-3: Experts' positions, their offshoring expertise, and countries of expertise

The 47 interviewed experts work for 36 different German companies. Thirteen experts or 28% work in the IT sector, 11 or 23% work in financial services, 6 or 13% work in the automotive industry, and 5 or 11% in the high tech industry. The remaining 12 experts work in other sectors such as transportation (3 experts), tourism (3 experts), logistics (2 experts), industrial goods (2 experts), utilities (1 expert), or telecommunications (1 expert). The left bar in Figure 2-4 illustrates the industry sectors in which the experts work. The right bar in Figure 2-4 shows how this corresponds to the industry sectors of the different companies where they are employed.

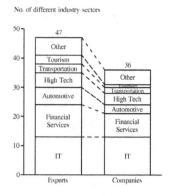

Figure 2-4: Industry sectors of experts and of their companies

Figure 2-3 and Figure 2-4 together show that we covered a diverse variety of experts' positions and personal expertise as well as different industry sectors in our interview sample. This is in line with our objective to ground our research on a broader empirical basis than previous studies.

E.2 Selection Criteria

We asked the experts to describe potential selection criteria for selecting applications or projects as candidates for offshore delivery. When they mentioned these criteria, we also asked for a short explanation of why they thought this specific criterion is important. We aggregated the criteria mentioned by analyzing the content in the software NVivo. The starting point for aggregation was our initial categorization resulting from the literature review. This initial understanding was a useful foundation for coding the experts' answers. We could code almost all their responses within this taxonomy. Only one criterion was totally new, which was *language*. Also one criterion, *labor intensity*, was not mentioned by the experts but exists in the literature. In Section E.3 (p. 98) we discuss this specific finding in greater detail.

None of the experts had problems in naming and describing evaluation criteria. During the interviews the mentioned criteria converged to a set, with ten criteria being mentioned more frequently than the citation frequency mean of 26% or 12 of all experts.

The three most frequently cited criteria were *size* (27 or 57% of all experts), followed by *codification* (22 or 47%), and *language* (22 or 47%). Eighteen experts or 38% mentioned *business criticality* and 17 or 36% *technology availability*. *Business specificity*, *complexity*, and *interaction* were each cited by 16 experts or 34%. Finally, 15 experts or 32% mentioned *modularity*, and 12 or 26% mentioned *process formalization* as evaluation criteria. Figure 2-5 illustrates the citation frequency of the criteria showing the criteria as bars and the bar height indicating their citation frequency. The dotted line marks the threshold of more than 26% of all experts (citation frequency mean). The criteria mentioned by more than 26% of all experts are highlighted in gray. The remaining criteria are white. The clear distinction between the two groups of criteria is remarkable. It seems that the ten most frequently cited criteria are perceived by experts as more important than the remaining ones.

The following subsections describe these ten most frequently cited evaluation criteria as perceived by our expert panel, together with representative quotes in order of their citation frequency.

No. of experts mentioning characteristic (n = 47)

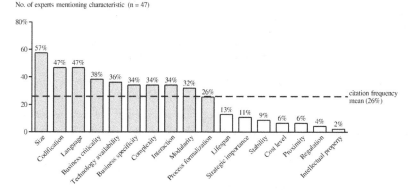

Figure 2-5: Citation frequency of selection criteria
(based on expert interviews, ordered by citation frequency)

E.2.1 Size

Size refers to the scope and duration of an application or a project. Experts mentioned that applications or projects must have a certain significant size and duration to be suitable for off-shore delivery.

The reason is that offshoring arrangements come with additional overhead in comparison to domestic sourcing arrangements. This overhead stems, for example, from communication, travel, or distant collaboration. Cost savings achieved from offshoring can only compensate for these additional overhead efforts if applications or projects have enough volume. Another reason cited is the fluctuation of staff in offshore countries. Fluctuation among offshore staff is usually high. Thus, delivery from the offshore country might be at risk if the application or project is too small and many members of the offshore staff leave at once.

> "From our perspective the size of a project is a decisive criterion. Projects that are too small do not make sense. The project rather needs a minimum size [for offshoring] to work." (Manager, Automotive Sector)

> "The project needs a certain size, a critical mass. […] But it has to be something, a size, where it makes sense… the time and effort for interfaces that you need to implement for communication. So that it pays off afterwards." (Senior Manager, Logistics Sector)

> "You have to take care that you have a multi-project team of approximately 10 to 20 people who can compensate for each other, since fluctuation in India is tremendously high." (Senior Manager, IT Sector)

E.2.2 Codification

Codification refers to the degree of documentation of an application or the level of requirements specification on a project level. Experts mentioned that applications or projects exhibiting a high degree of codification are more suitable for offshore delivery.

If the level of codification is high, i.e., documentation is up to date and complete, it is easier for offshore staff to understand applications or tasks. Otherwise they have to create a sufficient level of codification by themselves which implies higher effort and cost. Additionally, complete and unambiguous documentation avoids misunderstandings between client staff and offshore staff.

> "A very important criterion from my perspective is how well the whole application is documented from a functional or business point of view as well as technically. That is a very important criterion." (Senior Manager, Financial Services Sector)

> "[…] already during system analysis, you have to document in a way that there is no opportunity for misinterpretations. Because afterwards, communication is only performed via telephone conferences or similar channels […]" (Employee, Financial Services Sector)

> "The more ambiguous something is I hand over, the worse the result I get back. That is even worse with nearshoring." (Manager, IT Sector)

E.2.3 Language

Language comprises the language spoken between client staff and staff of the service provider from the offshore country. It also includes the language in which documentation and specifications are written. Experts perceived applications or projects where English is the operating language as being more suitable for offshoring.

If the operating language is not English, translations create additional effort and communication inefficiencies which increase time to fulfill certain tasks. In addition, insufficient language skills increase the risk of misunderstandings between client and offshore staff. This lowers productivity, delivery quality, and increases the risk of failure.

> "Usually, sooner or later the project language will be English; the whole communication is supposed to be in English – otherwise you will incur enormous transition costs." (Senior Manager, IT Sector)

> "But one question also is what kind of documentation exists? Is it only in German? Do we still have to maintain it in German in the future? That is already bad. If it only exists in German, we can cope with it – we will have it trans-

lated. But when we have to maintain it in German in the future – it's impossible. You do not have to think about [offshoring] anymore. That would be nonsense." (Senior Manager, IT Sector)

E.2.4 Business Criticality

Business criticality refers to the importance of an application or a project for fulfilling daily business operations. Experts mentioned that low criticality for business makes applications or projects more suitable for offshoring.

The reasons are that high business criticality increases the corresponding application or project risk. If problems in service delivery occur, problem resolution might take longer in comparison to regular domestic sourcing. Such problems might impact business operations. Consequently, when business critical applications or projects are offshored, more effort has to be invested to ensure stable delivery. These additional efforts impact delivery costs and thus partially offset savings generated from offshoring.

> "The more critical or the higher the strategic importance of an application, the less I would transfer it to offshore." (Senior Manager, Tourism Sector)

> "[…] such [offshoring] projects tend to fail from time to time. Therefore, it is important that it is not the most critical application. For example, do not initially offshore an ERP system." (Manager, IT Sector)

E.2.5 Technology Availability

Technology availability describes the availability of required technology skills in the marketplace. In the experts' opinions, applications or projects with common technology, i.e., not too proprietary, not too exotic, and not too new, are more suitable for offshore delivery.

This is because skills for uncommon technology are harder to find in offshore countries, thus making delivery in such cases impossible. Regarding new technology, experts perceive that new technology spreads slower to offshore countries, which makes corresponding skills harder to find.

> "Technology is an aspect also as to what can our colleagues in India and Armenia offer us. The older a technology is, the more difficult it is to find skilled people there." (Senior Manager, IT Sector)

> "Certainly, it is important that you focus on standards. It is certainly easier to find a java developer than something exotic." (Senior Manager, Logistics Sector)

"Then, of course, technology. [...] They are always a bit behind us technically. [...] That means the newer a technology is, the more it speaks against a near-shore partner." (Manager, High Tech Sector)

E.2.6 Business Specificity

Business specificity comprises the internal business process knowledge or proprietary industry knowledge inherent in an application or a project. Some researchers refer to this as domain knowledge. Applications or projects with a low degree of inherent business specificity are considered more suitable for offshoring by the experts.

A main reason for this perception is that business process or industry knowledge inherent in an application or project needs to be transferred to offshore staff in the course of service delivery. The more complex and proprietary the knowledge is, the more time and effort knowledge transfer requires. This leads to additional costs and prolongs delivery.

"Meaning, is it rather a technical thing? The more technical a project is, meaning the less business know-how it requires, the easier I can transfer it or parts of it." (Employee, Automotive Sector)

"Very specific, functionally highly complex things, when I am thinking of such projects [...] where complexity is more related to business specifics, then I would refrain from offshoring." (Senior Manager, Financial Services Sector)

"An additional aspect is the overall process know-how that is required. Thus, is it a task that has its main focus in IT or is utility-related process know-how required?" (Senior Manager, Utilities Sector)

E.2.7 Complexity

Complexity refers to an application's or project's number and size of interfaces, number of users and sites involved or characteristics of inputs and outputs. Experts perceive applications or projects with a low degree of complexity as being more suitable for offshoring.

In the experts' view, transfer of knowledge to offshore staff requires more time and effort when applications or projects are complex. This leads to additional costs and longer transition periods.

"If you have a very complex application at the beginning you have to allow for more time. If you do not have that time then it speaks – from my perspective – against [offshoring]." (Senior Manager, IT Sector)

"You can gauge a task's complexity. The less complex the better it is." (Executive, Financial Services Sector)

E.2.8 Interaction

Interaction describes the required degree of personal contact between client staff and offshore staff for performing daily operations regarding the application or project. In the experts' views, applications or projects that require only a low degree of personal interaction are more suitable for offshore delivery.

A high degree of required interaction, for example by personal face-to-face contacts, creates additional costs and overhead. Additionally, language issues may become more prevalent if communication has to be increased due to interaction needs.

> "And it is very important for the success of projects – if you imagine you would follow a prototyping approach where you sat together with your client on a daily basis – then it does not make sense to employ [offshore] staff at this stage." (Senior Manager, Tourism Sector)

> "And, of course, it is important, if it is a software development project, a very consulting-intensive one – that is a criterion for us to say we do not do it [offshore]." (Manager, Automotive Sector)

E.2.9 Modularity

Modularity subsumes the separability of applications or projects and their low degree of interdependency with other ones. Experts perceive applications or projects that show a high degree of modularity as more suitable for offshoring.

If an application or a project exhibits low modularity, more information on interfaces and tasks needs to be transferred to offshore staff. This again increases the required effort for knowledge transfer, transition times and in the end delivery costs. Apart from that, applications or projects with a low degree of modularity often require onsite work, for example integration tests. This may make offshore delivery impossible or require additional travel activities for offshore staff to do parts of the work onsite.

> "There are often interdependencies, even more in software development. If it is not possible to work on an uncoupled task in an application's development, then it does not become totally impossible but more risky." (Employee, Industrial Goods Sector)

> "If I got some change request running through the overall system. If I got many change requests and – because many teams are working on this application – it has a high impact on the other teams, then it requires a lot communication between the teams. And that is not so easy considering the distance. Then

it is often the case that something is neglected which leads to problems." (Executive, Financial Services Sector)

E.2.10 Process Formalization

Process formalization describes the degree of standardization, specification, and structure of the development and maintenance processes in a respective application or project. In the experts' perceptions, applications or projects with a high degree of process formalization are more suitable for offshoring.

The main reason for this perception is that offshoring represents some form of distributed collaboration that can be performed more easily if the modes of interaction are already formalized. If formalized and standardized processes are already in place, it facilitates the transfer of work to offshore staff.

> "If the software development processes in an organization or in a multinational enterprise are already structured and explicitly designed in a way that everything is clear and, for example, multi-project management is established, architecture management exists, then it [i.e., offshoring] is easier […]."(Manager, IT Sector)

> "What degree of standardization does the organization exhibit? And [with what degree of standardization] do they conduct projects? The higher the degree of standardization, the easier it is to transfer things abroad." (Senior Manager, Transportation Sector)

E.2.11 Other Criteria

As displayed in Figure 2-5 (p. 93) there were seven more criteria mentioned less frequently than the average citation frequency. These were *lifespan, strategic importance, stability, cost level, proximity, regulation,* and *intellectual property.* Considering their lower citation frequency, we do not describe them in greater detail at this stage since experts' perception of them is similar to that in the literature (c.f. Table 2-1, p. 79).

E.3 Comparison with Prior Research on Selection Criteria

Using the citation frequency as an indicator of the perceived importance of the evaluation criteria, we can compare the findings from the literature analysis with the expert interviews. Figure 2-6 illustrates this analysis graphically by contrasting the relative citation frequencies of the literature analysis (left) with the citation frequencies of the expert interviews (right). Each bar represents one criterion. They are sorted in descending order based on expert citation frequencies.

It becomes obvious that size and codification are cited more frequently by our expert panel than in the literature. Language is a completely new criterion not mentioned in the analyzed literature at all. In contrast to that, strategic importance and stability are less frequently cited by the experts in comparison to the literature. Labor intensity is only mentioned in the literature but not by our experts.

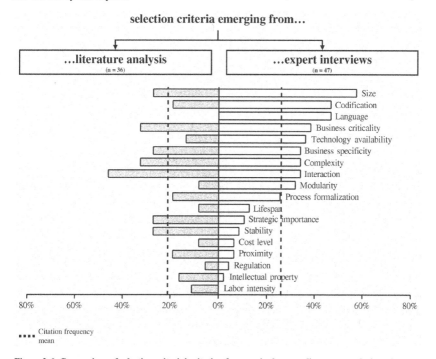

Figure 2-6: Comparison of selection criteria's citation frequencies between literature analysis and expert interviews

The appearance of language as a new criterion may be explained by cultural aspects. The literature is primarily influenced by research originating from English-speaking countries. Thus, language itself is usually not mentioned as an aspect to be considered in a special way. This marks a difference from the situation in Germany where language differences represent an issue. The reason is that English proficiency at German client organizations seems not to be high. However, the operating language in an offshore arrangement should be English because German is simply not widespread among offshore service providers. Therefore, sufficient English proficiency on the client side is perceived to increase offshore suitability.

The importance of language might also explain the perceived higher importance of size and codification. The language gap increases communication and collaboration overhead. Consequently, larger offshoring volumes and durations in the affected applications or projects are required so that savings can compensate for this additional overhead. Simultaneously, a high degree of codification helps to overcome the language gap for both parties, the knowledge transfer is made easier, and properly codified communication helps to avoid misunderstandings due to language issues.

E.4 Comparison with Theoretical Views

This section compares the findings from the expert interviews with our initial expectations drawn from the theoretical views as described in Section B.1 (p. 75). We perform this criterion comparison in order of their citation frequency in the interviews.

Initially, we did not expect the appearance of size as being the most frequently cited criterion by our expert panel. It rather relates to the potential transaction (TCE) which focuses on the decision of whether to use the market or produce internally. A certain application or project size and duration might yield savings that offset associated higher transaction costs, thus making the use of a market transaction instead of internal production feasible. However, this argument only represents a weak link to TCE due to the unclear impact of size on asset specificity and uncertainty.

This is different with the second most frequently cited criterion which is codification. We expected this criterion to emerge, because high degrees of codification lower the related uncertainty associated with TCE and make the inherent knowledge explicit, thus supporting knowledge transfer (KBV). Finally, high degrees of codification minimize cultural challenges because the need for unstructured cultural interaction is lower since all parties can rely to a certain degree on the structured and codified information.

The association of language to culture is obvious because language itself represents a core facet of any culture. However, we did not expect language to be one of the top-most cited criteria since we expected that there would be a higher degree of English proficiency at German corporations. This was apparently not the case (or at least at the organizations our experts worked for) and thus language became an important criterion from their perspective.

Business criticality was raised by implications drawn from the research-based view (RBV) and we also expected it to appear in a prominent position. However, the results from our sampled cases challenge its perceived importance, since the cases showed that business critical applications or projects were also offshored successfully (c.f. Section E.5, p. 102).

Not surprisingly, the emergence of technology availability was anticipated based on TCE. Availability of technology in the marketplace is directly related to asset specificity. Thus, a high degree of technology availability makes offshoring (in terms of offshore outsourcing) feasible in the marketplace.

Similarly, a low degree of business specificity increasing offshore suitability was expected by all four theoretical views. Related to TCE, business specificity directly impacts asset specificity. Thus, lower degrees of business specificity also lower asset specificity and thus make usage of the offshore sourcing market more viable. Regarding RBV, a low degree of business specificity is an indication that a resource (in this case the application or project) might be less important for the business, thus its delivery can be transferred. With respect to KBV, low business specificity limits the amount of firm-specific knowledge that needs to be transferred and increases the chance that respective knowledge is already available outside the domestic onshore organization. Finally, as a result, the need for communication might be lower, thus easing cultural interaction.

A comparable analysis applies to complexity, since low degrees of complexity also lower uncertainty (TCE), lower the amount of inherent explicit and implicit knowledge (KBV), and thus potentially decrease the amount of required cultural interaction. It does not, however, apply to RBV because complexity per se does not necessarily contribute to a project's or application's importance as a resource to the business.

The criterion interaction can be best related to TCE and cultural aspects. If personal interaction in the course of service delivery is not required, it decreases asset specificity. Additionally, low degrees of required personal interaction with business clients or members of the IT department, for example, lower potential adverse effects arising from cultural differences.

Modularity covers a similar aspect but with a stronger technological view. We did not expect modularity to arise as a separate criterion, but argue that it can be best related to TCE. The rationale is that if modularity on a technological level is high, the degree of asset specificity is decreased, thus making offshore outsourcing of applications or projects more viable.

Process formalization, as the last of the most cited criteria, can be best explained from the perspective of TCE, KBV, and cultural aspects. Regarding TCE, a high degree of process formalization lowers the associated uncertainty of applications or projects. Similarly, for KBV, this increases the degree of explicit knowledge which makes knowledge transfer easier. Furthermore, high degrees of process formalization can avoid difficulties arising from cultural aspects, because roles, responsibilities, tasks, and interaction in general are clearly defined and structured.

Finally, briefly covering some of the remaining less frequently cited criteria, strategic importance and intellectual property were perceived as less important by our expert panel. This is notable, because these two criteria describe key aspects constituting RBV. Perhaps RBV provides a less applicable approach for analyzing and understanding these sourcing decisions in comparison to other views. (Watjatrakul, 2005)

Combining the observations described above, we can tentatively deduce that TCE, KBV, and cultural aspects explain several of the selection criteria as mentioned by our expert panel. RBV, however, solely contributes business criticality and business specificity. Other RBV-specific key constructs such as strategic importance are not cited frequently by the experts.

Table 2-5 illustrates in tabular form how the most frequently cited criteria (first column) with their corresponding citation frequency (second column) can be related to the four theoretical views TCE (third column), RBV (fourth column), KBV (fifth column), and culture (sixth column). We placed a solid checkmark at the intersections where a criterion can be obviously attributed to a theoretical view. The gray checkmark for criterion size indicates that the relation can be inferred only in the broadest sense.

	Citation frequency	TCE	RBV	KBV	Culture
Size	57%	✓			
Codification	47%	✓		✓	✓
Language	47%				✓
Business criticality	38%		✓		
Technology availability	36%	✓			
Business specificity	34%	✓	✓	✓	✓
Complexity	34%	✓		✓	✓
Interaction	34%	✓			✓
Modularity	32%	✓			
Process formalization	26%	✓		✓	✓

Table 2-5: Mapping of most frequently cited criteria to theoretical views

E.5 Criteria Contribution to Offshoring Success

As part of our interviews, we asked each expert to illustrate the evaluation criteria she or he mentioned by using one or more brief case examples from his or her professional experience (c.f. Section D.1, p. 86). The intention was to deepen our understanding of the criteria, their application in practice, and their importance.

For each sampled case, we asked the experts to briefly describe the scope of the application or project and its technological context. Subsequently, we wanted to know what criteria were applied to select this respective application or project for offshore delivery and how it performed regarding the criteria, i.e., whether the application or project was considered offshore-suitable or offshore-unsuitable in light of each criterion. Finally, we inquired whether the case had been perceived as successful from a client perspective, considering the classical project-related dimensions time, budget, and scope. Operationalizing success in terms of individuals' success perception is in line with our qualitative-exploratory research approach (Balaji & Ahuja, 2005; Erickson & Ranganathan, 2006).

In total, the experts described 64 case examples. Of those, 39 or 61% were perceived to be successful and correspondingly 25 or 39% were perceived to be unsuccessful. Applying the same threshold level as in the analysis of the experts' criteria citation, Figure 2-7 illustrates which criteria were cited by more than 26% of all successful cases (left part of figure) and by more than 26% of the unsuccessful cases (right part of figure).

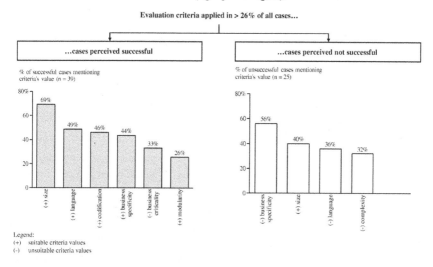

Figure 2-7: Perceived case success related to suitability of selection criteria

Sixty-nine percent of the successful cases (left graph) had a size suitable for offshoring. Forty-nine percent exhibited suitable language, 46% suitable degrees of codification, 44% advantageously low levels of business specificity, and 26% adequate degrees of modularity. Interestingly, 33% of the successful cases showed levels of business criticality which should have made them unsuitable for offshore delivery, i.e., these applications or projects were rather business critical but were nevertheless perceived to be successful.

Looking at the unsuccessful cases (right graph), 56% exhibited unsuitable levels of business specificity, 36% had unsuitable language, and 32% had unsuitable degrees of complexity. Remarkably, 40% of unsuccessful cases had an adequate size but still failed.

Comparing these results, it seems that business specificity has a high impact on case failure. It is the most frequently cited criterion in unsuccessful cases. The experts' statements showed that applications or projects with high business specificity come with increased risk, overhead, and require unexpected additional efforts for initial knowledge transfer and during delivery.

In contrast to that, business criticality seems to be less important. Although 38% of the experts mentioned business criticality as an evaluation criterion in the interviews (it is the fourth ranked criterion by citation frequency, c.f. Figure 2-5, p. 93), the case examples do not clearly support this: one third of all successful case examples showed inadequate levels of business criticality. Our interview partners stated that business criticality often stems from rather specific characteristics of an application or project. It might be possible to mitigate these rather critical characteristics by certain managerial and operational actions, so that business criticality is not per se an inhibitor for offshoring.

Finally, suitable size seems to be a necessary but not a sufficient criterion for an application's or project's offshore suitability: 69% of all successful cases came with suitable size. However, 40% of all unsuccessful cases also had a suitable size but failed nevertheless. An interpretation could be that size might be a prerequisite for offshoring success (i.e., to compensate for offshoring overhead) but it might not offset impacts of other unsuitable criteria.

The other mentioned criteria such as language, codification, modularity, or complexity show impacts on application or project success as previously expected, based upon the literature review and the expert interviews.

E.6 Criteria Importance in Relation to Offshoring Expertise

In the last part of our study, we asked all interviewed experts to answer a short survey. The survey included the ten most frequently cited evaluation criteria as they emerged from the interviews. In the survey, we asked each expert to put himself in the role of an external third who consults an organization that wants to do offshoring. We then asked the expert to assign a rating from 1 ("unimportant") to 7 ("very important") to each criterion according to its importance for selecting suitable applications or projects for offshoring, considering the organization's offshoring expertise. We asked this question twice: once assuming an organization with no to low offshoring expertise, and once assuming an organization with medium to high offshoring expertise. For details regarding the data collection procedure, please refer to Section D.2 (p. 88) and for the survey sheet itself and the variable naming, please refer to the Appendix (pp. 126-130).

Since the survey is rather simplistic, our initial analysis consisted of a means analysis by comparing the score means for each criterion assigned to organizations with assumed no to low offshoring expertise versus organizations with assumed medium to high offshoring expertise. Figure 2-8 illustrates the results. The ten most frequently cited criteria are presented on the x-axis in order of their citation frequencies from the expert interviews. The values on the y-axis represent the individual score mean values. The white bars represent values assuming an organization with no to low offshoring expertise. The black bars represent the values assuming an organization with medium to high offshoring expertise. The Appendix provides additional statistics regarding mean, minimal and maximal values, and standard deviation (p. 131).

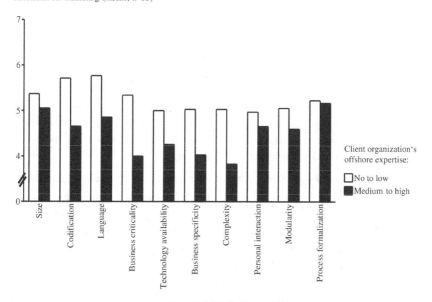

Figure 2-8: Perceived criteria importance in relation to
different offshoring expertise levels (all experts)

As expected from our reflections based on different theoretical views (c.f. Section B.1, p. 75), the survey respondents assigned on average lower importance ratings when an organization with medium to high offshoring expertise was assumed. Furthermore, criteria size, codification, and language get higher importance scores than all the remaining variables (no to low expertise) or at least most of them (medium to high expertise). This supports our findings from the expert interviews that used citation frequency as a proxy for criteria importance. Additionally, we can observe that certain criteria's importance do not seem to be so sensitive towards an increase in offshoring expertise: the importance ratings for size, personal interaction, modularity, and process formalization do not differ very much between the two offshoring expertise levels.

However, before delving deeper into the interpretation, it is necessary to address two obvious aspects. First, all criteria importance mean scores lay close together between value 3.8 and 5.8. This raises the question whether the criteria are really of different importance. Second, the differences of the importance scores between the two expertise levels are similar for six of the ten variables (codification, language, business criticality, technology availability, business specificity, and complexity). At this stage, we could conclude that the discriminatory and explanatory power of the survey results might be low and that our analysis provided only minor additional insight. However, since our qualitative findings seemed to be unambiguously clear, we wanted to better understand these results.

Therefore, we contacted a random selection of the experts who answered the survey and discussed these results with them. It turned out that – although all experts unanimously understood the criteria and the questions – experts with less personal offshoring expertise (between one and three years) said that it had been difficult for them to assign importance scores imagining an organization with medium to high offshoring expertise. This represents a structural expertise gap: a person with low personal expertise can hardly judge the importance of a selection criterion for an organization with high expertise.

Having understood this aspect in our data, we decided to analyze the results segmented by the experts' personal offshoring expertise. Therefore, we compared the importance scores assigned by experts with one to three years personal expertise assuming an organization with no to low offshoring expertise to the importance scores assigned by experts with more than three years personal expertise assuming an organization with medium to high offshoring expertise. By doing so we ensured a mapping of expertise and avoided any structural expertise gap.

Figure 2-9 illustrates the results. Corresponding to Figure 2-8 (p. 105), the ten most frequently cited criteria are presented on the x-axis in order of their citation frequencies from the expert interviews. The values on the y-axis represent the individual score mean values. The white bars represent values assuming an organization with no to low offshoring expertise (calculated from the scores assigned by experts with one to three years personal offshoring expertise). The black bars represent the values assuming an organization with medium to high offshoring expertise (calculated from the scores assigned by experts with more than three years personal offshoring expertise). The Appendix provides additional statistics regarding mean, minimal and maximal values, and standard deviation for the two data segments (p. 132).

Perceived criteria importance for evaluating
candidates for offshoring (means, n=19*, n=16**)

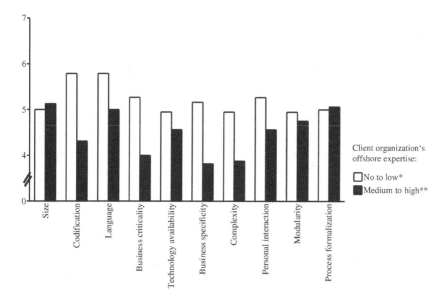

* rated by experts with 1 to 3 yrs. offshoring expertise
** rated by experts with more than 3 yrs. offshoring expertise

**Figure 2-9: Perceived criteria importance in relation to
different offshoring expertise levels (experts differentiated by levels of expertise)**

Most of the findings are similar to our initial analysis: apart from minor differences, the criteria importance scores are – as expected – lower for an organization with medium to high offshoring expertise. Furthermore, the situation that all importance scores lay between 3.8 and 5.8 did not change. Also, criteria codification and language are perceived as being more important than other criteria (no to low expertise). This is in line with our qualitative findings. However, this observation does not apply to the same extent to the medium to high expertise dimension where, for example, personal interaction, modularity, and process formalization get higher importance scores than codification. Nevertheless, considering the low number of responses and the simple structure of the survey, we do not perceive this as a strong contradiction because we rather rely on the richer and more profound results from the expert interviews which clearly showed that these criteria seem to be of less importance.

Similar to our original findings, the importance scores for size, modularity, process formalization, and additionally for technology availability do not differ very much between the two off-

108   Analysis

shoring expertise levels. However, as intended by this segmental analysis, the other differences of the importance scores between the two expertise levels became more accentuated. The criteria codification, business criticality, business specificity, and complexity seem to be clearly less important assuming an organization with medium to high offshoring expertise.

We used this segmented data set to analyze whether the differences in the importance scores of criteria codification, business criticality, business specificity, and complexity are statistically significant. A Kolmogorov-Smirnov test of normality (c.f. Appendix, p. 133) indicated that most of the survey data shows a non-normal distribution (a distribution can be assumed to be non-normal if $p < .05$). Since we want to compare the data segments, and normal distribution cannot be assumed in both segments, we cannot apply test methods based on the assumption of a normal distribution. Therefore, we used a non-parametric method to test for significant differences in importance scores.

The Mann-Whitney test as a non-parametric test is equivalent to the independent t-test. It is a rather common non-parametric test and was first developed by Wilcoxon (1945) for samples of similar size and later extended by Mann & Whitney (1947) for different sample sizes. It can be used to analyze whether the differences between the assigned importance scores are significant. The test builds on ranked data and the rank sums and compares their distribution to the known distribution of a test statistic U to determine whether the two samples belong to the same population. (Field, 2005; Siegel & Castellan, 1988)

The Mann-Whitney test results (c.f. Table 2-6) show that perceived importance scores for codification ($p < .05$; $r = -.424$), business criticality ($p < .05$; $r = -.469$), business specificity ($p < .05$; $r = -.469$), and complexity ($p < .05$; $r = -.366$) are significantly lower for organizations with assumed medium to high offshoring expertise. All effects (r) are between -.5 and -.3 and thus of medium size (Cohen, 1992). The effect size for business criticality and business specificity is close to a large effect.

	SIZE	CODIFICATION	LANGUAGE	CRITICALITY	TECHNOLOGY	SPECIFICITY	COMPLEXITY	INTERACTION	MODULARITY	FORMALIZATION
Mann-Whitney U	150.000	78.000	99.000	70.000	126.000	70.000	88.000	115.500	127.000	147.000
Wilcoxon W	340.000	214.000	235.000	206.000	262.000	206.000	224.000	251.500	263.000	337.000
Z	-.068	-2.509	-1.806	-2.776	-.890	-2.773	-2.164	-1.232	-.855	-.175
r	-.011	-.424	-.305	-.469	-.150	-.469	-.366	-.208	-.145	-.030
Asymp. Sig. (2-tailed)	.946	.012	.071	.005	.374	.006	.030	.218	.392	.861
Exact Sig. [2*(1-tailed Sig.)]	.961	.014	.082	.006	.403	.006	.034	.230	.422	.883

Table 2-6: Mann-Whitney test for criteria importance scores in relation to offshoring expertise

Apparently, the importance of selection criteria size, technology availability, personal interaction, modularity, and process formalization does not change significantly in relation to an organization's offshoring expertise. Regarding size, technology availability, and personal interaction, an explanation is that even at high levels of offshoring expertise organizations incur extra costs for offshore delivery. So it is still necessary to have a minimum size and duration for an application or a project in order to achieve expected economic benefits. Regarding technology availability, it is clear that offshoring is hardly possible if the technology cannot be obtained in the marketplace. Similarly, the need for personal interaction is also rather independent from accumulated expertise or shared knowledge in an offshoring arrangement and cannot be eased. With regard to the other two criteria modularity and process formalization, it is impossible to find an equivalent obvious explanation. Some experts mentioned that modularity and process formalization are imperatives of IT service delivery at all levels of offshoring expertise. However, apart from these expert statements we could not think of an additional adequate interpretation.

The picture is different for the four criteria that showed significant statistical differences between offshoring expertise levels. Obviously, experts perceive that negative effects to offshore suitability caused by codification, business criticality, business specificity, and complexity can be eventually offset by the growing offshoring expertise of an organization. Potential explanations can be drawn from the KBV or TCE with increased knowledge and trust being built up between the two interacting parties on- and offshore. This increased level of shared knowledge lowers additional costs for knowledge transfer, thus making the degree of codification less important and even allowing business-critical and business-specific applications or projects previously considered unsuitable for offshoring to be sourced from abroad. Additionally, higher levels of trust and existing experiences from previous offshore arrangements create a higher confidence on the client side so that the willingness to offshore business critical applications or projects is increased.

Finally, language in this two-tailed test also does not exhibit statistical significant differences. Obviously, English as an operating language for offshoring is of equal importance for successful offshore delivery, independent from the organization's offshoring expertise.

Based on these observations, we can draw conclusions in addition to our previous findings. Despite the existing offshoring expertise, it seems suitable to focus on applications or projects with a minimum size and duration and where the technology is available in the marketplace. This fosters our previous perception of size as a necessary but not sufficient criterion for success. The importance of language in terms of English as an operating language seems to decrease slightly but this decrease is not statistically significant. In contrast to that, codification, business criticality, specificity, and complexity seem to become less important for selecting suitable applications or projects for offshoring when an organization has more offshoring expertise. However, one should still consider the impact of these criteria on offshoring success as presented in the case studies. For example, business specificity was cited as one of the main failure reasons in our case study samples.

F Conclusions

F.1 Main Contributions

Not found in the analyzed literature, language represents a new evaluation criterion only mentioned by the expert panel. Additionally, the perceived criteria importance varies between the literature and the experts. As described earlier, this might result from cultural differences specific to Germany. However, the experts' perceptions do not contradict the literature completely: apart from language and labor cost, both mention the same criteria and to some extent similar degrees of importance, i.e., regarding business criticality, complexity, or interaction (c.f. Figure 2-6, p. 99).

The sampled case studies represented a practitioner-oriented review of the described characteristics. To a large extent they confirmed the findings from interview analysis, for example, the importance of suitable size, language, and codification for case success. However, we observed interesting and interpretable deviations, such as the previously unexpected high importance of business specificity for case failure and the effectively lower importance of business criticality in practice. Additionally, suitable size is indicated as a necessary criterion by the cases. However, size rather seems to be an essential prerequisite but not a sufficient criterion for success.

With respect to our initial expectations drawn from different theoretical views we see that primarily TCE, KBV, and cultural aspects relate to the identified selection criteria. RBV, however, solely contributes business criticality and business specificity. Other RBV-specific key constructs such as strategic importance are not cited frequently by the experts.

Looking at the importance scores assigned to the criteria by the experts in the survey, we also see that codification and language are rated as the most important criteria. Additionally, codification, business criticality, business specificity, and complexity are perceived significantly less important with the growing offshoring expertise of an organization. It seems that organizations can handle adverse effects for applications or projects resulting from these criteria better with growing offshoring expertise. Noticeably, size, technology availability, and personal interaction do not show significant differences in importance. Probably, as indicated by our interviews, a certain size and duration seems always be required for savings to offset additional overhead incurred by offshoring. Availability of technology is also independent from expertise, because if a technology is not available in the offshoring marketplace, the corresponding project's offshoreability stays low. Similarly, the need for personal interaction cannot be mitigated by accumulated expertise and is therefore an equally important criterion at the two levels of expertise.

Reflecting on our paper's relevance for management practice, we can draw some tentative advice from our findings. First, it seems to make sense to consider sizeable application or project candidates for offshoring. These candidates should be documented and specified well in order to ensure a high degree of codification. Additionally, applications or projects where involved staff has a certain proficiency in English, or where documentation is already available in English, seem to be more suitable. Apart from that, applications or projects with low degrees of business specificity should be preferred. Business criticality appears not to be an inhibitor per se because suitable actions can mitigate this aspect. Finally, as the survey analysis suggests, an organization with medium to high offshoring expertise can put less emphasis on the selection criteria codification, business criticality, business specificity, and complexity when evaluating application or project candidates for offshoring.

F.2 Limitations

Our study exhibits limitations in certain dimensions. Regarding our sample, we performed an arbitrary selection of interview partners that might not be representative of our basic population.

Regarding the criteria, it is clear that they are not fully mutually exclusive and free of overlaps. However, we decided against a further aggregation in order to obtain richer results by avoiding loss of too much information from our data.

Furthermore, we decided to collect a rather large number of 64 small cases instead of detailing a few cases selected on the basis of an explicit replication logic as it is usually done in case study research. As a consequence, we relied on the brief case descriptions by our experts and could not, for example, triangulate each case using different sources and different kinds of material. Our intention was to increase sample size on account of detail level. Thus, we could capture expert experience arising from various industry sectors, career levels, and with different offshore countries.

Other limitations arise from our research approach. We could have biased the interviewed experts despite using a pre-formulated and semi-structured interview guide and not telling our interview partners any research results or expectations beforehand. Apart from that, the impact of the identified criteria on success in terms of statistical significance and strength are aspects that cannot be properly addressed with qualitative research.

The most obvious limitations and improvement potential probably arise from the survey and thus the quantitative part of our research. The survey itself was rather simplistic and the sample size 35 is low, which limits the power of the applied tests. An increase of participants, maybe also beyond our initial expert sample, could have provided stronger insights. In this context, it is also clear that it would have been better to ask for importance ratings from experts not just *assuming* an organization with a certain offshoring expertise level but experts who work for organizations that actually *have* this expertise level. Thus, we could have avoided the structural expertise gap described earlier and made the data basis more reliable.

Finally, our regional focus was Germany and German corporations. It is unclear whether the presented evaluation criteria would apply similarly to a non-German environment. This might limit our findings' generalizability to other countries or language areas.

F.3 Opportunities for Future Research

The previously described limitations suggest opportunities for further research. One could evaluate the actual importance of application or project selection on success since there are other influencing factors for offshoring success such as vendor selection, contract design or project management. Comparing and evaluating the impact of these factors on success could result in valuable insights.

Additionally, further research in these areas could be enriched by a greater methodological variety, for example, by a quantitative study using a broader data set, a more detailed measurement instrument, and a more sophisticated analysis method. Another option would be to detail our findings by performing an in-depth case study or a comparison of cases.

Finally, in order to understand the influence of a specific culture or language area, one could repeat our research design in an international context in other countries and compare the findings among results from different countries.

Appendix

Literature-Derived Offshore Selection Criteria

Characteristic	Studies
Business criticality	Amoribieta et al., 2001; Bitkom, 2005; Cusick & Prasad, 2006; Klingebiel, 2006; Kumar & Willcocks, 1996; Matzke, 2007; Menon, 2005; Meyerolbersleben, 2005; Schaffer, 2006; Srivastava & Theodore, 2005; Wiener, 2006; William et al., 2006
Business specificity	Akmanligil & Palvia, 2004; Bruhn, 2004; Kakumanu & Portanova, 2006; Kuni & Bhushan, 2006; Matzke, 2007; McLaughlin & Fitzsimmons, 1996; Meyerolbersleben, 2005; Murthy, 2004; Pu Li & Kishore, 2006; Wiener, 2006
Codification	Jennex & Adelakun, 2003; Kuni & Bhushan, 2006; Menon, 2005; Mirani, 2007; Rajkumar & Mani, 2001; Ravichandran & Ahmed, 1993; Wiener, 2006
Complexity	Cusick & Prasad, 2006; Jennex & Adelakun, 2003; Kumar & Willcocks, 1996; Kuni & Bhushan, 2006; Matzke, 2007; McLaughlin & Fitzsimmons, 1996; Meyerolbersleben, 2005; Mirani, 2007; Ramarapu, Parzinger, & Lado, 1997; Ravichandran & Ahmed, 1993; Scheibe, Mennecke, & Zobel, 2006; Wiener, 2006
Cost level	Cusick & Prasad, 2006; Matzke, 2007; William et al., 2006
Intellectual property	BIHK, 2002; Meyerolbersleben, 2005; Murthy, 2004; Schaffer, 2006; Stack & Downing, 2005; William et al., 2006
Interaction	Amoribieta et al., 2001; Apte et al., 1997; Ben & Claus, 2005; BIHK, 2002; Cusick & Prasad, 2006; Jennex & Adelakun, 2003; Kumar & Willcocks, 1996; McLaughlin & Fitzsimmons, 1996; Meyerolbersleben, 2005; Mirani, 2007; Ramarapu et al., 1997; Ravichandran & Ahmed, 1993; Schaffer, 2006; Scheibe et al., 2006; Smith, Mitra, & Narasimhan, 1996; Wiener, 2006; Yan, 2004
Labor intensity	McLaughlin & Fitzsimmons, 1996; Ramarapu et al., 1997; Srivastava & Theodore, 2005; Wiener, 2006
Lifespan	Kumar & Willcocks, 1996; Meyerolbersleben, 2005; Ramarapu et al., 1997
Modularity	Mirani, 2007; Sayeed, 2006; Wiener, 2006
Process formalization	Apte, 1992; BIHK, 2002; Kuni & Bhushan, 2006; Meyerolbersleben, 2005; Mirani, 2007; Ramarapu et al., 1997; William et al., 2006
Proximity	Apte et al., 1997; Bruhn, 2004; Hirschheim et al., 2005; Meyerolbersleben, 2005; Scheibe et al., 2006; Stack & Downing, 2005; William et al., 2006
Regulation	Kuni & Bhushan, 2006; Stack & Downing, 2005
Size	Akmanligil & Palvia, 2004; Amoribieta et al., 2001; Bitkom, 2005; Bruhn, 2004; Cusick & Prasad, 2006; Ferguson, Kussmaul, McCracken, & Robbert, 2004; Kumar & Willcocks, 1996; Menon, 2005; Rajkumar & Mani, 2001; Schaffer, 2006
Stability	Bitkom, 2005; Bruhn, 2004; Ferguson et al., 2004; Jennex & Adelakun, 2003; Kumar & Willcocks, 1996; Kuni & Bhushan, 2006; Matzke, 2007; Meyerolbersleben, 2005; Mirani, 2007; Wiener, 2006
Strategic importance	Akmanligil & Palvia, 2004; Apte & Mason, 1995; Apte et al., 1997; Bitkom, 2005; Klingebiel, 2006; Kumar & Willcocks, 1996; Menon, 2005; Meyerolbersleben, 2005; Wiener, 2006; Yan, 2004
Technology availability	Amoribieta et al., 2001; Bitkom, 2005; Ramarapu et al., 1997; William et al., 2006; Yan, 2004

Company Lists

Top 100 Companies Germany

Company	Turnover 2005 (in € Millions)
DaimlerChrysler	149,776
Volkswagen	95,268
Siemens	75,445
Deutsche Telekom	59,604
Eon	56,399
Metro	55,722
BMW	46,656
Deutsche Post	44,594
BASF	42,745
ThyssenKrupp	42,064
RWE	41,819
Rewe-Gruppe	41,700
Robert Bosch	41,461
Schwarz-Gruppe	40,000
Edeka-Gruppe	38,060
Deutsche BP	37,432
Aldi-Gruppe	36,210
Bayer	27,383
Franz Haniel	25,892
Ford of Europe	25,507
Deutsche Bahn	25,055
Shell Deutschland Oil	24,300
Tengelmann-Gruppe	22,200
RAG Energie	21,869
Phoenix-Gruppe	19,894
TUI	19,619
Deutsche Lufthansa	18,065
Bertelsmann	17,890
Karstadt-Quelle	15,454
Hochtief	14,854
Adam Opel	14,700
MAN	14,671
Otto-Gruppe	14,570

Company	Turnover 2005 (in € Millions)
Continental	13,837
Energie Baden-Württemberg	12,057
Henkel	11,974
ZF Friedrichshafen	10,833
Vattenfall Europe	10,543
Boehringer Ingelheim	10,311
Total Deutschland	9,885
Linde	9,501
Heraeus Metall	9,311
Lekkerland	9,085
Tchibo	8,788
SAP	8,512
Marquard & Bahls	8,473
Vodafone Deutschland	8,440
Schaeffler-Gruppe	7,950
Fresenius	7,889
Heidelberg-Cement	7,803
Thomas Cook	7,661
EWE-Konzern	7,444
BSH Bosch Siemens Hausgeräte	7,340
Salzgitter	7,152
Lanxess	7,150
Bilfinger Berger	7,061
Oetker-Gruppe	7,029
Würth	6,914
Infineon	6,759
Adidas	6,636
Porsche	6,574
Baywa	6,537
Anton Schlecker	6,043
Merck Chemie	5,870
Alfred C. Toepfer International	5,778
Airbus Deutschland	5,770
IBM Deutschland	5,658
Motorola Deutschland	5,443
Hewlett-Packard Deutschland	5,400

Company	Turnover 2005 (in € Millions)
Südzucker	5,347
Benteler	5,315
Schering	5,308
Brenntag Holding	5,286
Klöckner & Co.	4,964
Freudenberg-Gruppe	4,837
Helm	4,745
Sanofi–Aventis in Deutschland	4,600
OMV Deutschland	4,587
GEA-Gruppe	4,498
Philips Deutschland	4,428
Strabag	4,341
Mahle	4,122
Unternehmensgruppe Knauf	3,900
VNG Verbundnetz Gas	3,810
Ingram Micro Holding	3,800
Nestlé	3,769
Globus-Handelshof	3,760
Procter & Gamble Deutschland	3,703
Stadtwerke München	3,700
Stadtwerke Köln	3,647
Agravis Raiffeisen	3,629
Heidelberger Druckmaschinen	3,586
Voith	3,551
SCA Hygiene Products	3,484
Rheinmetall Rüstung	3,454
Andreae-Noris Zahn	3,383
dm - Drogerie Markt	3,327
Remondis	3,305
Roche Deutschland Pharma	3,295
Altana Chemie	3,272

Source: http://www.sueddeutsche.de/imperia/md/content/pdf/wirtschaft/top100deutschland2005.pdf

Top 20 Banks

Company	Balance sheet total 2005 (in € Millions)
Deutsche Bank	992,161
HypoVereinsbank	493,523
Dresdner Bank	461,372
Commerzbank	444,861
LBBW	404,915
DZ Bank Konzern	401,628
KfW Bankengruppe	341,143
Bayern LB	340,854
WestLB	264,955
Eurohypo	234,303
Nord LB	197,810
HSH Nordbank	185,065
Helaba	164,422
Hypo Real Estate Holding	152,460
Bankgesellschaft Berlin	144,520
Deutsche Postbank	140,280
NRW.Bank	128,115
Deka-Bank Deutsche Girozentrale	114,982
Sachsen-Finanzgruppe	97,171
Hypothekenbank in Essen	92,781

Source: http://www.sueddeutsche.de/imperia/md/content/pdf/wirtschaft/topbanken2005.pdf

Top 20 Insurance Companies

Company	Insurance premiums 2005 (in € Millions)
Allianz-Gruppe	100,897
Münchener-Rück-Gruppe	38,199
Talanx	15,418
AMB-Generali-Gruppe	12,815
R+V-Versicherungsgruppe	8,466
Debeka-Gruppe	6,717
Axa-Konzern	6,402
Zurich-Gruppe Deutschland	6,228
Versicherungskammer Bayern	5,434
HUK-Coburg-Versicherungsgruppe	4,732
Signal-Iduna-Gruppe	4,613
Gerling Beteiligungs-GmbH	4,561
Gothaer Konzern	3,809
DBV-Winterthur-Gruppe	3,668
Provinzial-Nord-West-Konzern	3,088
Wüstenrot & Württembergische-Konzern	3,035
Kölnische-Rück-Gruppe	2,999
Nürnberger Versicherungsgruppe	2,994
SV Sparkassen-Versicherung	2,863
Verbund Alte-Leipziger-Hallesche	2,691

Source: http://www.sueddeutsche.de/imperia/md/content/pdf/wirtschaft/topversicherungen2005.pdf

Top 20 IT Companies

Company	Turnover 2005 (in € Millions)
IBM Global Business Services	1,015
Accenture GmbH	645
Atos Origin GmbH	500
Lufthansa Systems AG	476
CSC	450
SAP SI Systems Integration AG	325
Capgemini Deutschland Holding GmbH	297
LogicaCMG Deutschland GmbH & Co. KG	235
Softlab Group	216
msg systems ag	203
ESG Elektroniksystem- und Logistik Gruppe	192
IDS Scheer AG	155
IT-Services and Solutions GmbH	149
sd&m Software Design & Management AG	135
Materna GmbH	122
SerCon GmbH	115
Unisys Deutschland GmbH	110
TietoEnator Deutschland GmbH	102
C1 Group	100
GFT Technologies AG	81

Source: http://www.luenendonk.de/download/press/LUE_ITB_2007_f010607.pdf

Cover Letter as Used in XING

Sehr geehrter Herr/Frau XY,

über Ihr XING „ich biete"-Feld bin ich auf Sie als Offshoring Experte aufmerksam geworden.

Mein Name ist Markus Westner. Derzeit forsche ich an der TU Dresden und European Business School im Bereich IT Off-/Nearshoring (siehe auch http://www.it-offshoring.org). Dabei liegt unser Fokus auf dem Off-/Nearshoring von Anwendungsentwicklung und -wartung aus Deutschland heraus.

Im Rahmen des Forschungsvorhabens untersuchen wir, ob es bestimmte anwendungsspezifische Faktoren gibt, die die „Off-/Nearshorbarkeit" von Anwendungen beeinflussen und welche Faktoren dies sein könnten. Im Rahmen der Gespräche würden wir deshalb gerne ihre Expertise einbeziehen und verstehen, welche Art von Anwendungen deutsche Firmen verlagern.

Würden Sie als Experte aus der Praxis für ein 20 bis 30-minütiges Gespräch zur Verfügung stehen? Wenn ja, dann würde ich mich sehr über Ihre Rückantwort freuen. Meine Kontaktdaten sind unten angegeben.

Im Gegenzug würden wir Ihnen die späteren Ergebnisse des Forschungsvorhabens sowohl im Volltext als auch in Form einer Management-Präsentation zur Verfügung.

Selbstverständlich werden alle Ihre Angaben 100% anonym behandelt – wir sind wirklich nur an Ihrer Erfahrung als Experte interessiert und nicht an unternehmensspezifischen Aspekten.

Weitere Informationen finden Sie unter:

http://www.it-offshoring.org/071127-is-outshoring-interview-request.pdf

Mit freundlichen Grüßen

Markus Westner

Characteristics of All Interviewed Experts in Comparison to the Subset of Experts who Answered Research Phase Two's Survey

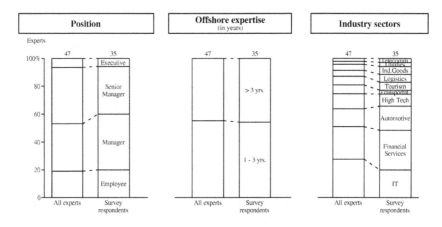

Interview Guideline

- In welcher Position befinden Sie sich in Ihrem Unternehmen?
- Bitte beschreiben Sie Ihre Erfahrung im Bereich IS Offshoring...
  - ...qualitativ.
  - ...hinsichtlich Anzahl der Projekte, an denen Sie beteiligt waren.
  - ...hinsichtlich Anzahl der Jahre.
- Ist die geeignete Auswahl von Applikationen und Projekten aus Ihrer Sicht wichtig für den Erfolg eines Offshoring Vorhabens?
- Stellen Sie sich eine/n CIO/IT-Abteilungsleiter/in vor, der/die IT Offshoring machen will. Er/Sie will Projekt/Applikationskandidaten für Offshoring identifizieren. Was könnten aus Ihrer Sicht Evaluationskriterien sein und warum?
- Wenn Sie an eine bestimmte Offshore-Applikation bzw. ein bestimmtes Offshore-Projekt aus Ihrer Erfahrung bzw. an dem Sie beteiligt waren denken...
  - ...was war die Zielsetzung des Projektes?
  - ...welche Technologien waren involviert?
  - ...wenn wir an die o.g. Evaluationskriterien denken: wie hat die Applikation bzw. das Projekt gegenüber diesen Evaluationskriterien abgeschnitten?
  - ...wurde die Applikation bzw. das Projekt als Erfolg erachtet in Bezug auf Zeit, Budget und Umfang/Ergebnis?

List of Interviewed Experts and Corresponding Companies

Company ID	Industry sector	Expert ID	Position	Offshore expertise (years)	Countries
1	IT Services	23	Senior Manager	3	India, Armenia
2	Financial Services	24	Manager	2	India
3	Automotive	6	Senior Manager	8	India
4	Financial Services	2	Manager	8	Czech Republic
		43	Senior Manager	3	Czech Republic
5	Automotive	16	Employee	4	India
		18	Manager	10	India
		33	Manager	3	Malaysia
6	Financial Services	11	Senior Manager	3	India
7	Transportation	13	Senior Manager	1	India
		41	Senior Manager	12	India, Philippines
8	Financial Services	1	Manager	4	India
		3	Employee	4	India
9	Financial Services	12	Executive	5	Czech Republic
10	Logistics	20	Senior Manager	2	India
		40	Senior Manager	7	Czech Republic
11	Utilities	36	Senior Manager	3	Hungary
12	IT Services	8	Manager	4	n/a
13	Financial Services	14	Senior Manager	1	Latvia
14	Automotive	7	Manager	3	India
		9	Manager	2	India
15	IT Services	26	Executive	2	India
16	Financial Services	27	Employee	7	Moldavia
17	High Tech	25	Manager	2	Russia
18	Financial Services	31	Senior Manager	4	India
19	IT Services	28	Executive	4	Slovakia
20	IT Services	44	Senior Manager	2	n/a
21	IT Services	21	Manager	2	Russia
22	High Tech	22	Employee	3	India

Company ID	Industry sector	Expert ID	Position	Offshore exper- tise (years)	Countries
		32	Manager	7	Malaysia
23	IT Services	37	Employee	3	India
24	Telecommunication	10	Senior Manager	2	India
25	Transportation	29	Manager	4	Poland
26	High Tech	39	Senior Manager	n/a	Armenia
27	Industrial Goods	38	Employee	3	Romania
28	Financial Services	5	Manager	6	India
		46	Employee	3	India
29	IT Services	19	Manager	4	India, Hungary, Po- land
30	High Tech	45	Manager	4	Philippines
31	IT Services	34	Senior Manager	2	India
32	Industrial Goods	17	Manager	2	Ukraine
33	IT Services	42	Senior Manager	4	India, Romania
34	IT Services	47	Senior Manager	2	India
35	Tourism	4	Senior Manager	3	India
		30	Employee	1	India
		35	Employee	2	India
36	IT Services	15	Senior Manager	5	India

Survey

Question #1

Stellen Sie sich vor, Sie beraten ein Unternehmen im deutschsprachigen Raum, das keine oder wenig IT Off-/Nearshoring Erfahrung hat.

„Wenig" Erfahrung würde auf ein Unternehmen zutreffen, das einen Ad-hoc Ansatz für das IT Off-/Nearshoring verfolgt, in dem es wenig Koordination und Wissensaustausch zu IT Off-/Nearshoring zwischen Abteilungen und noch keine kohärente IT Off-/Nearshoring Sourcing Strategie bzw. Richtlinie gibt. Kostenreduktion wäre in einem solchen Unternehmen der Haupttreiber für IT Off-/Nearshoring.

Diese Organisation mit keiner oder wenig IT Off-/Nearshoring Erfahrung will nun geeignete Projekt-/Applikationskandidaten für Off-/Nearshoring identifizieren. Nachfolgend finden Sie die zehn Kriterienausprägungen, die sich aus den Experteninterviews ergaben, zur Evaluation möglicher Kandidaten.

Welche Kriterienausprägung würden Sie diesem Unternehmen empfehlen zu verwenden, um möglichst geeignete Projekt-/Applikationskandidaten für Off-/Nearshoring zu identifizieren? Bitte vergeben Sie einen Wert zwischen 1 (unwichtig) bis 7 (sehr wichtig) für jede einzelne Kriterienausprägung.

Bitte wählen Sie die zutreffende Antwort aus:

	Unimportant				Very important		
	(1)	(2)	(3)	(4)	(5)	(6)	(7)
Significant **size and duration** of project/application							
High degree of **codification** I.e., regarding documentation or requirements specification							
English is operating **language** I.e., regarding language spoken between client employees and service provider employees, language of documentation and specifications							
Low **business criticality** I.e., regarding importance of project/application for fulfilling daily business operations							
Sufficient **technology availability** I.e., regarding availability of skills in the marketplace, for example technology not too proprietary, not too exotic, not too new							
Low degree of **business specificity** I.e., regarding inherent internal business process knowledge or proprietary industry knowledge							

	Unimportant				Very important		
	(1)	(2)	(3)	(4)	(5)	(6)	(7)

Low degree of **complexity**
I.e., regarding number and size of interfaces, number of users and sites involved, or characteristics of inputs and outputs

Low degree of required personal **interaction**
I.e., regarding required personal contact during development and/or maintenance among team members or client employees and provider employees

High degree of **modularity**
I.e., regarding modularity and separability of application/project and connection with other applications/projects

High degree of **process formalization**
I.e., regarding development or maintenance activities' degree of standardization, specification and structure

Question #2

Stellen Sie sich vor, Sie beraten ein Unternehmen im deutschsprachigen Raum, das mittel oder viel IT Off-/Nearshoring Erfahrung hat.

„Mittlere" Erfahrung würde auf eine Organisation zutreffen, in der es schon erste organisatorische Strukturen gibt, um die IT Off-/Nearshore-Aktivitäten zu managen und bspw. Anreize etabliert sind, damit IT Off-/Nearshoring genutzt wird. Neben der Kostenreduktion ist ein weitere Treiber für IT Off-/Nearshoring, dass sich die IT Abteilung auf höherwertigere Aufgaben konzentrieren kann.

„Viel" Erfahrung würde auf eine Organisation zutreffen, in der IT Off-/Nearshoring integraler Bestandteil der Sourcing-Strategie ist, Kernaktivitäten der Firma off-/neargeshored werden und eine strategische Partnerschaft mit Off-/Nearshore Service Providern besteht.

Diese Organisation mit mittel oder viel IT Off-/Nearshoring Erfahrung will nun geeignete Projekt-/Applikationskandidaten für Off-/Nearshoring identifizieren. Nachfolgend finden Sie die zehn Kriterienausprägungen, die sich aus den Experteninterviews ergaben, zur Evaluation möglicher Kandidaten.

Welche Kriterienausprägung würden Sie diesem Unternehmen empfehlen zu verwenden, um möglichst geeignete Projekt-/Applikationskandidaten für Off-/Nearshoring zu identifzieren? Bitte vergeben Sie einen Wert zwischen 1 (unwichtig) bis 7 (sehr wichtig) für jede einzelne Kriterienausprägung.

Bitte wählen Sie die zutreffende Antwort aus:

	Unimportant					Very important	
	(1)	(2)	(3)	(4)	(5)	(6)	(7)
Significant **size and duration** of project/application							
High degree of **codification** I.e., regarding documentation or requirements specification							
English is operating **language** I.e., regarding language spoken between client employees and service provider employees, language of documentation and specifications							
Low **business criticality** I.e., regarding importance of project/application for fulfilling daily business operations							
Sufficient **technology availability** I.e., regarding availability of skills in the marketplace, for example technology not too proprietary, not too exotic, not too new							

	Unimportant				Very important		
	(1)	(2)	(3)	(4)	(5)	(6)	(7)

Low degree of **business specificity**
I.e., regarding inherent internal business process knowledge
or proprietary industry knowledge

Low degree of **complexity**
I.e., regarding number and size of interfaces, number of users
and sites involved, or characteristics of inputs and outputs

Low degree of required personal **interaction**
I.e., regarding required personal contact during development
and/or maintenance among team members or client employees and provider employees

High degree of **modularity**
I.e., regarding modularity and separability of applica-
tion/project and connection with other applications/projects

High degree of **process formalization**
I.e., regarding development or maintenance activities' degree
of standardization, specification and structure

Variable Naming

In statistic analysis	Criteria	Offshoring expertise
SIZE_LOW	Significant size and duration	No to low
CODIFICATION_LOW	High degree of codification	No to low
LANGUAGE_LOW	English is operating language	No to low
CRITICALITY_LOW	Low business criticality	No to low
TECHNOLOGY_LOW	Sufficient technology availability	No to low
SPECIFICITY_LOW	Low degree of business specificity	No to low
COMPLEXITY_LOW	Low degree of complexity	No to low
INTERACTION_LOW	Low degree of required personal interaction	No to low
MODULARITY_LOW	High degree of modularity	No to low
FORMALIZATION_LOW	High degree of process formalization	No to low
SIZE_HIGH	Significant size and duration	High to medium
CODIFICATION_HIGH	High degree of codification	High to medium
LANGUAGE_HIGH	English is operating language	High to medium
CRITICALITY_HIGH	Low business criticality	High to medium
TECHNOLOGY_HIGH	Sufficient technology availability	High to medium
SPECIFICITY_HIGH	Low degree of business specificity	High to medium
COMPLEXITY_HIGH	Low degree of complexity	High to medium
INTERACTION_HIGH	Low degree of required personal interaction	High to medium
MODULARITY_HIGH	High degree of modularity	High to medium
FORMALIZATION_HIGH	High degree of process formalization	High to medium

Descriptive Statistics

All Experts

	N	Minimum	Maximum	Mean	Std. Deviation
SIZE_LOW	35	1	7	5.37	1.573
CODIFICATION_LOW	35	2	7	5.71	1.250
LANGUAGE_LOW	35	2	7	5.77	1.457
CRITICALITY_LOW	35	2	7	5.34	1.474
TECHNOLOGY_LOW	35	3	7	5.00	1.188
SPECIFICITY_LOW	35	3	7	5.03	1.294
COMPLEXITY_LOW	35	3	7	5.03	1.382
INTERACTION_LOW	35	1	7	4.97	1.636
MODULARITY_LOW	35	2	7	5.06	1.349
FORMALIZATION_LOW	35	2	7	5.23	1.285
SIZE_HIGH	35	2	7	5.06	1.327
CODIFICATION_HIGH	35	1	7	4.66	1.846
LANGUAGE_HIGH	35	2	7	4.86	1.593
CRITICALITY_HIGH	35	3	6	4.00	.840
TECHNOLOGY_HIGH	35	1	7	4.26	1.502
SPECIFICITY_HIGH	35	2	6	4.03	1.200
COMPLEXITY_HIGH	35	2	7	3.83	1.294
INTERACTION_HIGH	35	2	7	4.66	1.514
MODULARITY_HIGH	35	3	7	4.60	1.218
FORMALIZATION_HIGH	35	2	7	5.17	1,317

Experts with One to Three Yrs. Experience Rating Criteria Importance for Organization with No to Low Offshoring Experience

	N	Minimum	Maximum	Mean	Std. Deviation
SIZE_LOW	19	1	7	5.00	1.599
CODIFICATION_LOW	19	3	7	5.79	1.228
LANGUAGE_LOW	19	2	7	5.79	1.475
CRITICALITY_LOW	19	2	7	5.26	1.628
TECHNOLOGY_LOW	19	3	7	4.95	1.026
SPECIFICITY_LOW	19	3	7	5.16	1.344
COMPLEXITY_LOW	19	3	7	4.95	1.393
INTERACTION_LOW	19	1	7	5.26	1.628
MODULARIZATION_LOW	19	2	7	4.95	1.353
FORMALIZATION_LOW	19	2	7	5.00	1.374

Experts with Less than Three Yrs. Experience Rating Criteria Importance for Organization with Medium to High Offshoring Experience

	N	Minimum	Maximum	Mean	Std. Deviation
SIZE_HIGH	16	3	7	5.13	1.310
CODIFICATION_HIGH	16	1	7	4.31	1.815
LANGUAGE_HIGH	16	2	7	5.00	1.506
CRITICALITY_HIGH	16	3	5	4.00	.730
TECHNOLOGY_HIGH	16	2	7	4.56	1.413
SPECIFICITY_HIGH	16	2	6	3.81	1.109
COMPLEXITY_HIGH	16	2	7	3.88	1.360
INTERACTION_HIGH	16	2	7	4.56	1.750
MODULARIZATION_HIGH	16	3	7	4.75	1.238
FORMALIZATION_HIGH	16	2	7	5.06	1.289

Test for Normal Distribution of Data

Experts with One to Three Years Expertise

Tests of Normality[b]

	Kolmogorov-Smirnov[a]			Shapiro-Wilk		
	Statistic	df	Sig.	Statistic	df	Sig.
SIZE	.184	19	.089	.917	19	.099
CODIFICATION	.305	19	.000	.825	19	.003
LANGUAGE	.241	19	.005	.805	19	.001
CRITICALITY	.201	19	.042	.877	19	.019
TECHNOLOGY	.191	19	.068	.917	19	.101
SPECIFICITY	.208	19	.030	.903	19	.054
COMPLEXITY	.147	19	.200*	.906	19	.062
INTERACTION	.254	19	.002	.867	19	.013
MODULARITY	.252	19	.002	.885	19	.026
FORMALIZATION	.237	19	.006	.918	19	.104

a. Lilliefors Significance Correction

*. This is a lower bound of the true significance.

b. EXPERIENCE <= 3 (FILTER) = Selected

Experts with More than Three Years Expertise

Tests of Normality[b]

	Kolmogorov-Smirnov[a]			Shapiro-Wilk		
	Statistic	df	Sig.	Statistic	df	Sig.
SIZE	.163	16	.200*	.922	16	.182
CODIFICATION	.182	16	.165	.932	16	.259
LANGUAGE	.188	16	.136	.895	16	.066
CRITICALITY	.250	16	.009	.820	16	.005
TECHNOLOGY	.191	16	.122	.936	16	.300
SPECIFICITY	.192	16	.117	.933	16	.269
COMPLEXITY	.213	16	.050	.916	16	.145
INTERACTION	.189	16	.130	.870	16	.027
MODULARITY	.228	16	.026	.902	16	.087
FORMALIZATION	.293	16	.001	.881	16	.040

a. Lilliefors Significance Correction

*. This is a lower bound of the true significance.

b. EXPERIENCE <= 3 (FILTER) = Not Selected

134   References

References

Akmanligil, M., & Palvia, P. (2004). Strategies for global information systems development. *Information & Management, 42*(1), 45–59.

Amoribieta, I., Bhaumik, K., Kanakamedala, K., & Parkhe, A. D. (2001). Programmers abroad: A primer on offshore software development. *McKinsey Quarterly*, (2), 128–139.

Apte, U. M. (1992). Global outsourcing of information systems and processing services. *The Information Society, 7*, 287–303.

Apte, U. M., & Mason, R. O. (1995). Global disaggregation of information-intensive services. *Management Science, 41*(7), 1250–1262.

Apte, U. M., Sobol, M. G., Hanaoka, S., Shimada, T., Saarinen, T., & Salmela, T., et al. (1997). IS outsourcing practices in the USA, Japan, and Finland: A comparative study. *Journal of Information Technology, 12*(4), 289–304.

Aron, R., & Singh, J. V. (2005). Getting offshoring right. *Harvard Business Review, 83*(12), 135–143.

Balaji, S., & Ahuja, M. K. (2005). Critical team-level success factors of offshore outsourced projects: A knowledge integration perspective. In R. Sprague Jr. (Ed.), *Proceedings of the 38th Annual Hawaii International Conference on System Sciences* (pp. 52–59). Los Alamitos, CA: IEEE CS Press.

Barney, J. (1991). Firm resources and sustained competitive advantage. *Journal of Management, 17*(1), 99–120.

Ben, E. R., & Claus, R. (2005). Offshoring in der deutschen IT Branche. *Informatik Spektrum, 28*(1), 34–39.

Benbasat, I., Goldstein, D. K., & Mead, M. (1987). The case research strategy in studies of information systems. *MIS Quarterly, 11*(3), 368–386.

BIHK (2002). *Offshore IT für den Mittelstand: Leitfaden zur Schaffung und Sicherung von Arbeitsplätzen durch offshore IT-Entwicklung im Rahmen der Internationalisierung des Mittelstandes in Bayern.* Retrieved March 07, 2007, from http://www.software-offensive-bayern.de/pdf/OffshoreIT.pdf.

Bitkom (2005). *Leitfaden Offshoring.* Retrieved March 07, 2007, from http://www.bitkom.org/files/documents/BITKOM_Leitfaden_Offshoring_31.01.2005.pdf.

Boudreau, M.-C., Gefen, D., & Straub, D. W. (2001). Validation in information systems research: A state-of-the-art assessment. *MIS Quarterly, 25*(1), 1–16.

Bruhn, O. (2004). Offshore-Outsourcing: Von der Idee zum Projekterfolg. In J. Borchers & R. Kneuper (Eds.), *Software Management 2004. Outsourcing und Integration, Fachtagung des GI-Fachausschusses Management der Anwendungsentwicklung und -wartung im Fachbereich Wirtschaftsinformatik* (pp. 34–39). Bad Homburg: GI.

Carmel, E., & Agarwal, R. (2002). The maturation of offshore sourcing of information technology work. *MIS Quarterly Executive, 1*(2), 65–78.

Carmel, E., & Nicholson, B. (2005). Small firms and offshore software outsourcing: High transaction costs and their mitigation. *Journal of Global Information Management, 13*(3), 33–54.

Chua, A.-L., & Pan, S. (2006). Knowledge transfer in offshore insourcing. In W. Haseman, D. W. Straub, & S. Klein (Eds.), *Proceedings of the 27th International Conference on Information Systems* (pp. 1039–1054). Milwaukee, WI.

Coase, R. (1937). The nature of the firm. *Economica, 4*(November), 386–405.

Cohen, J. (1992). A power primer. *Psychological Bulletin, 112*(1), 155–159.

Creswell, J. W. (1994). *Research design: Qualitative and quantitative approaches.* Thousand Oaks, CA: Sage.

Cusick, J., & Prasad, A. (2006). A practical management and engineering approach to offshore collaboration. *IEEE Software, 23*(5), 20–29.

Dibbern, J., Goles, T., Hirschheim, R., & Jayatilaka, B. (2004). Information systems outsourcing: A survey and analysis of the literature. *The Data Base for Advances in Information Systems, 35*(4), 6–102.

Dibbern, J., Winkler, J., & Heinzl, A. (2006). *Offshoring of application services in the banking industry: A transaction cost analysis,* from Universität Mannheim: http://wifo1.bwl.uni-mannheim.de/fileadmin/files/publications/Working_Paper_16-2006.pdf.

Erber, G., & Sayed-Ahmed, A. (2005). Offshore outsourcing: A global shift in the present IT industry. *Intereconomics, 40*(2), 100–112.

Erickson, J. M., & Ranganathan, C. (2006). Project management capabilities: Key to application development offshore outsourcing. In *Proceedings of the 39th Annual Hawaii International Conference on System Sciences* (pp. 199–208). Hawaii.

Ferguson, E., Kussmaul, C., McCracken, D. D., & Robbert, M. A. (2004). Offshore outsourcing: Current conditions & diagnosis. In D. Joyce, D. Knox, W. Dann, & T. L. Naps (Eds.), *Proceedings of the 35th SIGCSE Technical Symposium on Computer Science Education* (pp. 330–331). Norfolk, VA.

Field, A. (2005). *Discovering statistics using SPSS* (2nd edition). London: Sage.

Fish, K. E., & Seydel, J. (2006). Where IT outsourcing is and where it is going: A study across functions and department sizes. *Journal of Computer Information Systems, 46*(3), 96–103.

Gannon, B., & Wilson, D. (2007). IS offshoring: A proposed maturity model of offshore IS suppliers. In H. Österle, J. Schelp, & R. Winter (Eds.), *Proceedings of the 15th European Conference on Information Systems* (pp. 950–960). St. Gallen.

Gurung, A., & Prater, E. (2006). A research framework for the impact of cultural differences on IT outsourcing. *Journal of Global Information Technology Management, 9*(1), 24–43.

Heeks, R., Krishna, S., Nicholsen, B., & Sahay, S. (2001). Synching or sinking: Global software outsourcing relationships. *IEEE Software, 18*(2), 54–60.

Hirschheim, R., Loebbecke, C., Newman, M., & Valor, J. (2005). Offshoring and its implications for the information systems discipline. In D. Avison, D. Galletta, & J. I. DeGross (Eds.), *Proceedings of the 26th International Conference on Information Systems* (pp. 1003–1018). Las Vegas, NV.

Hofstede, G. (1980). *Culture's consequences: International differences in work-related values.* Beverly Hills, CA: Sage.

Jahns, C., Hartmann, E., & Bals, L. (2006/7). Offshoring: Dimensions and diffusion of a new business concept. *Journal of Purchasing and Supply Management, 12*(4), 218–231.

Jennex, M. E., & Adelakun, O. (2003). Success factors for offshore system development. *Journal of Information Technology Cases and Applications, 5*(3), 12–31.

Kakumanu, P., & Portanova, A. (2006). Outsourcing: Its benefits, drawbacks and other related issues. *Journal of American Academy of Business, 9*(2), 1–7.

Kim, S., & Chung, Y. (2003). Critical success factors for IT outsourcing implementation from an interorganizational relationship perspective. *Journal of Computer Information Systems, 43*(4), 81–90.

Klingebiel, N. (2006). Offshoring: Varianten und Wirkungseffekte von Dienstleistungsverlagerungen. *Wirtschaftswissenschaftliches Studium : Wist ; Zeitschrift für Ausbildung und Hochschulkontakt, 35*(9).

Kumar, K., & Willcocks, L. (1996). Offshore outsourcing: A country too far? In J. D. Coelho, J. Tawfik, W. König, H. Krcmar, R. O'Callaghan, & M. Sääksjarvi (Eds.), *Proceedings of the 4th European Conference on Information Systems* (pp. 1309–1325). Lisbon, Portugal.

Kumar, N., & Palvia, P. (2002). A framework for global IT outsourcing management: Key influence factors and strategies. *Journal of Information Technology Cases and Applications, 4*(1), 56–75.

Kuni, R., & Bhushan, N. (2006). IT application assessment model for global software development. In *Proceedings of International Conference on Global Software Engineering (ICGSE)* (pp. 92–100). Florianopolis, Brazil.

Mann, H. B., & Whitney, D. R. (1947). On a test of whether one of two random variables is stochastically larger than the other. *Annals of Mathematical Statistics, 18*, 50–60.

Maskell, P., Pedersen, T., Petersen, B., & Dick-Nielsen, J. (2007). Learning paths to offshore outsourcing: From cost reduction to knowledge seeking. *Industry & Innovation, 14*(3), 239–257.

Mata, F., Fuerst, W., & Barney, J. (1995). Information technology and sustained competitive advantage: A resource-based analysis. *MIS Quarterly, 19*(4), 487–505.

Matzke, P. (2007). Offshoring - nicht um jeden Preis. *Computerwoche, 30*, 28–29.

Mayring, P. (2002). *Einführung in die qualitative Sozialforschung: Eine Anleitung zum qualitativen Denken*. Weinheim: Beltz.

McLaughlin, C. P., & Fitzsimmons, J. A. (1996). Strategies for globalizing service operations. *International Journal of Service Industry Management, 7*(4), 43–57.

Menon, M. (2005). A strategic decision framework for offshoring IT services. *Journal of Global Business*, (Spring), 89–95.

Mertens, P. (2005). *Die (Aus-)Wanderung der Softwareproduktion: Eine Zwischenbilanz*. Erlangen: Univ. Erlangen-Nürnberg Inst. für Informatik.

Meyerolbersleben, S. (2005). *IT-Offshoring: Was geht? Was geht nicht?* Retrieved January 25, 2007, from http://www.ecin.de/strategie/offshoring/print.html.

Mirani, R. (2006). Client-vendor relationships in offshore applications development: An evolutionary framework. *Information Resources Management Journal, 19*(4), 72–86.

Mirani, R. (2007). Procedural coordination and offshored software tasks: Lessons from two case studies. *Information & Management, In Press, Corrected Proof*.

Moczadlo, R. (2002). *Chancen und Risiken des Offshore-Development: Empirische Analyse der Erfahrungen deutscher Unternehmen*. Retrieved November 07, 2006, from http://www.competence-site.de/offshore.nsf/8FB68EAB823EF285C1256D72005BBCD1/$File/studie_offshore_prof_moczadlo.pdf.

Murthy, S. (2004). The impact of global IT outsourcing on IT providers. *Communications of the AIS, 2004*(14), 543–557.

Nicholson, B., & Sahay, S. (2004). Embedded knowledge and offshore software development. *Information & Organization, 14*(4), 329–365.

Niederman, F., Kundu, S. K., & Salas, S. (2006). IT software development offshoring: A multi-level theoretical framework and research agenda. *Journal of Global Information Management, 14*(2), 52–74.

Nonaka, I., & Takeuchi, H. (1995). *The knowledge-creating company: How Japanese companies create the dynamics of innovation*. New York: Oxford Univ. Press.

Orlikowski, W. J., & Baroudi, J. J. (1991). Studying information technology in organizations: Research approaches and assumptions. *Information Systems Research, 2*(1), 1–28.

Penrose, E. (1959). *The theory of the growth of the firm*. New York: Blackwell.

Polanyi, M. (1983). *The tacit dimension*. Gloucester, MA: Smith.

Pu Li, J., & Kishore, R. (2006). Offshore or not?: An transaction cost economics analysis. In I. Garcia & R. Trejo (Eds.), *Proceedings of the 12th Americas Conference on Information Systems* (pp. 3140–3147).

Rajkumar, T., & Mani, R. (2001). Offshore software development: The view from Indian suppliers. *Information Systems Management, 18*(2), 63–73.

Ramarapu, N., Parzinger, M. J., & Lado, A. A. (1997). Issues in foreign outsourcing. *Information Systems Management, 14*(2), 27–31.

Ravichandran, R., & Ahmed, N. (1993). Offshore systems development. *Information & Management, 24*(1), 33–40.

Sayeed, L. (2006). A qualitative investigation of IS offshore sourcing. In I. Garcia & R. Trejo (Eds.), *Proceedings of the 12th Americas Conference on Information Systems* (pp. 3199–3206).

Schaaf, J., & Weber, J. (2005). *Offshoring report 2005: Ready for take-off.* Retrieved November 06, 2006, from http://www.dbresearch.de/PROD/DBR_INTERNET_DE-PROD/PROD0000000000188986.pdf.

Schaffer, E. M. (2006). A decision table: offshore or not? *Interactions, 13*(2), 32–33.

Scheibe, K. P., Mennecke, B. E., & Zobel, C. W. (2006). Creating offshore-ready IT professionals: A global perspective and strong collaborative skills are needed. *Journal of Labor Research, 27*(3), 275–290.

Siegel, S., & Castellan, N. J. (1988). *Nonparametric statistics for the behavioral sciences* (2nd edition). New York: McGraw-Hill.

Smith, M. A., Mitra, S., & Narasimhan, S. (1996). Offshore outsourcing of software development and maintenance: A framework for issues. *Information & Management, 31*(3), 165–175.

Srivastava, S., & Theodore, N. (2005). A long jobless recovery: Information technology labor markets after the bursting of the high-tech bubble. *WorkingUSA, 8*(3), 315–326.

Stack, M., & Downing, R. (2005). Another look at offshoring: Which jobs are at risk and why? *Business Horizons, 48*(6), 513–523.

Wade, M., & Hulland, J. (2004). Review: the resource-based view and information systems research: Review, extension, and suggestions for future research. *MIS Quarterly, 28*(1), 107–142.

Watjatrakul, B. (2005). Determinants of IS sourcing decisions: A comparative study of transaction cost theory versus the resource-based view. *Journal of Strategic Information Systems, 14*(4), 389–415.

Westner, M. (2007). *Information systems offshoring: A review of the literature* (Dresdner Beiträge zur Wirtschaftsinformatik No. 51/07). Dresden.

Westner, M., & Strahringer, S. (2008). Evaluation criteria for selecting offshoring candidates: An analysis of practices in German businesses. *Journal of Information Technology Management, 19*(4), 16–34.

Wiener, M. (2006). *Critical success factors of offshore software development projects: The perspective of German-speaking companies.* Wiesbaden: Dt. Univ.-Verl.

Wilcoxon, F. (1945). Individual comparisons by ranking methods. *Biometrics, 1*(f), 80–83.

William, A., Mayadas, F., & Vardi, M. Y. (2006). *Globalization and offshoring of software: A report of the ACM job migration task force.* Retrieved December 12, 2006, from Association for Computing Machinery: http://www.acm.org/globalizationreport.

Williamson, O. E. (1985). *The economic institutions of capitalism.* New York: Free Press.

Winkler, J., Dibbern, J., & Heinzl, A. (2006). Success in offshoring of application development – does culture matter? In J. Ljunberg & M. Andersson (Eds.), *Proceedings of the 14th European Conference on Information Systems* (pp. 1640–1650). Goteborg.

Yan, Z. (2004). Efficient maintenance support in offshore software development: A case study on a global e-commerce project. In D. Damian, F. Lanubile, E. Hargreaves, & J. Chisan (Eds.), *Proceedings of the 3rd International Workshop on Global Software Development* (pp. 12–18). IEEE CS Press.

Yin, R. (1996). *Case study research: Design and methods* (2nd edition). Beverly Hills, CA: Sage.

ZEW (2007). *IKT-Umfrage 2007: Internetwirtschaft weiter auf dem Vormarsch,* from Zentrum für Europäische Wirtschaftsforschung GmbH: ftp://ftp.zew.de/pub/zew-docs/div/IKTRep/IKT_Report_2007.pdf.

Determinants of Success in IS Offshoring Projects[*]

[*] An earlier and shorter version of this paper was presented on June 10, 2009, at the European Conference on Information Systems (ECIS): Westner, M. (2009). Antecedents of success in IS offshoring projects: Proposal for an empirical research study. In *Proceedings of the 17th European Conference on Information Systems (in press)*. Verona.

Abstract: Recent studies indicate that companies engaged in IS offshoring are not fully satisfied with their engagements' performances. This paper examines determinants of IS offshore project success at German companies. It develops a research model and empirically tests it by using structural equation modeling. Specifically, it examines the direct impact of *offshoring expertise* and *trust in offshore service provider (OSP)* on success, as well as the indirect impact mediated by *project suitability, knowledge transfer,* and *liaison quality*. Results show that offshoring expertise plays only a minor role in explaining success and the mediating constructs. Trust in OSP, on the other hand, has a small direct positive impact on success as well as a medium to large impact on the mediating constructs. Project suitability, knowledge transfer, and liaison quality have a small positive direct impact on success. The paper's originality stems from its empirical-confirmatory research approach and its operationalization attempt for offshoring expertise, project suitability, and liaison quality.

Keywords: Offshoring, nearshoring, outcome, success, information systems, information technology, success factors, PLS

Table of Contents

Figures and Tables.. 144

A   Introductions 148

    A.1   Background and Motivation.. 148

    A.2   Research Questions 149

    A.3   Research Focus.. 150

    A.4   Paper Structure 150

B   Theoretical Foundations.. 151

    B.1   IS Offshoring Implementation Process 151

    B.2   Reference Theories for Success Determinants.. 153

C   Research Model.. 154

    C.1   Overview 154

    C.2   Offshore Project Success... 154

    C.3   Exogenous Determinants of Offshore Project Success 155

        C.3.1   Offshoring Expertise 155

        C.3.2   Trust in Offshore Service Provider 156

    C.4   Endogenous Determinants of Offshore Project Success 157

        C.4.1   Project Suitability.. 157

        C.4.2   Knowledge Transfer.. 158

        C.4.3   Liaison Quality.. 159

D   Methodology 161

    D.1   Research Approach.. 161

    D.2   Research Design 161

    D.3   Measurement Instrument.. 161

    D.4   Statistical Procedures.. 169

E   Data Collection 171

    E.1   Data Source 171

    E.2   Response Rate 172

F   Analyses and Results.. 174

    F.1   Response Structure 174

        F.1.1   Response Time 174

        F.1.2   Non-Response Bias 174

        F.1.3   Missing Values 176

    F.2   Descriptive Analyses 176

        F.2.1   Participants... 176

        F.2.2   Projects.. 178

        F.2.3   Construct Indicators 189

    F.3   Offshore Project Success Analyses of Variances.............................. 197

        F.3.1   Subgroup Comparisons 197

        F.3.2   Pre-Test of Research Model... 205

    F.4   Structural Equation Model Analysis 221

        F.4.1   Quality Criteria.. 221

        F.4.2   Quality Assessment of Measurement Model 226

        F.4.3   Quality Assessment of Structural Model 236

        F.4.4   Model Adequacy 239

        F.4.5   Subgroup Analysis 240

G   Discussion of Results... 242

    G.1   Exogenous Determinants of Offshore Project Success 242

        G.1.1   Offshoring Expertise 242

        G.1.2   Trust in Offshore Service Provider 243

    G.2   Endogenous Determinants of Offshore Project Success 244

        G.2.1   Project Suitability... 244

        G.2.2   Knowledge Transfer... 244

        G.2.3   Liaison Quality... 245

H   Conclusions... 246

H.1   Contributions 246

H.2   Managerial Implications 246

H.3   Limitations 247

H.4   Directions for Future Research 247

Appendix 249

References 289

Figures and Tables

Figure 3-1: Research model on determinants of offshore project success. 154

Figure 3-2: Screenshot of the web-based survey instrument 168

Figure 3-3: Survey response rate 173

Figure 3-4: Survey response times 174

Figure 3-5: Job positions of study participants 177

Figure 3-6: Experience levels of study participants 178

Figure 3-7: Industry sectors where projects were conducted 179

Figure 3-8: Employee demographics of companies where projects were conducted 180

Figure 3-9: Reasons for doing projects near-/offshore 181

Figure 3-10: Embededness of projects in corporate program 182

Figure 3-11: Countries of delivery 183

Figure 3-12: Ownership structure regarding OSP 184

Figure 3-13: Application development and maintenance share 185

Figure 3-14: Project sizes and offshore shares 185

Figure 3-15: Consulting support for projects 186

Figure 3-16: Distribution of first versus recent projects 187

Figure 3-17: Finishing dates of projects 187

Figure 3-18: Study participants' roles in the project 188

Figure 3-19: Residential location of participants 189

Figure 3-20: Indicator values for construct offshore project success (SUCCESS) 190

Figure 3-21: Indicator values for perceived importance of success determinants 191

Figure 3-22: Indicator values for self-perceived levels of constructs 192

Figure 3-23: Indicator values for construct offshoring expertise (EXP) 193

Figure 3-24: Indicator values for construct trust in OSP (TRUST) 194

Figure 3-25: Indicator values for construct project suitability (SUITA) 195

Figure 3-26: Indicator values for construct knowledge transfer (KNOWT) 196

Figure 3-27: Indicator values for construct liaison quality (LIASO) 197

Figure 3-28: Relationship of offshoring expertise and offshore project success 207

Figure 3-29: Relationship of offshoring expertise and project suitability............................ 208

Figure 3-30: Relationship of offshoring expertise and knowledge transfer......................... 210

Figure 3-31: Relationship of offshoring expertise and liaison quality................................. 211

Figure 3-32: Relationship of trust in OSP and knowledge transfer 213

Figure 3-33: Relationship of trust in OSP and liaison quality 214

Figure 3-34: Relationship of trust in OSP and offshore project success.............................. 215

Figure 3-35: Relationship of project suitability and offshore project success 217

Figure 3-36: Relationship of knowledge transfer and offshore project success................... 218

Figure 3-37: Relationship of liaison quality and offshore project success........................... 220

Figure 3-38: Adapted research model with one-factor operationalization of knowledge
transfer... 230

Figure 3-39: Adapted research model with two-factor operationalization of knowledge
transfer... 230

Figure 3-40: Additional assessment of formative measurement model for project
suitability... 235

Figure 3-41: PLS results for one-factor model.. 236

Figure 3-42: PLS results for two-factor model 238

Table 3-1: Overview of measurement indicators from previous studies............................. 162

Table 3-2: Measurement indicators for construct offshoring expertise [EXP] 163

Table 3-3: Measurement indicators for construct trust in OSP [TRUST]............................ 163

Table 3-4: Measurement indicators for construct project suitability [SUITA].................... 164

Table 3-5: Measurement indicators for construct knowledge transfer [KNOWT] 165

Table 3-6: Measurement indicators for construct liaison quality [LIAISO]........................ 165

Table 3-7: Measurement indicators for construct offshore project success [SUCCESS] 166

Table 3-8: Reasons cited for non-participation 172

Table 3-9: Reasons for exclusion of data items 173

Table 3-10: Mean differences of offshoring expertise indicator EXP4 between first and
recent projects 198

Table 3-11: Mean differences of offshore project success indicator values between first
and recent projects 198

Table 3-12: Mean differences of offshore project success indicator values between
nearshore and offshore projects 199

Table 3-13: Mean differences of offshore project success indicator values between
projects delivered by an internal or partially owned OSP and projects
delivered by an external OSP 200

Table 3-14: Mean differences of offshoring expertise indicator EXP4 between stand-
alone projects and projects conducted as part of a larger offshoring program .. 201

Table 3-15: Mean differences of offshore project success indicator values between stand-
alone projects and projects conducted as part of a larger offshoring program .. 201

Table 3-16: Mean differences of offshore project success indicator values between small
projects and large projects regarding labor months 202

Table 3-17: Mean differences of offshore project success indicator values between
projects with low offshore share and projects with high offshore share 203

Table 3-18: Mean differences of offshore project success indicator values between
projects with no consulting support and projects with consulting support 204

Table 3-19: Overview of subgroup comparison results 205

Table 3-20: Correlation of surrogate constructs 206

Table 3-21: Significances of overall success mean differences for different offshoring
expertise levels 208

Table 3-22: Significances of project suitability mean differences for different offshoring
expertise levels 209

Table 3-23: Significances of knowledge transfer mean differences for different offshoring
expertise levels 211

Table 3-24: Significances of liaison quality mean differences for different offshoring
expertise levels 212

Table 3-25: Significances of knowledge transfer mean differences for different trust
levels 213

Table 3-26: Significances of liaison quality mean differences for different trust levels 215

Table 3-27: Significances of overall success mean differences for different trust levels 216

Table 3-28: Significances of overall success mean differences for different levels of project suitability 217

Table 3-29: Significances of overall success mean differences for different levels of knowledge transfer 219

Table 3-30: Significances of overall success mean differences for different liaison quality levels 220

Table 3-31: Overview of ANOVA test results 221

Table 3-32: Quality criteria: unidimensionality 222

Table 3-33: Quality criteria: convergent validity 223

Table 3-34: Quality criteria: discriminant validity 224

Table 3-35: Quality criteria: construct reliability 224

Table 3-36: Quality criteria: formative construct 225

Table 3-37: Quality criteria: structural model 226

Table 3-38: Assessment of unidimensionality with exploratory factor analysis 227

Table 3-39: Assessment of convergent validity for one-factor model 231

Table 3-40: Assessment of convergent validity for two-factor model 232

Table 3-41: Assessment of discriminant validity for one-factor model 232

Table 3-42: Assessment of discriminant validity for two-factor model 233

Table 3-43: Assessment of construct reliability 233

Table 3-44: Quality assessment of formative indicators 234

Table 3-45: Structural paths and effect sizes for one-factor model 237

Table 3-46: Structural paths and effect sizes for two-factor model 239

Table 3-47: Model differences for projects delivered by an internal or partially owned OSP and projects delivered by an external OSP 241

A Introductions

A.1 Background and Motivation

Information systems (IS) offshoring describes the transfer of IS services to an offshoring service provider (OSP) in a near or far away country.[1] This OSP can be an internal subsidiary (so-called captive offshoring), a partially owned unit, or an external service provider (so-called offshore outsourcing). The services themselves are partially or totally transferred. (Carmel & Agarwal, 2002; Hirschheim, Loebbecke, Newman, & Valor, 2005; Jahns, Hartmann, & Bals, 2006/7; Mirani, 2006; Niederman, Kundu, & Salas, 2006; Rajkumar & Mani, 2001; Srivastava, Teo, & Mohapatra, 2008)

High labor cost differentials in comparison to western countries and the resulting cost savings are the main reasons why companies engage in IS offshoring. Accordingly, the market volume for offshoring of IS services has been growing fast in the last few years, with India being the most popular offshoring destination (Knapp, Sharma, & King, 2007; Metters & Verma, 2008; Poornima, 2008). Application development and maintenance activities, where labor constitutes a significant share of total costs, are especially likely to be performed offshore (Bitkom, 2005; Boes, Schwemmle, & Becker, 2004; William, Mayadas, & Vardi, 2006). However, recent studies among companies worldwide indicate that a large number of companies that engaged in IS offshoring are not fully satisfied with their engagements' performances (Bright, 2008; Computerwoche, 2008).

The situation is especially noticeable in Germany. There, offshoring levels are rather low: only 6% of all companies source IS services from abroad in contrast to 64% that already use domestic IS outsourcing (Schaaf & Weber, 2005; ZEW, 2007). Additionally, German companies also experience difficulties in performing IS offshoring successfully (Prehl, 2008). This seems to be due to language and cultural barriers (Dibbern, Winkler, & Heinzl, 2006; Mertens, 2005; Moczadlo, 2002; Wiener, 2006).

IS offshoring is worth being researched as a domain of its own because it has specific characteristics that distinguish it from the well-researched field of IS outsourcing. In IS offshoring, service delivery occurs under the additional condition of distance between service provider and consumer in terms of physical distance, time zone differences, or cultural differences. Additionally, complexity increases due to the higher degree of geographical dispersion among team members. Finally, IS offshoring arrangements often create additional organizational challenges because offshore staff partially replaces domestic onshore staff.

---

[1] For readability reasons we consistently use the term *offshoring* in this paper. Offshoring thereby subsumes near- and offshoring, i.e., the transfer either to a nearby or distant country with regard to Germany.

(Chua & Pan, 2008; Holmström Olsson, Conchúir, Ågerfalk, & Fitzgerald, 2008; Ranganathan & Balaji, 2007; Rottman & Lacity, 2008; Srivastava et al., 2008; Winkler, Dibbern, & Heinzl, 2008)

Research in IS offshoring has been growing in the last years and journals such as the *MIS Quarterly* (2008, vol. 32, issue 2) or *Information Systems Frontier* (2008, vol. 10, issue 2) have recently published issues addressing the phenomenon. IS offshoring research, in contrast to IS outsourcing research, is primarily case study based and qualitative, which shows that it is still in its initial, theory-building stage (Dibbern, Goles, Hirschheim, & Jayatilaka, 2004; King & Torkzadeh, 2008). The research situation is furthermore characterized by studies that employ a project or organizational level of analysis, focus on India as an offshoring destination, and investigate success or outcome factors as research topics (King & Torkzadeh, 2008).

A.2 Research Questions

Our study examines determinants of IS offshore project success at German companies. Therefore, our general research objective is:

- What are determinants of success for IS offshore projects?

Specifically, we focus on selected success determinants that we derive from the implementation process for IS offshoring. Our research questions are:

- Do *offshoring expertise, trust in OSP, project suitability, knowledge transfer*, and *liaison quality* directly impact offshore project success, and if so, to what extent?

- Is the direct impact of *trust in OSP* and *offshoring expertise* on success mediated by *project suitability, knowledge transfer*, and *liaison quality*, and if so, to what extent?

We employ a confirmatory-quantitative research approach to address these questions. In this sense we follow the current state in IS offshoring research to focus on success/outcome factors with projects being the unit of analysis. However, we add original content through our research model that partially builds upon recent research results but also incorporates new aspects. We ensure methodological originality by gathering a broad empirical dataset and by analyzing the research model with structural equation modeling as a method for analysis. Finally, we address the paucity of research that quantitatively investigates offshoring in the context of German businesses.

For management practice, the study analyzes the influence of the above-mentioned determinants on success. The study indicates which determinants have a material, i.e., statistical significant and sizeable, impact on success for IS offshore projects. Furthermore, the study's results show the determinants' relative importance. Practitioners can use this information to determine on which aspects they should focus when implementing an IS offshore project in order to increase the project's likelihood of success.

A.3 Research Focus

We focus our research along four dimensions: the regional focus is Germany; we focus on the offshore consuming client's perspective; the unit of analysis is offshoring projects, i.e., not the arrangement or relationship between service consumer and provider in total; and we focus on application development or maintenance projects.

A.4 Paper Structure

Based on the implementation process for IS offshoring, Section B develops five determining constructs of offshore project success which are: offshoring expertise; trust in OSP; project suitability; knowledge transfer; and liaison quality. Afterwards, it relates these determinants to reference theories. Section C describes the research model, the main dependent construct offshore project success, and its determinants. Section D explains the applied research approach and the corresponding research design. It also contains the measurement instrument and outlines the statistical procedures we used for analyses. Section E describes the data collection process. Section F contains the main analyses of the essay. Section F.1 focuses on the response structure regarding time to respond, non-response bias, and missing values. The following section, F.2, comprises descriptive analyses regarding the survey participants, projects, and the actual construct indicator values. Section F.3 compares several subgroups regarding differences of offshore project success and pre-tests the research model. Section F.4 contains the actual core analysis of the research model using Partial Least Squares (PLS). Based on the analyses results, Section G discusses the findings. Finally, Section H concludes this study by highlighting its contributions to theory and practice, as well as its specific limitations and potential directions for future research.

B Theoretical Foundations

We derive potential success determinants for IS offshore projects by using the implementation process for IS offshoring as a starting point for our considerations. Employing this process perspective, we ensure practitioner-relevant and outcome-oriented research constructs. Subsequently, we relate the identified constructs to existing reference theories.

B.1 IS Offshoring Implementation Process

A literature analysis shows that there are five stages in the implementation process of IS offshoring arrangements (Westner, 2007). These are the *initiation* of IS offshoring with the actual decision to offshore or not, the *selection of a vendor* for delivery, the *transition* of the service delivery to the service provider, the *delivery* of the transferred service, and the *finalization* with an assessment regarding the project's outcomes (Erber & Sayed-Ahmed, 2005; Murray & Crandall, 2006). This implementation process exhibits similarities to the implementation process in the field of IS outsourcing: in their extensive literature review Dibbern et al. (2004) find *vendor selection, relationship building and structuring,* and *relationship management* as key aspects of how to implement IS outsourcing arrangements.

However, not all of the previously described implementation stages are of equal relevance when deriving determinants of offshore project success. Regarding the initiation stage, an important aspect is the identification of suitable project candidates for offshoring. This is one of the first activities in an IS offshoring arrangement. Once identified, these offshoring candidates represent the core objects in the subsequent implementation of IS offshoring. Therefore, research and practice indicate that the identification of suitable project candidates is a main step in pursuing an IS offshoring endeavor (Aron & Singh, 2005; Chua & Pan, 2006; Kumar & Palvia, 2002). Accordingly, the study focuses on project suitability as a success determinant emerging from the initiation stage.

The subsequent vendor selection stage is less important for the scope of our research. First, we employ a definition of IS offshoring that embraces offshoring to an external third party (offshore outsourcing), as well as offshoring to an internal subsidiary (captive offshoring). Therefore we cannot always expect the existence of a separate vendor selection stage since there might be no vendor-client relationship at all, for example in a captive offshore arrangement. Second, our unit of analysis is the individual project. If a project is part of a larger offshoring program at a company, vendor selection might have happened before the project was initiated. Thus, there would be no vendor selection stage in the direct context of the project. Considering this, we do not incorporate any aspects of the vendor selection stage into the research model.

In contrast to that, the transition stage is of greater importance for our research objective. The key part of the transition stage is the transfer of knowledge from domestic onshore staff to staff of the OSP (Carmel & Beulen, 2005; Erber & Sayed-Ahmed, 2005; Murray & Crandall, 2006). The importance of knowledge transfer thereby stems from the fact that in IS offshore arrangements OSP staff replaces domestic staff in order to gain benefits from labor cost differences (Chua & Pan, 2008; Ranganathan & Balaji, 2007). Therefore, all relevant knowledge for delivering the offshored services needs to be transferred to and understood by the OSP staff for successful offshoring. To account for this characteristic of offshoring during the transition-stage, we incorporate the aspect of knowledge transfer in the research model.

The delivery stage comprises the activities related to the provisioning of offshored services, such as project management, change management, or software engineering. Research results show that in IS offshoring, specific challenges arise from the globally dispersed work environment as well as from cultural differences. Therefore, researchers stress the importance of collaboration quality between domestic and offshore staff (Dhar & Balakrishnan, 2006; Kumar & Willcocks, 1996; Nicklisch, Borchers, Krick, & Rucks, 2008; Rottman, 2008). Close collaboration increases liaison quality and helps to overcome the above-mentioned challenges regarding distance and culture. Therefore, we include the aspect of collaboration, i.e., liaison quality, between staff in IS offshore projects as a success determinant in the study.

The last stage of the implementation process, finalization, is less relevant to our research objective. Since it happens after a project's end and addresses issues such as project wrap-up or documentation of lessons-learned, it has no direct impact on project success. Therefore, we do not deduct a success determinant from this stage.[2]

Guided by the implementation process of IS offshoring, we identified project suitability, knowledge transfer, and liaison quality as success determinants relevant for our research objective. The following section relates these three determinants to existing reference theories and derives the other two considered success determinants, offshoring expertise and trust in OSP.

---

[2] One could argue that results from the finalization stage increase organizations' and individuals' levels of offshoring expertise and therefore have a positive impact on *future* projects. We share this view and also perceive offshoring expertise as a success determinant. Section B.2 derives this determinant from a theoretical perspective instead of a process perspective.

B.2 Reference Theories for Success Determinants[3]

The initially derived success determinant project suitability primarily relates to transaction cost economics (TCE). TCE states that asset specificity, uncertainty, and frequency impact production and transaction costs, thus influencing transactions' structures at companies (Apte, 1992; Dibbern et al., 2006; Kumar & Palvia, 2002). Projects with a high degree of asset specificity and uncertainty (frequency is not considered on the project level, c.f. Westner & Strahringer, 2008) might incur unexpected additional costs making them unsuitable for offshoring and thus lowering their chance for successful delivery.

Success determinant knowledge transfer relates to the knowledge-based view (KBV). KBV states that organizations possess knowledge and that this knowledge needs to be managed properly to be successful. With regard to IS offshoring, knowledge pertinent to applications can be explicit, such as software documentation, technical specification, or standardized development processes, but it can also be tacit, such as practices like norms of communication or non-specified processes and activities (Chua & Pan, 2006; Nicholson & Sahay, 2004). Successful knowledge transfer thereby depends on the exchange of explicit and tacit knowledge as well as the absorptive capacity of the knowledge receiver – in this case the OSP staff. Furthermore, knowledge is accumulated over time in the form of expertise. Individuals and organizations can build upon this expertise when conducting offshoring. Thus, we consider offshoring expertise as an additional success determinant in our study.

Liaison quality as a success determinant can be related to social theories, namely social exchange theory and relationship theories. Social theories conceptualize the activities between two or more persons as exchanges. Thereby, reciprocity, balance, cohesion, and power determine the attributes of the exchanges (Dibbern et al., 2004; Emerson, 1972). Relationship theories focus on interaction between parties with the aim of a joint accomplishment. These interactions are motivated by the understanding that a specific accomplishment can be achieved better jointly instead of using another form of exchange (Dibbern et al., 2004; Klepper, 1995). High levels of liaison quality indicate that cooperating partners attempt to jointly achieve offshore project success. Moreover, trust is often embedded in relations and represents an important factor in social exchanges (Park & Im, 2007; Young-Ybarra & Wiersema, 1999). Trust is moreover considered as a key success factor in customer-supplier arrangements (Park & Im, 2007; Westner, 2007; Zaheer, McEvily, & Perrone, 1998). Therefore, we include trust in OSP as a success determinant within our study.

---

[3] See also Essay 1 (Westner, 2007) and Essay 2 (Westner & Strahringer, 2008) in this thesis for a detailed illustration of reference theories.

C Research Model

This section describes the applied research model and illustrates the five success determinants in greater detail, with a special focus on findings from existing research.

C.1 Overview

The research model argues that offshoring expertise has a direct positive effect on offshore project success. Additionally, it is positively associated with a project's suitability for offshoring, knowledge transfer, and liaison quality which act as mediators for offshore project success. Trust in the OSP is positively associated with knowledge transfer, liaison quality, and offshore project success. Figure 3-1 illustrates the model. A plus (+) symbol in the model denotes a positive relation between constructs. The subsequent sections develop and describe the model's constructs and their relationships.

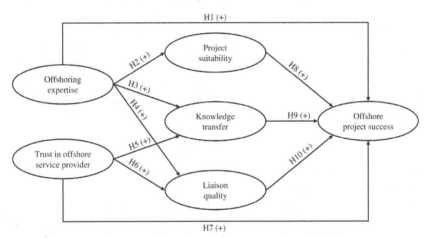

Figure 3-1: Research model on determinants of offshore project success.

C.2 Offshore Project Success

Offshore project success is the dependent construct in the research model. As Erickson & Ranganathan (2006) show, success can be understood and measured in multiple ways, including "the organization's satisfaction with the results of outsourcing (Grover, Cheon, & Teng, 1996), an expectations fulfillment view (Lacity & Willcocks, 1998), a cost/benefit approach (Wang, 2002), a psychological contract perspective on fulfilled obligations (Koh, Soon Ang, & Straub, 2004), and a strategic fit view of success (Lee, Miranda, & Kim, 2004)" (Erickson & Ranganathan, 2006, p. 202).

Several studies measure success as the satisfaction of outcomes, sometimes calibrated by initial expectations (Balaji & Ahuja, 2005; Grover et al., 1996; Dahlberg & Nyrhinen, 2006; Wüllenweber, Beimborn, Weitzel, & König, 2008). In their extensive review of IS outsourcing success definitions and measures, Dahlberg & Nyrhinen (2006) find that satisfaction with outcomes can be evaluated along four categories: strategic factors, economic factors, technological factors, and social factors. Additionally, overall satisfaction forms a part of their success definition.

Strategic, economic, technological and social outcome factors may also apply to projects but they are not applicable in all cases. For example one might think of projects that completely lack a specific strategic proposition. Since a project is by definition an effort bound by schedule, budget, functionality, and quality (Erickson & Ranganathan, 2006), it rather makes sense to use these dimensional factors together with overall satisfaction as an operationalization of offshore project success.

Therefore, this paper interprets the dependent construct offshore project success as the perceived satisfaction with the outcome of the offshore project in total, and with the dimensions of schedule, budget, functionality, and quality in particular.

C.3 Exogenous Determinants of Offshore Project Success

C.3.1 Offshoring Expertise

We define expertise as a certain degree of individual or organizational experience in managing or conducting offshoring in a more efficient and thus successful manner. In organizational research this is commonly referred to as learning curve or experience curve effects (Day & Montgomery, 1983; Ghemawat, 1985).

As mentioned earlier, delivery in an offshoring context raises multiple challenges for all involved parties. Individuals as well as organizations can benefit from best practices and experiences they have had in past engagements. Thus they can cope better with offshore-specific challenges.

The positive impact of expertise on diverse activities of the offshore process and directly on offshore project success has already been addressed in research. Carmel & Agarwal (2002) develop a maturity model for companies engaging in offshoring and give recommendations on how to move along this maturity curve. In a study of an eight-year offshore outsourcing alliance, Kaiser & Hawk (2004) describe how the alliance evolved towards a more beneficial cosourcing model, for both the consumer and the supplier. Similarly, Mirani (2006) shows how increasing expertise leads to a change in the offshoring relationship from rather simple to more sophisticated arrangements. Rottman & Lacity (2006) in their study of offshoring practices at 21 U.S. companies, also find positive effects of expertise on offshoring success. Apart from these studies, there is a paucity of research regarding the impact of expertise on success in the field of IS offshoring.

Higher levels of organizational and individual expertise help to cope with the potential challenges of offshoring and thus increase the probability of project success. Thus, expertise has a positive impact on all three mediating constructs because, based on past experiences, it is rather likely a company selects projects which are most suitable for offshoring. Additionally, the organization and the individuals know how to manage knowledge transfer and improve liaison quality based on their expertise. Thus, we hypothesize:

H1: IS offshoring expertise is positively and directly associated with offshore project success.

H2: IS offshoring expertise is positively associated with project suitability.

H3: IS offshoring expertise is positively associated with knowledge transfer.

H4: IS offshoring expertise is positively associated with liaison quality.

C.3.2   Trust in Offshore Service Provider

We define trust as the "expectation that an actor (1) can be relied on to fulfill obligations [...], (2) will behave in a predictable manner, and (3) will act and negotiate fairly when the possibility for opportunism is present" (Zaheer et al., 1998, p. 143). Trust can thereby take the form of interpersonal or interorganizational trust. Interpersonal trust is trust placed by the individuals in their individual opposite member. Interorganizational trust is trust placed in the partner organization by the members of a focal organization (Lee, Huynh, & Hirschheim, 2008; Zaheer et al., 1998). Since we focus on offshore projects as the unit of analysis and not the overall arrangement between client and OSP, we employ the interpersonal trust perspective for the course of our study.

Trust is important within an IS offshoring context because it is a facilitator and precondition for activities such as knowledge transfer, but also for collaboration among team members in general. Trust thereby increases the room to maneuver within an arrangement beyond the specifications of a contract. If individuals or organizations trust their counterparts, they are more willing to cooperate and to put in extra effort if needed. (Lee et al., 2008)

In IS outsourcing research, the role of trust as an important arrangement attribute has been widely recognized. Higher levels of trust seem to positively influence the relationship between client and vendor (Grover et al., 1996; Lee & Kim, 1999; Winkler et al., 2008). Recent empirical-confirmatory studies show that trust is positively related to the extent of knowledge sharing (Lee et al., 2008) and that trust, mediated by cooperative learning, has a significant positive influence on knowledge transfer (Park & Im, 2007). With respect to IS offshoring research, trust is mentioned as a critical success factor regarding the interface between offshore consumer and supplier (Jennex & Adelakun, 2003). Kaiser & Hawk (2004) confirm this in a case study and perceive the creation of trust as a best practice for successful offshoring because it facilitates collaboration between on- and offshore staff. Thus, offshore staff becomes productive in a short time and projects progress faster. Winkler et al. (2008) show that trust positively influences the degree of connectedness between an offshore consumer and a service provider in their aim to achieve specified goals. Rottman (2008) illustrates how trust facilitates the knowledge transfer within an offshoring arrangement because it increases the willingness to share knowledge and collaborate.

Apparently, trust seems to influence knowledge transfer because individuals are more likely to share knowledge if they trust each other. This is especially important when it comes to implicit and thus sticky knowledge. Additionally, trust fosters and facilitates collaboration, communication, and – more generally – increases liaison quality among team members. Thus we hypothesize:

H5: Trust in OSP is positively associated with knowledge transfer.

H6: Trust in OSP is positively associated with liaison quality.

Similar to the hypotheses concerning the construct offshoring expertise, we could hypothesize a direct effect of trust on offshore project success. However, the studies mentioned above and other non-IS research (c.f. literature overview by Lee et al., 2008) do not support such an association. They do not link levels of trust directly to success or outcome but rather examine the impact of trust on constructs such as relationship or partnership quality, thus assuming a fully mediated effect. We nevertheless include a potential direct impact of trust on offshore project success in the model. However, because the theoretical backing is weak, we treat it with the necessary prudence regarding its direct impact in the model on success and later interpretation of results:

H7: Trust in OSP is positively and directly associated with offshore project success.

C.4 Endogenous Determinants of Offshore Project Success

C.4.1 Project Suitability

We define project suitability for offshoring as the sense that a project's attributes and its task characteristics make it more amenable for delivery in a dispersed, inter-cultural environment, i.e., in an offshoring setting.

Research in IS outsourcing has shown that there is a link between the function being outsourced and arrangement success (Fisher, Hirschheim, & Jacobs, 2008). They suggest focusing on routinely performed and non-core functions. Applying the lens of transaction cost theory and operations management models, Stratman (2008) finds that well understood, standardized service processes that are non-core are best candidates for successful offshoring. Stringfellow, Teagarden, & Nie (2008) show that it is more challenging to offshore complex, loosely defined and non-standardized tasks that require complex judgments and implicit knowledge. If projects or tasks show these characteristics, offshore delivery incurs additional costs which might threaten project success. King (2008) suggests a framework for determining whether an IS activity should be considered for offshoring. He posits that activities should be kept in-house if they require proximity and the risk of offshoring is too great, or if the activity is too business-critical. Schaffer (2006) develops a similar framework that suggests refraining from offshoring projects which are very short, require a tremendous amount of personal interaction, are of high security and extreme criticality for the business. Mirani (2006) states that small applications or components of low complexity, for which specifications can be communicated completely, and whose development process is highly structured, are more likely to be successfully delivered in an offshore arrangement.

Since most of these studies are conceptual in nature or rely on a small set of empirical data, we carried out a qualitative pre-study with 47 German offshoring experts from different companies to find out whether project suitability is actually important for project success and what the respective evaluation criteria could be (Westner & Strahringer, 2008). In the interviews, these experts confirmed that a project's characteristics and its suitability for offshoring have an impact on later project success. Criteria such as project size, project duration, operating language, degree of codification, and business specificity were most frequently mentioned as determining a project's suitability for offshoring with regard to successful delivery. If projects have a certain minimum size and duration, the project language is English, the degree of codification is high, and business specificity or required domain knowledge is low, it takes less time and effort to make OSP staff fully productive. Therefore we hypothesize:

H8: Project suitability is positively associated with offshore project success.

C.4.2 Knowledge Transfer

Following Davenport & Prusak (1998) and Lee et al. (2008) we define knowledge as "a fluid mix of experience, values, contextual information and expert insight that provides a framework for evaluating and incorporating new experiences and information" (Lee et al., 2008, p. 149). Knowledge transfer as an outcome is the result of the exchange of knowledge as a systematic activity between individuals and organizations (Chua & Pan, 2008; Wang, Tong, & Koh, 2004) and the ability to absorb the knowledge, to apply it, and to use it in project delivery (Orlikowski, 2002; Oshri, Kotlarsky, & Willcocks, 2007).

To profit from the economic benefits of offshoring, offshore staff must actually replace more expensive onshore staff (Chua & Pan, 2008). Accordingly, all project-relevant explicit and implicit knowledge needs to be transferred to offshore staff. This knowledge transfer happens at the beginning of an offshoring project but is also a continuous activity during the whole project. Correspondingly, offshoring process models used in the industry and proposed by research recognize knowledge transfer as a specific activity (Bugajska, 2007; Carmel & Beulen, 2005; Oshri et al., 2007; Voigt, Novak, & Schwabe, 2007).

Applying this perspective, the importance of knowledge transfer becomes obvious and has also been addressed in research. A case study by Chua & Pan (2008) examines how a financial institution transferred knowledge within a captive offshoring arrangement, and highlights knowledge transfer's importance for successful service delivery. Another case study, by Oshri et al. (2007) from the OSP perspective, investigates best practices for managing dispersed knowledge among on- and offshore sites and acknowledges that knowledge transfer is a key part of successful offshoring. Previously, Ganesh & Moitra (2004) identified knowledge transition and the absorptive capacity of the OSP as one of the critical success factors for successful service transition in the context of business process outsourcing and offshoring. Rottman & Lacity (2008) develop best practices to ensure success in IS offshoring. Most of these best practices are fundamentally linked to facilitate and ensure successful knowledge transfer. Finally, in one of the few recent empirical-confirmatory studies, Lee et al. (2008) examine IS outsourcing arrangements between Korean firms and find significant support for the hypothesis that knowledge sharing is positively related to the success of outsourcing.

Thus, we can conclude that if knowledge transfer is successful, offshore staff is more productive because it has the required know-how to perform project tasks and onshore staff can be replaced as initially planned because it does not hold exclusive knowledge anymore. Based on this understanding we hypothesize that:

H9: Knowledge transfer is positively associated with offshore project success.

C.4.3   Liaison Quality

We define liaison quality as the degree of connectedness between onshore and OSP staff in the aim to achieve specified goals, i.e., in our case, a project's objectives (Winkler et al., 2008). Liaison between staff should incorporate reciprocity and closeness (Xu & Yao, 2006).

The environmental circumstances of IS offshoring delivery have negative impacts on liaison quality. Due to distance, communication frequency between team members decreases, collaboration is aggravated, and individuals tend to feel they are not equal members of a team (Herbsleb & Mockus, 2003; Xu & Yao, 2006).

Therefore, research in IS offshoring emphasizes the importance of liaison quality on offshoring success. Erickson & Ranganathan (2006) highlight the need for clear roles, responsibilities, communication mechanisms, and conflict resolution in the management of global virtual teams. Rottman (2008) recognizes liaison quality's impact on success and suggests building personal connections between OSP staff and client staff, for example by regular site visits and face-to-face meetings. Furthermore, he proposes to integrate offshore staff into onshore staff and synchronize training of offshore employees with internal training efforts. Similarly, Heeks, Krishna, Nicholsen, & Sahay (2001) find that a high degree of congruence between provider and client improves chances for project success regarding schedule and budget. They recommend building bridging relationships between involved team members, and using straddlers, i.e., dedicated individuals who are responsible for facilitating and moderating the interaction between on- and offshore staff. Levina & Vaast (2008) mention that liaison quality lessens negative effects of distance and thereby improves performance. They mention good onshore middle managers, frequent communication, constructive communication, and the efficient usage of technology as practices to improve liaison quality. Other research shows congruent findings and mentions the positive effect of liaison quality on performance achieved by liaison engineers and personal relationships (Kobitzsch, Rombach, & Feldmann, 2001), facilitation of informal communication (Herbsleb & Mockus, 2003), the presence of expert intermediaries, and supplier presence on-site (Carmel & Nicholson, 2005).

Achieving satisfactory levels of liaison in an offshore project setting seems to be challenging due to the negative effects of cultural and physical distance. However, liaison between on- and offshore staff is vital for collaboration, working efficiency, and productivity. Thus liaison quality directly impacts offshore project success and we hypothesize:

H10: Liaison quality is positively associated with offshore project success.

D Methodology

D.1 Research Approach

The study at hand follows a confirmatory research approach. Confirmatory research attempts to test a priori specified relationships through structured scientific instruments of data gathering and analysis (Boudreau, Gefen, & Straub, 2001; Dibbern et al., 2004). In our study, we specify the assumed relationships in the form of distinct hypotheses based on findings from existing research (c.f. Section C, p. 154).

Our research is empirical and we use a survey design for data gathering. A survey design "provides a quantitative or numeric description of some fraction of the population – the sample – through the data collection process of asking questions [...]" (Creswell, 1994, p. 117). Regarding data analysis we use statistical methods including first generation statistics, such as descriptive statistics and the analysis of variance (ANOVA) method, and second generation statistics in the form of PLS structural equation modeling (Boudreau et al., 2001). Finally, our study's unit of analysis is the offshore application development or application maintenance project at German corporations.

D.2 Research Design

Our research design followed four phases. In phase one we developed the research model based on existing previous research and derived specific hypotheses (c.f. Section B, p. 151, and Section C, p. 154).

In phase two we designed an instrument to operationalize the constructs specified in the research model. As far as possible we relied on indicators used in previous studies. We pre-tested the resulting questionnaire with selected experts who had already participated in our previous qualitative study. Based on their feedback, we refined and finalized the questionnaire (c.f. Section D.3, p. 161).

In the following third phase, we identified potentially relevant experts on the social network XING and populated a database. Using this database we sent the questionnaire to all identified experts. This represented the data collection phase lasting for two months until March 2009 (c.f. Section E.1, p. 171).

Having finished the data collection, we analyzed the data in phase four and tested the research model and its corresponding hypotheses (c.f. sections F, p. 174, and G, p. 242).

D.3 Measurement Instrument

We used a survey design to gather data for the study. Apart from raising descriptive and demographic data, the survey primarily needs to measure the constructs of the research model in an adequate manner. As Section C (p. 154) illustrated, our variables are latent and cannot be measured directly. Thus, we have to generate a set of measurement indicators, or manifest variables, to operationalize each construct of the research model. Researchers suggest using indicators that were developed and applied in previous research in this operationalization process (Homburg & Giering, 1996). Accordingly, we used existing indicators as far as possible and adapted them if necessary. Table 3-1 illustrates the studies we used to develop the indicator set for the survey. The following paragraphs explain indicator selection and adaption for each construct.

Construct	Studies
Offshoring expertise [EXP]	Carmel & Agarwal, 2002; own
Trust in OSP [TRUST]	Lee et al., 2008
Project suitability [SUITA]	own
Knowledge transfer [KNOWT]	Lee et al., 2008; Simonin, 1999
Liaison quality [LIAISO]	Erickson & Ranganathan, 2006; Xu & Yao, 2006; own
Offshore project success [SUCCESS]	Erickson & Ranganathan, 2006; Grover et al., 1996; Wüllenweber et al., 2008

Table 3-1: Overview of measurement indicators from previous studies

Regarding offshoring expertise there is a paucity of research that attempts to measure expertise within a quantitative-confirmatory research design. Therefore, we relied on the frequently referenced IS offshore sourcing maturity framework suggested by Carmel & Agarwal to deduce specific indicators (Carmel & Agarwal, 2002). Based on their description of the four maturity stages we formulated two indicators addressing the general company related expertise (EXP2) and the more specific organizational and process related expertise (EXP3). EXP1 represents a self-developed indicator addressing the degree of individual expertise of each staff member. Finally, EXP4 directly addresses the overall level of self-perceived expertise. We included such a question type within each construct's indicator set in order to be able to perform analyses using these indicators as surrogate variables for our constructs (c.f. sections F.2.3.3, p. 191, and F.3.2, p. 205). Table 3-2 shows the indicators measuring offshoring expertise.

Indicator label	Question text
EXP1	At the time the project was started most project team members had already gathered work experience in near-/offshore arrangements.
EXP2	At the time the project was started our company had already performed many projects in near-/offshore arrangement.
EXP3	At the time the project was started our company had dedicated processes and organizational structures in place to plan, manage, and execute near-/offshore arrangements.
EXP4	Overall, at this time, we considered our level of offshoring expertise as being high.

Table 3-2: Measurement indicators for construct offshoring expertise [EXP]

Regarding operationalization of trust in OSP we primarily draw on the recent confirmatory study by Lee et al. (2008). The authors examine a trust-based relationship research model in the context of IS outsourcing among Korean firms and try to assess the impact of trust on perceived success mediated by knowledge transfer. Specifically, we use indicators one to five of their construct "customer's mutual trust" as our indicators TRUST1 to TRUST5. Similar to the previous construct offshoring expertise, we introduced an additional indicator TRUST6 that directly addresses the overall level of perceived trust in OSP. Table 3-3 shows the indicators for construct trust in OSP as used in the survey.

Indicator label	Question text
TRUST1	After starting to work with the offshore service provider we realized that its staff makes favorable decisions to us under any circumstances.
TRUST2	After starting to work with the offshore service provider we realized that its staff is willing to provide assistance to us without exception.
TRUST3	After starting to work with the offshore service provider we realized that its staff reliably provides pre-specified support.
TRUST4	After starting to work with the offshore service provider we realized that its staff is honest.
TRUST5	After starting to work with the offshore service provider we realized that its staff cares about us.
TRUST6	Overall, we had the impression that we could trust the offshore service provider staff.

Table 3-3: Measurement indicators for construct trust in OSP [TRUST]

For project suitability we had to define indicators ourselves since there is no known existing instrument from previous studies. We constructed these indicators on the basis of a previous qualitative study that examined factors to evaluate a project's suitability for offshoring (Westner & Strahringer, 2008). Including all 17 selection criteria, however, would overstretch the indicator set and would have made the resulting questionnaire items impractical for participants to answer. Therefore we focused on the most important criteria size (decomposed into volume regarding labor months (SUITA1) and project duration (SUITA2)), language

(SUITA3), and degree of codification (SUITA4). Considering the qualitative study's success/failure analysis we decided to additionally include a project's degree of business specificity (SUITA5) as an indicator because this aspect was most frequently cited as a failure reason. Again, we included an additional indicator SUITA6 that directly asks for the overall level of a project's perceived suitability for offshoring. Table 3-4 shows the indicators for construct project suitability as used in the survey.

Indicator label	Question text
SUITA1	The offshored project's volume in terms of man months was rather large.
SUITA2	The offshored project's duration was rather short (*reversely coded*).
SUITA3	The primary operating language of the project was English.
SUITA4	Most of the information and knowledge concerning the project was well documented.
SUITA5	The project required business-specific know-how of staff members (*reversely coded*).
SUITA6	Today, we would say the project was suitable for offshore delivery.

Table 3-4: Measurement indicators for construct project suitability [SUITA]

To measure knowledge transfer, we relied on indicators from two previous studies (Lee et al., 2008; Simonin, 1999). Lee et al. develop several indicators for explicit and implicit knowledge sharing. To keep the instrument concise we adopted a selection of five indicators from their set represented in indicators KNOWT1 to KNOWT5. Since the indicators of Lee et al. are rather activity focused, we added two indicators developed by Simonin that are more outcome oriented (KNOWT6 and KNOWT7). Finally, we included indicator KNOWT8 that directly asks for the overall satisfaction level with the knowledge transfer. Table 3-5 displays the indicators for construct knowledge transfer as used in the survey.

Indicator label	Question text
KNOWT1	During the project, with the offshore service provider staff we shared business proposals and reports.
KNOWT2	During the project, with the offshore service provider staff we shared manuals, models, and methodologies.
KNOWT3	During the project, with the offshore service provider staff we shared know-how from work experience.
KNOWT4	During the project, with the offshore service provider staff we shared each other's know-where and know-whom.
KNOWT5	During the project, with the offshore service provider staff we shared expertise obtained from education and training.
KNOWT6	The offshore service provider staff had learned a great deal about the project-related technology/process know-how.
KNOWT7	The offshore service provider staff had greatly reduced its know-how related reliance or dependence upon us since the beginning of the project.
KNOWT8	Overall, we were satisfied with the knowledge transition from us to offshore service provider staff within the project.

Table 3-5: Measurement indicators for construct knowledge transfer [KNOWT]

In contrast to trust in OSP and knowledge transfer, we could not directly adopt indicators for liaison quality from existing studies. However, two studies contain certain aspects of the construct (Erickson & Ranganathan, 2006; Xu & Yao, 2006). Regarding LIAISO1 we follow Erickson & Ranganathan and Xu & Yao who both emphasize the importance of communication. Concerning LIAISO2, LIAISO3, and LIAISO4 we follow the literature analysis of Xu & Yao regarding their operationalized construct "across team cohesion". The fifth indicator, LIAISO5, again directly asks for the overall satisfaction level with the liaison quality on the project. Table 3-6 displays the indicators for construct liaison quality as we used them in the survey.

Indicator label	Question text
LIAISO1	During the project our staff and offshore service provider staff communicated openly.
LIAISO2	During the project our staff and offshore service provider staff developed a mutual understanding of the respective ethnic and corporate cultures.
LIAISO3	During the project our staff and offshore service provider staff members each perceived themselves as equal and recognized members of the project team.
LIAISO4	During the project our staff and offshore service provider staff formed close individual working connections with each other.
LIAISO5	Overall, we were satisfied with the working liaison between our staff and offshore service provider staff.

Table 3-6: Measurement indicators for construct liaison quality [LIAISO]

Operationalizations of success can be frequently found in IS offshoring or outsourcing research (Erickson & Ranganathan, 2006; Grover et al., 1996; Wüllenweber et al., 2008). As outlined in Section C.2 (p. 154), success is commonly measured as the satisfaction with specific outcomes. Regarding the indicator set, we follow Erickson & Ranganathan and Wüllenweber et al. who measure a project's success by its participants' perceived satisfaction with the project outcomes regarding schedule, budget, functionality, and quality represented by SUCCESS1 to SUCCESS4. Additionally, we included an indicator addressing the overall satisfaction with a project's outcomes (SUCCESS5). Table 3-7 shows the employed indicators to measure construct offshore project success.

Indicator label	Question text
SUCCESS1	How satisfied was your organization with the project performance regarding time schedule.
SUCCESS2	How satisfied was your organization with the project performance regarding budget.
SUCCESS3	How satisfied was your organization with the project performance regarding expected functionality.
SUCCESS4	How satisfied was your organization with the project regarding expected quality.
SUCCESS5	How satisfied was your organization with the overall outcomes of our offshoring arrangement.

Table 3-7: Measurement indicators for construct offshore project success [SUCCESS]

We measure each construct's indicators using a 7-point likert-scale with anchors at both sides. This interval scale ranges from 1, *fully disagree, not important* or *not at all satisfied*, to 7, *fully agree, very important*, or *totally satisfied*. Survey data regarding demographics and descriptive data was primarily measured using nominal scales.

On the level of the measurement model, constructs can be measured either reflectively or formatively. The distinction of the two measurement modes is of significant importance because a construct's misspecification can lead to wrong results in the overall model. Nevertheless, misspecified measurement models can often be found in existing research and even in renowned journals (Diamantopoulos, Riefler, & Roth, 2008). Therefore, the decision about which measurement type to use must be carefully made. Jarvis, Mackenzie, Podsakoff, Mick, & Bearden (2003) for example suggest a criteria catalogue to support the decision of whether reflective or formative measurements are appropriate (Diamantopoulos et al., 2008; Eberl, 2006). However, as several authors state, the fundamental question whether to measure reflectively or formatively is the question regarding the causality direction between indicators and their construct (Diamantopoulos et al., 2008; Huber, Herrmann, Meyer, Vogel, & Vollhardt, 2007). With reflective measurements, the "causality is from the construct to the measures […]. A fundamental characteristic of reflective models is that a change in the latent variable causes variation in all measures simultaneously; furthermore, all measures in a reflective measurement model must be positively intercorrelated." (Diamantopoulos et al., 2008, pp. 1204–1205).

With formative measurements, "the indicators determine the latent variable which receives its meaning from the former." (Diamantopoulos et al., 2008, p. 1205). Additionally, formative indicators are not interchangeable and there are no specific expectations regarding their intercorrelation (Diamantopoulos & Winklhofer, 2001). Applying this lens to the previously defined indicators, it is obvious that construct project suitability is measured formatively by its indicators SUITA1 to SUITA5. Indicator SUITA6 represents a reflective measurement. We will therefore not include SUITA6 in the structural equation model. However, we purposely included it in the survey so that it can serve as an auxiliary variable in the descriptive analyses and in the pre-test of the research model. Regarding constructs knowledge transfer and trust in OSP, some indicators could be interpreted as formative according to the decision criterion above. However, Lee et al. (2008) define their measurement model as being purely reflective and we will therefore stick to their perception. Apart from that, all other constructs' indicators are reflective measurements.

Regarding the design quality of formative indicators, the most important criterion is content-related validity. It is recommended that formative indicators be based on thorough research, for example, the inclusion of expert interviews and several indicator refinement rounds (Diamantopoulos & Winklhofer, 2001; Rossiter, 2002). We fulfilled these requirements since the indicators are based on an extensive qualitative pre-study where these indicators emerged after several iterations of textual analysis (Westner & Strahringer, 2008).

For the general design of the survey, we followed recommendations described by Dillman (1978). The author suggests to (a) reward the respondent, (b) reduce cost to the respondent, and (c) establish trust.

We adhered to requirement (a) by stating the purpose of the research, the personal benefit to the participant of receiving a copy of the results, promising a management presentation within three months after finishing the survey, and by designing the mail contact in an individual and personal style. Regarding (b) we minimized the actual time- and money-related costs for participants by choosing an online questionnaire tool for the survey. Thus respondents did not have to use standard mail to send the questionnaire back. Additionally, we kept the questionnaire brief and concise, so that it could be answered within 10 to 15 minutes. Finally, regarding (c) we fostered perceived trust by referring to the sponsoring institutions, European Business School and TU Dresden, thus emphasizing that it is a scientific study. Furthermore, we assured anonymity of all submitted data.

Apart from these general design principles, we also adhered to more specific aspects of survey instrument creation. Regarding questionnaire wording, we used simple, unambiguous words.

Questions were formulated in a brief and concise way. We refrained from using suggestive questions, focused the questions on one topic, only asked for information presumably available to respondents, and provided complete and mutually exclusive response categories. Regarding sequencing of questions, we put simple questions that could be answered quickly and contained no confidential information at the beginning of the survey. This approach helps participants to get familiar with the questionnaire and increases their motivation to finish it. Additionally, we clustered similar questions by respective sequencing and textual formatting. Questions that asked for potentially confidential information, such as revenue or employee figures, were not mandatory. (Dillman, 1978; Schuhmann, 2000)

Having followed these quality criteria, we pre-tested the survey (Churchill, 1999) by distributing the questionnaire in the first round to academic staff at IS chairs of different universities and in the second round to industry experts and practitioners from our previous research (Westner & Strahringer, 2008). We specifically asked about validity, quality, and comprehensibility of the questions and their presentation. Since most indicators concerning the research model were deduced from previous studies, pre-test feedback was positive. Apart from minor wording changes, the structural quality of the survey instrument appeared to be consistent and of acceptable quality. Based on these pre-test results, we adapted and finalized the questionnaire and sent it out to all potential offshoring experts identified at XING. Figure 3-2 shows a screenshot of the survey instrument as presented on the web page. The Appendix (pp. 253-265) contains the complete instrument.

Figure 3-2: Screenshot of the web-based survey instrument

D.4 Statistical Procedures

For the descriptive analyses in the study (c.f. Section F.2, p. 176) we examine the sample data by using basic statistical procedures such as mean, median, and standard deviation.

Furthermore we analyze differences regarding offshore project success levels between different subgroups (c.f. Section F.3.1, p. 197). For these purposes we use the non-parametric Mann-Whitney test to test for significant differences (Mann & Whitney, 1947). The Mann-Whitney test is the non-parametric equivalent of the independent t-test for normal distributed data. The test builds on ranked data and the rank sums and compares their distribution to the known distribution of a test statistic U to determine whether the two samples belong to the same population. (Field, 2005; Siegel & Castellan, 1988)

Regarding the pre-test of the research model (c.f. Section F.3.2, p. 205), we apply ANOVA, i.e., analysis of variance techniques. With this procedure we test for significant differences of the dependent construct's value for different levels of the independent construct. ANOVA compares the amount of systematic variance to the amount of unsystematic variance producing an F-ratio. It is an omnibus test, i.e., ANOVA tests for an overall effect. This means that further tests are necessary to find out which groups (in our case which levels of the independent construct) are affected and show significant differences for the dependent construct. Therefore we use post-hoc tests, namely the Games-Howell procedure, if homogeneity of variance cannot be assumed and Hochberg's GT2, if homogeneity of variance can be assumed. (Backhaus, Erichson, Plinke, & Weiber, 2006; Field, 2005)

We test the research model by using structural equation modeling and the variance-based PLS technique. In contrast to covariance-based procedures which use a structural equation model to explain the covariation of all indicators, PLS attempts to calculate parameter estimates by minimizing the residual variances of both latent and observed dependent variables (Chin, 1998). The PLS algorithm first generates estimated values for the latent variables. It then refines these estimates iteratively by an alternating inner and outer approximation with regard to the structural and measurement models. Finally, it calculates the path coefficients based on these iteratively refined estimates (Huber et al., 2007).

With regard to their output results, covariance-based procedures provide "optimal estimations of the model parameters. Yet, there is an inherent indeterminacy in the procedure. [...] Thus, the ability to estimate scores for the underlying latent variables and in turn, be able to predict the observed indicators is not provided. [...] The PLS approach [...] starts off with a different goal: to help the researcher obtain determinate values of the latent variables for predictive purposes." (Chin, 1998, p. 301). This makes PLS more suitable for research questions that attempt to predict a target variable or explain its variation, for example, more management-focused research questions that are decision-relevant (Huber et al., 2007).

PLS does not require normally distributed data for its algorithm. However, this means that significances can only be calculated using auxiliary procedures such as Bootstrapping which calculates t-values based on the estimated distribution of the sample. Apart from that, PLS can incorporate formatively as well as reflectively measured constructs. Additionally, PLS does not demand identical distribution of residuals, i.e., it also works in case of heteroscedasticity. (Chin, 1998; Gefen, Straub, & Boudreau, 2000; Herrmann, Huber, & Kressmann, 2006; Huber et al., 2007; Hulland, 1999)

Several studies argue that PLS is especially suitable for small sample sizes (e.g., Huber et al., 2007; Lee et al., 2008). It is true that the PLS algorithm produces results even with low sample sizes (Chin, 1998). However, low sample sizes come with the disadvantage of a loss in statistical power. Consequently, recent journal articles reject the notion of PLS being able to handle small sample sizes exceptionally well and strongly recommend using sufficiently large samples in order to achieve relevant levels of statistical power (Goodhue, Lewis, & Thompson, 2006; Marcoulides & Saunders, 2006).

Considering the above-mentioned aspects, PLS is a suitable analysis procedure for our research model. The research questions address the determinants of offshore project success, so we take advantage of PLS's predictive purposes regarding model estimation. In addition, the sample data is not fully normal-distributed and – most important – the research model incorporates formative as well as reflective constructs. With regard to our sample size (n = 304), we achieve high levels of statistical power.[4] For conducting the actual analyses, we use the PLS algorithm as implemented by the software SmartPLS in release 2.0.M3 (Ringle, Wende, & Will, 2005).

---

[4] An a priori power analysis using the software G-Power 3 shows, that n = 92 is required to detect effects of medium size in our model at p < .05 with a probability of 80%. A post-hoc power analysis reveals that with our sample size we detect medium effects at p < .05 with almost 100% probability and small effects at p < .05 with probability of 43%. (Cohen, 1988; Erdfelder, 1996)

E Data Collection

E.1 Data Source

The unit of analysis for the study is the individual IS offshoring project. The population is IS offshoring projects conducted at German companies. However, to the best of our knowledge, there is no database that aggregates data for IS projects across Germany. Thus it is difficult to access the population as defined above in order to draw a statistical representative sample. Therefore, we had to rely on an alternative approach for data gathering.

We adopted a key-informant approach (Kumar, Stern, & Anderson, 1993; Phillips, 1981) and identified offshoring experts in Germany, asking them to contribute data about one specific completed IS offshoring project. We relied on the business social network XING[5] for expert identification. With regard to XING, we identified all people registered at XING who had an affiliation with near- or offshoring. Thus, the experts at XING are the survey population. Our sampling method is a convenient and non-stratified sampling (Fowler, 1988; van der Stede, Young, & Chen, 2005). This negatively impacts the study's external validity regarding its accurate representation of the population, i.e., the associated sampling error. However, from our perspective this approach is the only way to gather an adequate amount of cross-company data given the study's budget and time constraints.

We used the search string "offshor* OR nearshor* OR off-shor* OR near-shor*" in XING's "I offer" search field to identify experts with near- or offshore affiliation. The wildcard character "*" ensures that variations of the term are also found, such as offshor*ing* or offshor*e*. Furthermore, we limited the search to "Deutschland" in the "region" search field. We conducted the search from December 8-22, 2008. The search yielded 1,721 persons in total. However, these search results also contained experts with affiliations not related to IS, such as offshore financing, offshore oil drilling or natural resource exploitation, and offshore energy production, etc. Therefore we accessed all 1,721 XING profiles one by one, analyzed the expert's profile, and excluded those with non-IS related expertise. In the end 1,472 experts with a potentially relevant expertise remained.

We contacted every expert in the database with a personalized e-mail (c.f. Appendix pp. 251-252) using XING's e-mail functionality. XING limits the daily amount of e-mails one is allowed to send so this contact round lasted from January 4 to February 10, 2009. The e-mail contained an explanatory text on the study's rationale and a link to the web page that hosted the questionnaire. The subsequent reminder round lasted from February 11 to March

---

[5] URL: http://www.xing.com - as of April 20, 2009 XING has over seven million registered users and is one of the largest German business social networks (company information).

13, 2009. Experts were asked to participate in the survey within 14 days. We did not share the hypotheses or the research model with the participants beforehand.

In order to avoid any potential bias resulting from the incremental contacting, we determined the mail sequence randomly. We implemented this in the spreadsheet software Excel 2003 by assigning a random number to each expert in the database and then sorting ascending by this random number. This randomized list represented the final contact sequence.

Another source of bias might result from the point of time when the project had been conducted. Therefore, 50% of randomly selected experts were asked to contribute data from "one of the first finished projects", the remaining 50% were asked to contribute data from "one of the most recent finished projects". The applied randomization procedure was the same as described in the previous paragraph.

E.2 Response Rate

Of 1,472 e-mails we sent out, 997 experts or 67.7% did not react but 475 experts or 32.3% people did respond. Of those 475 experts, 142 did not participate in the survey. Table 3-8 illustrates the reasons cited for non-participation and the corresponding number of experts.

Cited reason	No. of experts
Expertise not coming from development or maintenance	42
Expert works for a provider	42
Expertise is insufficient	12
Expert cannot participate because of confidentiality reasons	9
Expert does not have time	9
Expert's expertise was generated outside Germany	6
Expert is not interested	5
Other reasons	17
Total	**142**

Table 3-8: Reasons cited for non-participation

Furthermore, we excluded 29 completed data items from experts who actually answered the questionnaire, but indicated that one or more of the research focus criteria did not apply to the data they provided. Table 3-9 shows the reasons why we excluded these data items, what the corresponding rationale was, and how many data items were actually affected.

Exclusion reason	Rationale	No. of data items
Items with project end after 2009.	Study only considers finished projects.	14
Items with reported project offshore-share of 2% or less.	Offshoring impact on the project as a whole is only marginal.	7
Items where experts stated that they did not provide information for one specific project but for their own total offshoring expertise.	Unit of analysis is individual offshoring projects.	5
Items that indicated projects with an application development vs. application maintenance share of 0% and 0%.	0%-0% distribution is not valid in the context of our study, because we only focus on development and maintenance.	3
Total		**29**

Table 3-9: Reasons for exclusion of data items

After this exclusion, 304 expert responses remained in scope for analysis purposes. This represents a response rate of 20.7% in relation to all 1,472 contacted experts which is illustrated in Figure 3-3.

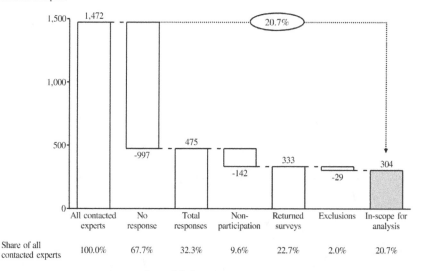

Figure 3-3: Survey response rate

F Analyses and Results

F.1 Response Structure

F.1.1 Response Time

As described in Section E.1 (p. 171) we sent out the survey invitation e-mails incrementally over a time period of several weeks. We calculate the response time as the difference in days between returned survey and first date of contact, i.e., the dispatching of the first invitation e-mail.[6]

In the end, 123 or 40.5% of all participants answered within 48 hours to our e-mail request; 218 or 71.7% participants responded within the given time limit of 14 days; 86 or 28.3% participants answered after 14 days. This indicates a rather high participation motivation among the experts. Figure 3-4 illustrates the distribution of the overall response time.

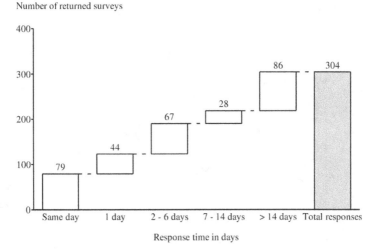

Figure 3-4: Survey response times

F.1.2 Non-Response Bias

Non-response bias, sometimes also referred to as non-response error, "occurs when some target respondents do not [take part in a survey], causing responses to be an unreliable representation of the selected sample" (van der Stede et al., 2005, pp. 669–670). Even with

---

[6] An anonymized tracking code included in the survey link enabled us to match the date of contact and data of questionnaire submission.

high survey response rates, strong hypothetical differences of the non-response group "can produce misleading conclusions that do not generalize to the entire population" (Rogelberg & Stanton, 2007, p. 196) and consequently limit a study's external validity. Therefore, it is an imperative to address the issues of non-response before, during, and after data collection. (King & He, 2005; van der Stede et al., 2005)

Before and during data collection, we followed recommended procedures to minimize non-response: we designed the survey instrument carefully (c.f. Section D.3, p. 161), we sent out reminder notes to all potential respondents, we provided sufficient response opportunities by using a web-based questionnaire tool, we emphasized the importance of respondents' participation as well as our high valuation for respondents' opinions, and promised to provide feedback on the study's results. (Rogelberg & Stanton, 2007)

After data collection, the three most common techniques to analyze potential non-response bias are the so-called *archival analysis, follow-up approach*, and *wave analysis* (Armstrong & Overton, 1977; King & He, 2005; Rogelberg & Stanton, 2007). Archival analysis compares characteristics of respondents and non-respondents based on data in an archival database. This was not a feasible option in the study, since we have no coherent and complete database from which to drew the sample. The follow-up approach tries to resurvey non-respondents, e.g., by calling them or writing a letter, and afterwards analyzing for differences in responses. We did not follow this approach because apart from the XING e-mail functionality we did not have further contact information making it impossible to use alternative communication channels to ensure timely answers to our follow-up. Therefore, we finally opted for wave analysis which compares survey data submitted by late respondents to data submitted by early respondents. The assumption behind wave analysis is that survey participants who respond late or only after a reminder note, resemble non-respondents. If survey data for early and late responders differs, this is an indication for the existence of non-response bias.

In order to perform a wave analysis, we subdivided the sample into two groups based on the time difference in days between dispatching the first contact e-mail and submission date of survey. The first group (early responders) contains all respondents who participated in the survey within the given time frame of 14 days. The second group (late responders) contains all respondents who participated after the given time frame of 14 days. As can be inferred from Figure 3-4 (p. 174), the early responder group consists of 218 items, the late responder group consists of 86 items.

After group formation, we tested for statistically significant differences in response data between the two groups. We thereby focused on the indicators that are directly relevant to the research model (EXP, TRUST, SUITA, KNOWT, LIAISO, SUCCESS). Since data is not normally distributed, i.e., a K-S test of normality resulted in $D(304)$ between .14 and .39, p <

.001 (c.f. Appendix, p. 249 for detailed test results) and group sizes are different, we used the non-parametric Mann-Whitney test (Mann & Whitney, 1947) instead of a t-test to test for differences between the two groups. The test showed no statistically significant differences between the two groups (c.f. Appendix, p. 250).

For reasons of result robustness, we changed the boundaries for the early responder and late responder groups. Instead of using day 14 as a cut-off limit, we tested for differences between early responders from day zero to six and late responders after day six. The group sizes changed to 190 early responders in Group 1, and to 114 late responders in Group 2 respectively. Again, a Mann-Whitney test showed no statistical significant differences between the two groups. Thus, we assume that the study is not affected by a significant non-response bias.

F.1.3 Missing Values

Missing values in data, also referred to as item non-response, occur when respondents omit survey questions and do not provide data for the respective question. Missing values can therefore represent a source of bias for a study's results. (van der Stede et al., 2005)

Since we used a web-based questionnaire tool for data gathering we could take technological provisions to ensure that all questions are filled out by study participants (so-called mandatory fields). Participants were not able to proceed within the questionnaire or submit it when data items were missing. Additionally, built-in validation rules prevented participants from entering obviously wrong values, such as text instead of figures.

Therefore, missing values did not occur in the data and we did not have to take corresponding correcting measures to account for them.

F.2 Descriptive Analyses

The following subsections contain descriptive analyses of the sample data regarding study participants, projects, and construct indicators. We use statistical measures such as median, mean, and standard deviation as well as illustrations to generate an initial understanding of the demographics and response patterns in the sample.

F.2.1 Participants

Study participants currently hold managerial positions (141 or 46% of all participants), are Vice Presidents / Directors (67 or 22% of all participants), and CXOs, i.e., CIOs, CEOs, or CTOs (17 or 6% of all participants). The remaining 79 participants (26%) work in other non-managerial roles. Figure 3-5 illustrates the current job positions held by study participants.

Your current position / job title

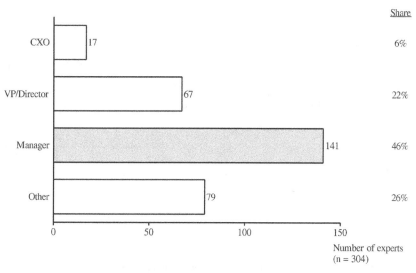

Figure 3-5: Job positions of study participants

Participants in the sample show a high level of experience in the field of IS in general and the field of IS offshoring in particular. Most of the participants (279 or 92%) have accumulated six or more years of personal experience in the field of IS. With regard to IS offshoring, 227 participants (75%) have three or more years of personal experience. Figure 3-6 illustrates the sample's experience profile. The left bar shows study participants' experience in the field of IS in general, the right bar shows study participants' experience specifically in IS offshoring.

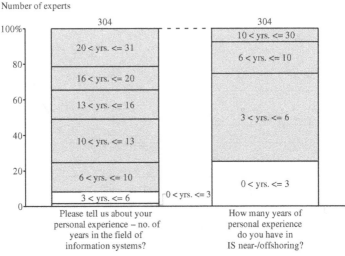

Number of experts

Yrs. = years

Figure 3-6: Experience levels of study participants

F.2.2 Projects

Following our key-informant approach, we asked each participant to provide data for one specific finished offshore project. This section reports on the characteristics of the reported project-related data.

Most projects were conducted at companies in the sectors[7] of telecommunications (91 projects), information technology (79 projects), and manufacturing (48 projects). Other sectors were banking and insurance (34 projects), transportation (25 projects), retail and distribution (24 projects), consulting (14 projects), healthcare (12 projects), public sector (9 projects), utilities (8 projects), construction (5 projects), and other sectors (20 projects). For 23 projects, study participants did not specify a sector. Figure 3-7 illustrates the distribution of industry sectors.

---

[7] Multiple answers were allowed for this question.

To which industry did your company belong?

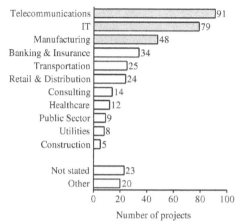

Note: Multiple answers possible.

Figure 3-7: Industry sectors where projects were conducted

Regarding company sizes, we asked for the number of employees and the number of internal IS staff of the company at the time the project was conducted. Data shows that primarily large companies populate the sample: 109 projects (36%) were executed at companies with more 25,000 employees, 34 projects (11%) at companies with 5,001 to 25,000 employees, and 35 projects (12%) at companies with 1,001 to 5,000 employees. The left graph in Figure 3-8 shows the distribution of employees across different categories.

Similarly, the number of internal IS staff was rather high: 67 projects (22%) were conducted at companies with more than 5,000 internal IS employees, 30 projects (10%) at companies with 1,001 to 5,000 internal IS employees, and 41 projects (13%) at companies with 251 to 1,000 internal IS employees. The right graph in Figure 3-8 illustrates the distribution of internal IS staff members across different categories.

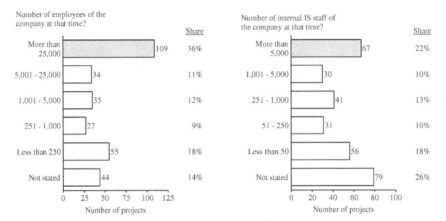

Figure 3-8: Employee demographics of companies where projects were conducted

The three main reasons for doing parts or the entire project offshore were cost reduction (285 projects), strategic reasons (159 projects), and perceived resource shortage (115 projects).[8] This is in line with existing research that mentions similar reasons why companies do IS offshoring (Apte, Sobol, Hanaoka, Shimada, Saarinen, & Salmela et al., 1997; Bitkom, 2005; Carmel & Agarwal, 2001; Prikladnicki, Audy, & Evaristo, 2004; Rao, Poole, Raven, & Lockwood, 2006; Smith, 2006; William et al., 2006). Figure 3-9 illustrates which reasons study participants mentioned for engaging in IS offshoring.

---

[8] Multiple answers were allowed for this question.

Descriptive Analyses   181

What was the main reason for doing parts
or the entire project near-/offshore?

Note: Multiple answers possible.

Figure 3-9: Reasons for doing projects near-/offshore

In their *sourcing of IT work offshore stage model (SITO)*, Carmel & Agarwal mention that offshoring activities at companies usually start on an ad-hoc single project basis and evolve towards a more coherent integrated sourcing strategy over time (Carmel & Agarwal, 2002). Therefore, we wanted to know whether the project for which data was submitted was part of a larger offshoring program. Most projects (207 projects or 68%) were carried out within the context of a larger offshoring program. Ninety-two projects (30%) were stand-alone projects. Only five participants could not tell if the project for which they submitted data was part of a program. These results indicate that companies were at stage three (*Proactive Cost Focus*) or stage four (*Proactive Strategic Focus*), rather than stage two (*Offshore Experimenter*) within the framework suggested by Carmel & Agarwal.

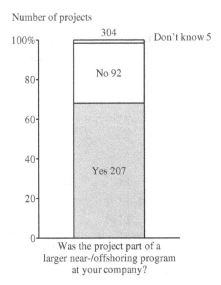

Figure 3-10: Embededness of projects in corporate program

Our previous research already indicated that in Germany IS services are primarily offshored to India rather then countries which are closer (Westner & Strahringer, 2008). This perception was supported by the data: 171 projects (56%) were delivered from India. India thus represents the most frequently mentioned single delivery country in the sample. Other countries serve less frequently as delivery countries, such as Russia (16 projects or 5%), Poland and Romania (each with 14 projects or 5%), Hungary (11 projects or 4%), Belarus (10 projects or 3%), and various other countries. The left bar in Figure 3-11 shows the large share of India as delivery country, the right bar illustrates the other countries' shares as delivery countries.

Number of projects

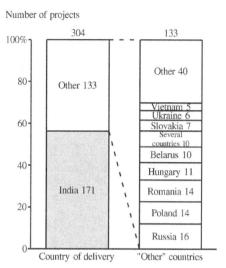

From which country were the
near-/offshoring services delivered?

Figure 3-11: Countries of delivery

Many studies define offshoring in the narrow sense of offshore outsourcing. Outsourcing implies that the service provider is an external third party. However, we examine offshoring in a broader sense, not limited to a certain ownership structure. In order to make this aspect transparent in the data, we asked for the relationship of the client to the offshore service provider. Data shows that 135 projects (44%) were delivered by an external third party company, 125 projects (41%) were delivered by an internal subsidiary, and 44 projects (14%) by a partially owned subsidiary, for example a joint venture. Figure 3-12 shows the ownership structure regarding the service providers in the sample.

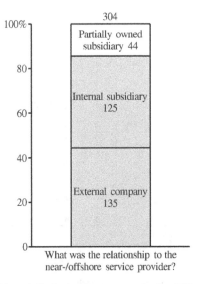

Figure 3-12: Ownership structure regarding OSP

Only offshoring of application development or maintenance services were within the scope of our research. Development activities were more common within the sample. Figure 3-13 illustrates this graphically: the y-axis depicts the relative distribution of development activities (in white) versus maintenance activities (in grey) in a project; the x-axis represents the total amount of all 304 projects. Figure 3-13 shows that most of the offshored activities were application development activities: 127 projects (42%) were projects consisting only of application development tasks. Existing research shows similar findings and mentions that application development activities are primarily suitable for offshoring (Apte et al., 1997; Fish & Seydel, 2006; Gopal, Sivaramakrishnan, Krishnan, & Mukhopadhyay, 2003; Wiener, 2006).

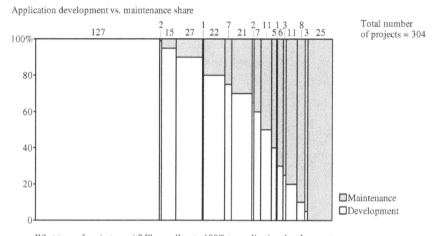

What type of project was it? Please allocate 100% to application development and application maintenance.

Figure 3-13: Application development and maintenance share

To assess project size, we asked for a project's volume in labor months. Most of the reported projects were smaller than 300 labor months (195 projects or 64%). The left bar in Figure 3-14 shows the project sizes in labor months. Looking at the offshored parts of the projects in terms of labor months in relation to a project's total volume in labor months, we can see that the majority of projects have an offshore share of 41% or more (213 projects or 70%). Thus, offshored project parts represented a significant amount of projects' overall volumes. The right bar in Figure 3-14 illustrates the actual offshore shares of all 304 reported projects.

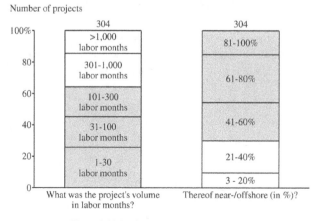

Figure 3-14: Project sizes and offshore shares

Most projects (219 projects or 72%) did not have additional consulting support during project execution. Of the 85 projects (28%) with consulting support, 38 study participants (13%) were one of those consultants. This shows that most study participants were employees in the line organization of the company where the project was conducted.

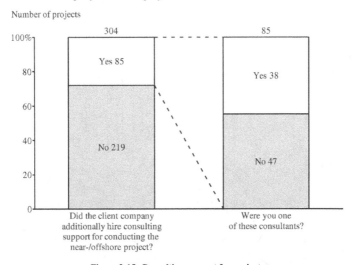

Figure 3-15: Consulting support for projects

As Section E.1 (p. 171) describes, we asked 50% of contacted experts to report data on "one of the most recent projects" and the other 50% to report data on "one of the first projects" from their individual offshore expertise. Analyzing participants' returned questionnaires the 50/50 allocation still remains: 155 study participants (51%) submitted data for one of their first IS offshoring projects; 149 study participants (49%) submitted data for one of their most recent IS offshoring projects. This shows that – as intended by the randomized allocation – no specific participant-induced project time selection dominates the sample. Figure 3-16 illustrates the distribution of most recent versus first projects.

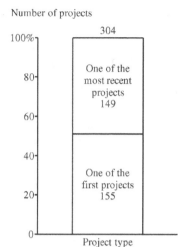

Figure 3-16: Distribution of first versus recent projects

Although the distribution between first and most recent projects was almost equal, the majority of reported projects (220 projects or 72%) were finished between 2007 and 2009. Only 84 projects (28%) were finished before 2007. For study participants, offshore application development or maintenance projects seems to have occurred recently. Figure 3-17 illustrates the relative shares of projects with different finishing dates.

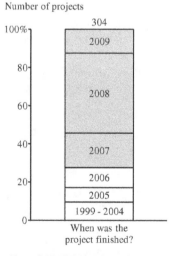

Figure 3-17: Finishing dates of projects

As Figure 3-18 shows, 258 (85%) study participants were in managerial roles on the projects for which they submitted data. Only 46 (15%) said they were in non-managerial roles. This result indicates that we addressed the key informants regarding the projects in the sample because one can assume that individuals in managerial roles have access to the relevant project information we asked in the survey.

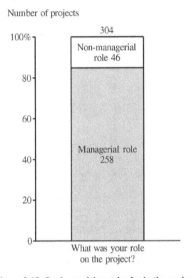

Figure 3-18: Study participants' roles in the project

Finally, we identified where survey participants actually resided while the project was conducted: 253 participants (83%) resided onshore, 35 participants (12%) equally on- and offshore, and only 16 participants (5%) exclusively offshore. This shows that the data incorporates, as originally intended, the German service-receiving, i.e., offshore-consuming, perspective on the topic. Figure 3-19 illustrates where study participants resided during project execution.

Number of projects

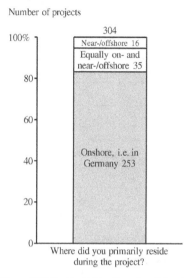

Figure 3-19: Residential location of participants

F.2.3   Construct Indicators

F.2.3.1   IS Offshore Project Success

We measured success by assessing participants' levels of satisfaction regarding a project's time schedule, budget, functionality, quality, and satisfaction with the overall outcome of the project. Figure 3-20 shows the data for each indicator together with the corresponding median values, mean values, and standard deviations (STDV). Mean values regarding the dimensions time schedule (SUCCESS1: mean = 4.38) and expected quality (SUCCESS4: mean = 4.24) are slightly lower in comparison to the other dimensions. However, the differences are only minor: mean indicator values do not differ much across the sample and range between 4.24 and 4.78. Overall, projects seem to be perceived to be successful, demonstrated by an overall outcome satisfaction with mean = 4.63 and median = 5 (SUCCESS5).

How satisfied was your organization with the
project performance regarding...

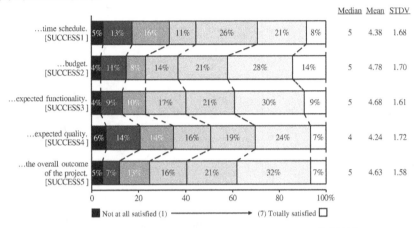

Figure 3-20: Indicator values for construct offshore project success (SUCCESS)

F.2.3.2   Perceived Importance of Constructs

Asked for the perceived importance of the research model's constructs, study participants
perceive trust in OSP, project suitability, knowledge transfer, and liaison quality as almost
equally important. Mean scores for these four constructs range from 5.98 (trust in OSP) to
6.08 (liaison quality). Results are rather different regarding construct offshoring expertise:
participants perceive offshoring expertise as less important for offshore project success and
rank it lower with mean = 5.54. Figure 3-21 shows the means, medians, and standard
deviations for the perceived importance of the five constructs for the successful execution of
an offshore project.

For the successful execution of a near-/offshore project,
how important do you consider each of the following?

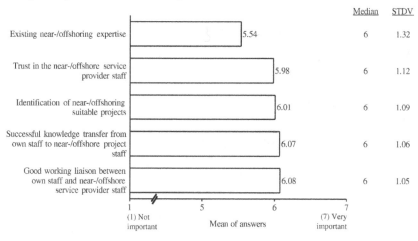

Figure 3-21: Indicator values for perceived importance of success determinants

F.2.3.3   Self-Perceived Levels of Constructs

Each construct indicator set in the survey included a question that attempted to measure the construct directly. This was always the last question of an indicator set. These questions directly asked for participants' self-perceived levels of offshoring expertise, trust in OSP, project suitability, knowledge transfer, liaison quality, and offshore project success. The corresponding indicator codes are EXP4, TRUST6, SUITA6, KNOWT8, LIAISO5, and SUCCESS5. We use these indicators' values as auxiliary constructs. Figure 3-22 shows the respective relative distribution of scores, the corresponding medians, means, and standard deviations.

Self-perceived levels of expertise, trust, project suitability,
knowledge transfer, and liaison quality

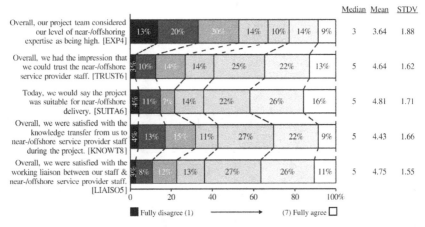

Figure 3-22: Indicator values for self-perceived levels of constructs

Self-perceived levels of trust in OSP, project suitability, knowledge transfer, and liaison quality are almost equal with mean values ranging from 4.43 (KNOWT8) to 4.81 (SUITA6) and the same median value of 5. Offshoring expertise (EXP4) represents the main difference: its mean value of 3.64 is lower. The same applies to its median value of 3. Apparently, project teams working on 53%[9] of all reported projects had little or no offshoring expertise before starting the project.

F.2.3.4   Determinants of Success

Offshoring Expertise

As stated above, indicator values for offshoring expertise score low in comparison to the other constructs' indicators. Figure 3-23 displays the corresponding data for the remaining expertise indicators EXP1, EXP2, and EXP3. The majority of project team members had no work experience in offshore arrangements (EXP1: median = 2; mean = 3.09) before the specific project. However, organizations seemed to be slightly more experienced: more companies had already performed projects in offshore arrangements (EXP2: median = 3; mean = 3.58), and even more had dedicated processes and structures in place to plan, manage, and execute offshore arrangements (EXP3: median = 4, mean = 3.77). This corresponds to the descriptive

---

[9] Relative shares of summed indicator EXP4 values one (13%), two (20%), and three (20%).

analyses where data indicated that companies in the sample have achieved a certain minimum level of offshore maturity (c.f. Figure 3-10, p. 182).

At the time the project was started...

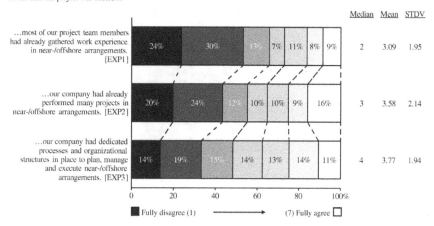

Figure 3-23: Indicator values for construct offshoring expertise (EXP)

Trust in OSP

Study participants perceived OSP staff as willing to provide assistance (TRUST2: median = 5; mean = 4.67), as honest (TRUST4: median = 5; mean = 4.73), and caring (TRUST5: median = 5; mean = 4.59). Scores are slightly lower for the question whether the OSP staff reliably provides pre-specified support (TRUST3: median = 4; mean = 4.16). The lowest mean values occurred for the question whether OSP staff makes favorable decisions under any circumstances (TRUST1: median = 4; mean = 3.73). It might be that the remark "under any circumstances" in the question text appeared rather extreme to study participants, thus resulting in lower indicator scores. Figure 3-24 illustrates the relative distribution of all indicator values, their corresponding median values, mean values, and standard deviations.

After starting to work with the near-/offshore service provider we
realized that its staff...

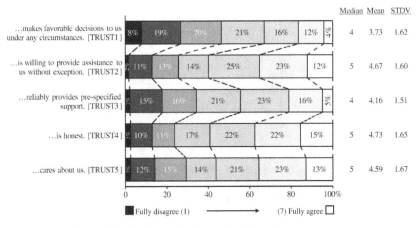

Figure 3-24: Indicator values for construct trust in OSP (TRUST)

Project Suitability

Indicator values for project suitability deviated strongly from other constructs' indicators.
Additionally, mean and median values differed among the five project suitability indicators.
For most of the projects in the sample the primary operating language was English (SUITA3:
median = 7; mean = 6.09); 81% of all projects reported indicator values of 6 and 7 to this
question. Projects seem to be rather large in terms of labor months (SUITA1: median = 5;
mean = 4.54) and – reciprocally – not short in duration (SUITA2: median = 3; mean = 3.25).
The degree of information and knowledge documentation regarding the project was medium
(SUITA4: median = 4; mean = 4.35). Finally, projects mostly required business-specific
know-how, i.e., domain knowledge, of staff members (SUITA5: median = 6; mean = 5.31),
thus making them less suitable for offshore delivery. Figure 3-25 illustrates the aggregated
indicator data for the construct project suitability.

Project suitability for near-/offshoring

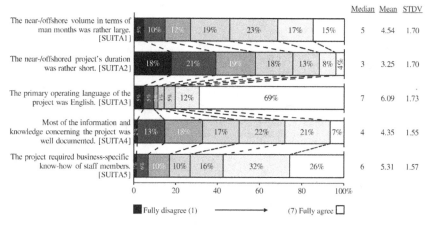

Figure 3-25: Indicator values for construct project suitability (SUITA)

Knowledge Transfer

Six of the seven indicators' values measuring knowledge transfer do only vary slightly. mean values range from 4.86 (KNOWT1) to 5.75 (KNOWT2 and KNOWT3) and median values of 5 and 6. The last question regarding whether the OSP staff had reduced its know-how related reliance or dependence since the beginning of the project (KNOWT7) marks the main difference with a mean value of 4.20 and median value of 4. Apparently knowledge was actually transferred using the mechanisms contained in the other questions, but OSP staff was only partially able to understand and apply it. Figure 3-26 illustrates this data graphically.

During the project, with the near-/offshore service provider staff we
shared...

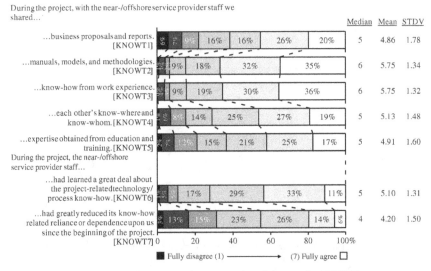

Figure 3-26: Indicator values for construct knowledge transfer (KNOWT)

Liaison Quality

Indicator values for liaison quality show a high degree of homogeneity: mean values are close
together ranging only from 4.85 (LIAISO4) to 4.93 (LIAISO2) with the same median values
of 5. Additionally, the relative distribution of scores within each indicator is similar, as can be
derived from Figure 3-27 which illustrates all indicator values with their median values, mean
values, and standard deviations.

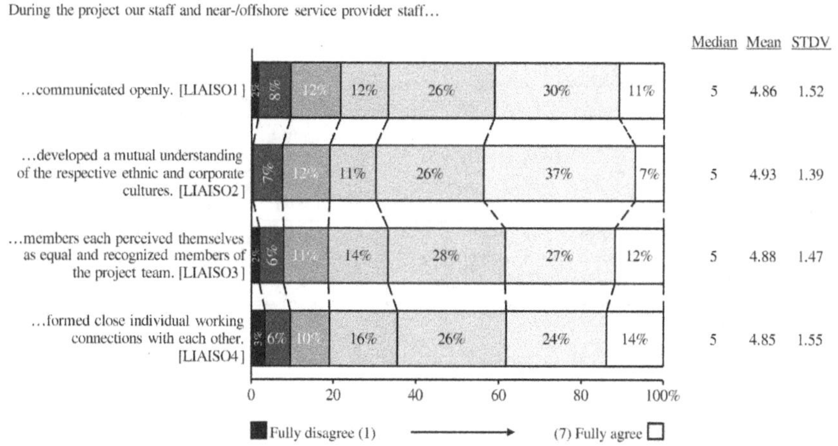

During the project our staff and near-/offshore service provider staff...

Figure 3-27: Indicator values for construct liaison quality (LIASO)

F.3 Offshore Project Success Analyses of Variances

F.3.1 Subgroup Comparisons

This section focuses on the main dependent construct offshore project success and analyzes whether and to what extent its indicator scores change for different subgroups. This deepens our understanding of the data and supports later interpretation. Since the data is not normally distributed, as shown earlier, we use the non-parametric Mann-Whitney test (Mann & Whitney, 1947) to assess significances of mean differences.

F.3.1.1 First versus Recent Projects

As described in Section E.1 (p. 171), we asked a randomly selected 50% of the contacted experts to provide data for one of the first IS offshore projects they participated in (Group 1), and the other 50% of the contacted experts to provide data for one of the most recent IS offshore projects (Group 2).

We would expect that the degree of expertise differs between the two groups and is higher in Group 2. The rationale is that during the first project, staff and organizations will have little or no offshoring expertise. This is different when it comes to more recent projects. More recent projects might of course also be first projects for some individual members of a project team, but other project members will have done offshore projects before and will have accumulated corresponding expertise. A statistical test confirms this assumption. As Table 3-10 illustrates, Group 2 (median = 4; mean = 3.97) shows higher values for self-perceived expertise than

Group 1 (median = 3; mean = 3.33). These differences are significant but the effect is only
small (U = 9423.50, p < .01, r = -.16).

	Mean values		
	Group 1	Group 2	
	First	Recent	
	projects	projects	
Statement	(n = 155)	(n = 149)	Difference
At the time the project was started...			
...overall, our project team considered our level of near-/offshoring expertise as being high. [EXP4]	3.33	3.97	-0.64 **

* p < .05   ** p < .01   *** p < .001

Table 3-10: Mean differences of offshoring expertise indicator EXP4
between first and recent projects

If, as hypothesized, levels of expertise have a strong impact on success, Group 2 (recent
project) indicator values for construct offshore project success should be higher than for
Group 1 (first project). Table 3-11 illustrates the mean values and the differences for the two
groups. It shows that indicator values are slightly higher for recent projects than for first
projects except for indicator SUCCESS3. However, the differences are not significant. This
could indicate that the impact of offshoring expertise on offshore project success is less strong
than expected.

	Mean values		
	Group 1	Group 2	
	First	Recent	
	projects	projects	
Statement	(n = 155)	(n = 149)	Difference
How satisfied was your organization with...			
...the project performance regarding time schedule. [SUCCESS1]	4.35	4.40	-0.04
...the project performance regarding budget. [SUCCESS2]	4.68	4.87	-0.19
...the project performance regarding expected functionality. [SUCCESS3]	4.77	4.59	0.18
...the project performance regarding expected quality. [SUCCESS4]	4.19	4.30	-0.11
...the overall outcome of the project. [SUCCESS5]	4.60	4.66	-0.06

* p < .05   ** p < .01   *** p < .001

Table 3-11: Mean differences of offshore project success indicator values
between first and recent projects

F.3.1.2   Nearshore versus Offshore Projects

The most frequently cited reason for engaging in IS offshoring is cost reduction (c.f. Figure 3-9, p. 181). Nearshoring, i.e., delivery from a country nearby, comes with certain advantages regarding travel, communication, and infrastructure costs. Additionally, one might assume that increased cultural proximity positively impacts project success. Consequently, we would expect higher indicator values for success at nearshore projects (Group 1) in comparison to offshore projects (Group 2).[10]

Table 3-12 illustrates the mean values of offshore project success indicators for nearshore and offshore projects. It shows that indicator values are indeed higher for nearshore projects. However, these differences are significant only for indicator SUCCESS3 (U = 8694.00, p < .05, r = -.14) and indicator SUCCESS5 (U = 8454.00, p < .01, r = -.16). Effect sizes are both small.

| | Mean values | | |
| | Group 1 Nearshore projects (n = 105) | Group 2 Offshore projects (n = 199) | |
Statement			Difference
How satisfied was your organization with…			
…the project performance regarding time schedule. [SUCCESS1]	4.52	4.30	0.23
…the project performance regarding budget. [SUCCESS2]	4.92	4.70	0.23
…the project performance regarding expected functionality. [SUCCESS3]	5.00	4.51	0.49 *
…the project performance regarding expected quality. [SUCCESS4]	4.51	4.10	0.41
…the overall outcome of the project. [SUCCESS5]	5.00	4.44	0.56 **

* p < .05   ** p < .01   *** p < .001

Table 3-12: Mean differences of offshore project success indicator values
between nearshore and offshore projects

F.3.1.3   Projects Delivered by Internal or Partially Owned OSP versus External OSP

Table 3-13 shows that indicator values for offshore project success are higher for projects that were conducted by an internal subsidiary or a partially owned OSP (Group 1) than for projects that were conducted by an external OSP (Group 2). Maybe there is less organizational friction

---

[10] For a classification of near- vs. offshore countries of delivery please refer to Appendix, p. 266.

and a higher degree of efficiency if projects are delivered by internal units of an organization, resulting in a higher degree of success. Differences are significant for indicator SUCCESS1 (U = 9458.00, p < .01, r = -.15), indicator SUCCESS3 (U = 9422.50, p < .01, r = -.15), indicator SUCCESS4 (U = 9734.50, p < .05, r = -.13), and indicator SUCCESS5 (U = 9891.00, p < .05, r = -.12). However, similar to the previous subgroup comparisons, effects were small for all four significant differences.

| | Mean values | | |
| | Group 1 | Group 2 | |
Statement	Internal / partially-owned (n = 169)	External company (n = 135)	Difference
How satisfied was your organization with…			
…the project performance regarding time schedule. [SUCCESS1]	4.61	4.08	0.53 **
…the project performance regarding budget. [SUCCESS2]	4.90	4.62	0.28
…the project performance regarding expected functionality. [SUCCESS3]	4.93	4.36	0.57 **
…the project performance regarding expected quality. [SUCCESS4]	4.45	3.99	0.46 *
…the overall outcome of the project. [SUCCESS5]	4.84	4.37	0.47 *

* p < .05   ** p < .01   *** p < .001

Table 3-13: Mean differences of offshore project success indicator values between projects delivered by an internal or partially owned OSP and projects delivered by an external OSP

F.3.1.4   Stand-Alone Projects versus Projects Embedded in Larger Offshore Program

We would expect that companies with offshore programs (Group 2) have accumulated more offshoring expertise than companies where offshore projects are executed on a stand-alone basis (Group 1). Indeed, as Table 3-14 displays, Group 1 shows slightly lower indicator values regarding self-perceived overall offshoring expertise (EXP4: median = 3; mean = 3.56) in comparison to Group 2 (median = 3; mean = 3.69). However, these differences are not significant.

	Mean values		
	Group 1 **Stand-alone/** **don't know**	**Group 2** **Larger** **program**	
Statement	**(n = 97)**	**(n = 207)**	**Difference**
At the time the project was started…			
…overall, our project team considered our level of near- /offshoring expertise as being high. [EXP4]	3.56	3.69	-0.13

* p < .05   ** p < .01   *** p < .001

Table 3-14: Mean differences of offshoring expertise indicator EXP4
between stand-alone projects and projects conducted as part of a larger offshoring program

In contrast to these findings, Table 3-15 shows that indicator values for offshore project success are actually higher for stand-alone projects (Group 1) than for projects that were embedded in a larger program (Group 2). However, these differences are not significant except for a small effect regarding indicator SUCCESS2 with mean = 4.99 for Group 1 and mean = 4.68 for Group 2 (U = 8620.00, $p < .05$, r = -.12).

	Mean values		
	Group 1 **Stand-alone/** **don't know**	**Group 2** **Larger** **program**	
Statement	**(n = 97)**	**(n = 207)**	**Difference**
How satisfied was your organization with…			
…the project performance regarding time schedule. [SUCCESS1]	4.49	4.32	0.18
…the project performance regarding budget. [SUCCESS2]	4.99	4.68	0.31 *
…the project performance regarding expected functionality. [SUCCESS3]	4.70	4.67	0.03
…the project performance regarding expected quality. [SUCCESS4]	4.41	4.16	0.25
…the overall outcome of the project. [SUCCESS5]	4.72	4.59	0.13

* p < .05   ** p < .01   *** p < .001

Table 3-15: Mean differences of offshore project success indicator values
between stand-alone projects and projects conducted as part of a larger offshoring program

F.3.1.5 Small versus Large Projects

Although offshore projects require a certain minimum size to compensate for additional offshore-related cost and overhead, augmenting size also increases project complexity which has a negative impact on offshore project success (Westner & Strahringer, 2008). Using the median value of project size in labor months (median = 150) as a group formation criterion, we compare small projects with a size of equal or less than 150 labor months (Group 1) and large projects with a size greater than 150 labor months (Group 2). Table 3-16 shows that offshore project success indicator values are higher for Group 1. However, there is only a small significant effect for indicator SUCCESS3 with mean values of 4.88 for Group 1 and 4.47 for Group 2 (U = 9855.00, p < .05, r = -.13).

	Mean values		
	Group 1	Group 2	
	Project <= 150	Project > 150	
	labor months	labor months	
Statement	(n = 155)	(n = 149)	Difference
How satisfied was your organization with…			
…the project performance regarding time schedule. [SUCCESS1]	4.54	4.21	0.33
…the project performance regarding budget. [SUCCESS2]	4.94	4.60	0.34
…the project performance regarding expected functionality. [SUCCESS3]	4.88	4.47	0.41 *
…the project performance regarding expected quality. [SUCCESS4]	4.42	4.06	0.36
…the overall outcome of the project. [SUCCESS5]	4.80	4.46	0.34

* p < .05   ** p < .01   *** p < .001

Table 3-16: Mean differences of offshore project success indicator values
between small projects and large projects regarding labor months

F.3.1.6   Projects with Low versus High Offshoring Share

The right bar in Figure 3-14 (p. 185) shows that the projects in the sample are not exclusively delivered from offshore. Projects are rather a combination of activities conducted offshore and onshore, i.e., in Germany. Offshoring thereby adds complexity to a project, e.g., with regard to distance, cultural aspects, or time zone differences, and thus increases the risk of project failure. We would therefore expect that projects with low shares of offshoring in terms of labor months tend to be more successful and show higher[11] indicator values for offshore project success. Table 3-17 shows that this does not seem to apply to the sample. The opposite

---

[11] Only indicator SUCCESS2, focusing on the budget perspective, might possibly show different scores because one could expect lower cost savings for lower offshore shares.

is the case: projects with offshore shares below 50% of total labor months (Group 1) have slightly lower success indicator values than projects with offshore shares of equal or greater than 50% of total labor months (Group 2). However, none of these differences is significant.

	Mean values		
Statement	Group 1 Offshoring share < 50% (n = 93)	Group 2 Offshoring share >= 50% (n = 211)	Difference
How satisfied was your organization with...			
...the project performance regarding time schedule. [SUCCESS1]	4.33	4.39	-0.06
...the project performance regarding budget. [SUCCESS2]	4.65	4.83	-0.19
...the project performance regarding expected functionality. [SUCCESS3]	4.51	4.76	-0.25
...the project performance regarding expected quality. [SUCCESS4]	4.16	4.28	-0.12
...the overall outcome of the project. [SUCCESS5]	4.55	4.67	-0.12

$* p < .05 \quad ** p < .01 \quad *** p < .001$

Table 3-17: Mean differences of offshore project success indicator values between projects with low offshore share and projects with high offshore share

F.3.1.7 Projects without versus with Consulting Support

A company can hire consultants in order to acquire external expertise and experience. By comparing projects without consulting support (Group 1) and projects with consulting support (Group 2) we can expect two equally viable results: either (a) projects with consulting support are actually more successful because projects benefit from consultants' expertise and experience or (b) projects with consulting support are actually less successful and prone to fail and therefore consultants are hired to improve delivery. Table 3-18 shows that projects without consulting support (Group 1) have higher mean scores than Group 2 regarding all five success indicators. So, hypothesis (b) seems to apply. These differences are significant for indicator SUCCESS2 (U = 7582.00, p < .05, r = -.15), indicator SUCCESS3 (U = 7700.00, p < .05, r = -.14), and indicator SUCCESS4 (U = 7874.50, p < .05, r = -.12) with small effects for each.

| | Mean values | | |
Statement	Group 1 No consulting support (n = 219)	Group 2 Consulting support (n = 85)	Difference
How satisfied was your organization with...			
...the project performance regarding time schedule. [SUCCESS1]	4.47	4.14	0.32
...the project performance regarding budget. [SUCCESS2]	4.93	4.38	0.56 *
...the project performance regarding expected functionality. [SUCCESS3]	4.82	4.32	0.50 *
...the project performance regarding expected quality. [SUCCESS4]	4.38	3.88	0.50 *
...the overall outcome of the project. [SUCCESS5]	4.75	4.33	0.42

* $p < .05$ ** $p < .01$ *** $p < .001$

Table 3-18: Mean differences of offshore project success indicator values between projects with no consulting support and projects with consulting support

F.3.1.8   Summary

Subgroup comparisons regarding offshore project success using subgroup formation criteria based on the sample's demographics yielded unclear results. Although success indicator values often differ in the expected directions, the number of statistically significant differences and corresponding effects sizes are small. The subgroups with the highest number of significant differences are projects delivered by an internal subsidiary or partially owned OSP versus projects delivered by an external OSP: four of five success indicators show significant differences, with success being higher for projects in the first group. Apparently, internal or partially owned OSPs are more successful in delivering offshoring projects. As already indicated in Section F.3.1.3 (p. 199), this might be due to less organizational friction, knowledge discrepancies, or a higher degree of efficiency of internal or partially owned OSPs. However, we need to consider that effects sizes are small for all four significant indicator mean value differences. The choice of OSP explains only a small portion of indicator variances for offshore project success which limits its relevancy. Table 3-19 provides an overview of the subgroup comparison results. It lists the actual subgroup comparison (first column), the direction of success indicator differences (second column), the number of significant differences (third column), and the corresponding effect sizes (fourth column).

Subgroup comparison	Observed success indicator values	Significant differences	Effect sizes
First versus recent projects	Slightly higher for recent projects	0	n/a
Nearshore versus offshore projects	Higher for nearshore projects	2	small
Projects delivered by internal or partially-owned OSP versus external OSP	Higher for projects delivered by internal or partially-owned OSP	4	small
Stand-alone projects versus projects embedded in larger offshoring program	Higher for stand-alone projects	1	small
Small versus large projects	Higher for small projects	1	small
Projects with low versus high offshoring share	Higher for projects with high offshoring share	0	n/a
Projects without versus with consulting support	Higher for projects without consulting support	3	small

Table 3-19: Overview of subgroup comparison results

F.3.2   Pre-Test of Research Model

F.3.2.1   Overview and Correlation Analysis

The last questions of each construct's indicator set directly asked for participants' self-perceived levels of offshoring expertise, trust in OSP, project suitability, knowledge transfer, liaison quality, and offshore project success (c.f. Section F.2.3.3, p. 191). In the following analyses, we use this indicator data (EXP4, TRUST6, SUITA6, KNOWT8, LIAISO5, and SUCCESS5) as surrogates for our constructs in order to pre-test the hypotheses from the research model.

For each hypothesis we perform a graphical and a quantitative analysis using the statistic software SPSS 16. We graphically analyze the relationship between independent and dependent constructs using a box plot. The box plot displays the values for the independent surrogate construct on the x-axis and shows the dependent surrogate construct's values on the y-axis.

Quantitatively, we test the significance of mean differences using ANOVA with post-hoc tests as implemented by SPSS. However, some assumptions of this test procedure are violated: sample sizes between the groups are unequal, data is not normally distributed, and the homogeneity of variance assumption is sometimes broken (Backhaus et al., 2006). Regarding the ANOVA test, we use Welch's F to account for unequal group sizes and the broken homogeneity of variance (Tomarken & Serlin, 1986; Welch, 1951). Regarding post-hoc tests, we account for different sample sizes by using either Hochberg's GT2 in case of homogeneity of variance or the Games-Howell procedure in case the homogeneity of variance assumption is broken (Field, 2005). By using ANOVA we assume asymptotic normal distribution of data. However, for reasons of result robustness and to account for not normally distributed data, we compare the ANOVA test results with the results from the non-parametric Kruskal-Wallis test that does not require normally distributed data (Kruskal & Wallis, 1952). The American Psychological Association (APA) states that "reporting and interpreting effect sizes [...] is essential to good research" (Wilkinson, 1999, p. 599). We adhere to this recommendation and report effect sizes where applicable.

An initial correlation analysis[12] indicates, what to expect from the analyses in the following subsections. Table 3-20 shows that all indicators are significantly positively correlated with each other. Correlation coefficients are low for the offshoring expertise indicator EXP4 and large for all other indicators, i.e., TRUST6, SUITA6, KNOWT8, LIAISO5, and SUCCESS5.

Correlations

			EXP4	TRUST6	SUITA6	KNOWT8	LIAISO5	SUCCES5
Spearman's rho	EXP4	Correlation	1.000	.238**	.300**	.250**	.237**	.246**
		Sig. (1-tailed)		.000	.000	.000	.000	.000
		N	304	304	304	304	304	304
	TRUST6	Correlation	.238**	1.000	.583**	.615**	.673**	.573**
		Sig. (1-tailed)	.000		.000	.000	.000	.000
		N	304	304	304	304	304	304
	SUITA6	Correlation	.300**	.583**	1.000	.635**	.627**	.647**
		Sig. (1-tailed)	.000	.000		.000	.000	.000
		N	304	304	304	304	304	304
	KNOWT8	Correlation	.250**	.615**	.635**	1.000	.763**	.728**
		Sig. (1-tailed)	.000	.000	.000		.000	.000
		N	304	304	304	304	304	304
	LIAISO5	Correlation	.237**	.673**	.627**	.763**	1.000	.731**
		Sig. (1-tailed)	.000	.000	.000	.000		.000
		N	304	304	304	304	304	304
	SUCCES5	Correlation	.246**	.573**	.647**	.728**	.731**	1.000
		Sig. (1-tailed)	.000	.000	.000	.000	.000	
		N	304	304	304	304	304	304

**. Correlation is significant at the 0.01 level (1-tailed).

Table 3-20: Correlation of surrogate constructs

---

[12] We use Spearman's rho because data is not normally distributed.

F.3.2.2   Offshoring Expertise

H1: Offshoring Expertise (+) → Offshore Project Success

Figure 3-28 illustrates the relationship of self-perceived offshoring expertise levels (EXP4, on x-axis) and perceived offshore project success (SUCCESS5, on y-axis). According to hypothesis H1 we expect that offshore project success indicator values gradually increase with higher offshoring expertise levels. However, this effect is not immediately recognizable: except for offshoring expertise levels six and seven, offshore project success indicator values are scattered widely.

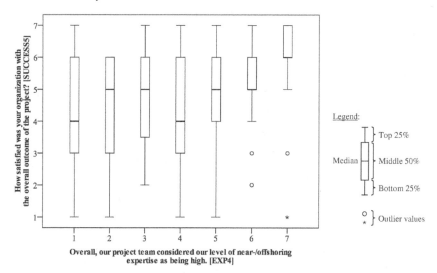

Figure 3-28: Relationship of offshoring expertise and offshore project success

Quantitatively, ANOVA shows that there is a significant marginal medium effect of expertise on levels of success (Welch's F (6, 118.37) = 5.598, p < .001, r = .30). This finding is also confirmed by a Kruskal-Wallis test (H(6) = 32.395, p < .001). However, as Table 3-21 shows, post-hoc tests using the Games-Howell procedure reveal that only a high offshoring expertise level of seven significantly increases perceived offshore project success in comparison to lower offshoring expertise levels of one to five.[13] Please refer to the Appendix (pp. 267-268) for documentation of the whole test procedure.

---

[13] Please note that this table and the subsequent tables in the section display significances, i.e., p-values. The "*" symbol is therefore redundant. However, we purposely included it to highlight p-values below .05, .01, and .001.

SUCCES5				EXP4			
Games-Howell	1	2	3	4	5	6	7
1	-	.999	.893	.996	.685	.357	.000***
2	.999	-	.974	.999	.812	.278	.000***
3	.893	.974	-	.993	.995	.753	.001**
4	.996	.999	.993	-	.892	.399	.000***
5	.685	.812	.995	.892	-	.996	.032*
6	.357	.278	.753	.399	.996	-	.065
7	.000***	.000***	.001**	.000***	.032*	.065	-

(left axis label: EXP4)

* $p < .05$ ** $p < .01$ *** $p < .001$

**Table 3-21: Significances of overall success mean differences
for different offshoring expertise levels**

H2: Offshoring Expertise (+) → Project Suitability

Figure 3-29 illustrates the relationship of self-perceived offshoring expertise levels (EXP4, on x-axis) and perceived project suitability (SUITA6, on y-axis). We expect that with increased offshoring expertise levels, more offshore suitable projects are selected, i.e., the higher the project suitability indicator values will be. Similar to hypothesis H1, this effect is not immediately recognizable: except for offshoring expertise levels of six and seven, project suitability indicators scatter widely.

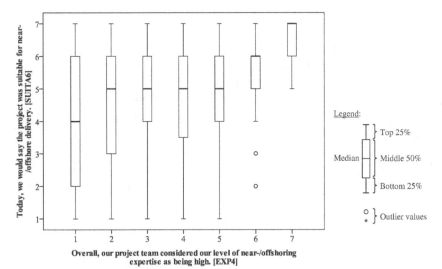

Figure 3-29: Relationship of offshoring expertise and project suitability

ANOVA shows that there is a significant medium effect of offshoring expertise on levels of project suitability (Welch's F(6, 122.21) = 15.414, p < .001, r = .34). A Kruskal-Wallis test confirms this result (H(6) = 39.477, p < .001). However, post-hoc tests with the Games-Howell procedure show that only the highest offshoring expertise, level seven, significantly increases project suitability in comparison to all other offshoring expertise levels. Table 3-22 illustrates these results. Please refer to the Appendix (pp. 269-270) for documentation of the whole test procedure.

SUITA6 Games-Howell		1	2	3	4	5	6	7
	1	-	.998	.839	.784	.648	.102	.000***
	2	.998	-	.961	.924	.812	.099	.000***
EXP4	3	.839	.961	-	1.000	.997	.464	.000***
	4	.784	.924	1.000	-	1.000	.828	.000***
	5	.648	.812	.997	1.000	-	.946	.000***
	6	.102	.099	.464	.828	.946	-	.001***
	7	.000***	.000***	.000***	.000***	.000***	.001***	-

*p < .05   **p < .01   ***p < .001

Table 3-22: Significances of project suitability mean differences
for different offshoring expertise levels

H3: Offshoring Expertise (+) → Knowledge Transfer

Figure 3-30 shows the relationship of self-perceived offshoring expertise (EXP4, on x-axis) and perceived satisfaction with knowledge transfer (KNOWT8, on y-axis). According to hypothesis H3, we expect levels of satisfaction with knowledge transfer to be higher for increased level of offshoring expertise. Although median values are higher for increased levels of offshoring expertise, indicator values for knowledge transfer do still scatter widely for all offshoring expertise levels and the assumed positive relationship is not immediately visible.

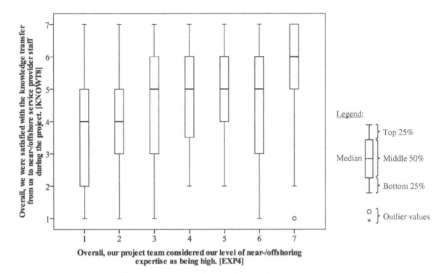

Figure 3-30: Relationship of offshoring expertise and knowledge transfer

ANOVA reveals that there is a significant but small effect of offshoring expertise on knowledge transfer (Welch's F (6, 118.29) = 4.735, p < .001, r = .29). A Kruskal-Wallis test confirms this result (H(6) = 27.643, p < .001). Similar to the pre-tests of hypotheses H1 and H2, post-hoc tests show that only an offshoring expertise value of seven in comparison to values of one, two, and three significantly increases knowledge transfer values. Table 3-23 illustrates the significant knowledge transfer mean differences for various offshoring expertise levels. We used Hochberg's GT2 for post-hoc tests since Levene's test shows that the assumption of homogeneity of variance applies. The Appendix (pp. 271-272) documents the whole test procedure.

KNOWT8				EXP4			
Hochberg	1	2	3	4	5	6	7
1	-	1.000	.503	.492	.450	.609	.000***
2	1.000	-	.815	.794	.739	.886	.000***
3	.503	.815	-	1.000	1.000	1.000	.035*
4	.492	.794	1.000	-	1.000	1.000	.094
5	.450	.739	1.000	1.000	-	1.000	.264
6	.609	.886	1.000	1.000	1.000	-	.067
7	.000***	.000***	.035*	.094	.264	.067	-

(left label: EXP4)

* p < .05   ** p < .01   *** p < .001

Table 3-23: Significances of knowledge transfer mean differences
for different offshoring expertise levels

H4: Offshoring Expertise (+) → Liaison Quality

Figure 3-31 illustrates the relationship between self-perceived offshoring expertise (EXP4, on x-axis) and perceived satisfaction with liaison quality (LIASO5, on y-axis). Following hypothesis H4 we expect higher levels of liaison quality for increasing levels of offshoring expertise. Similar to the previous sections, the impact is also not immediately visually recognizable: liaison quality indicator median values are equal for offshoring expertise values of one to six. Additionally, liaison quality indicator values scatter widely for all offshoring expertise levels except for two and seven.

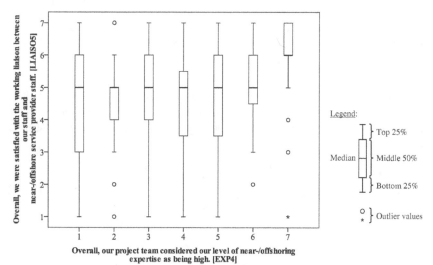

Figure 3-31: Relationship of offshoring expertise and liaison quality

ANOVA shows that there is a significant small effect of offshoring expertise on levels of liaison quality (Welch's F (6, 117.23) = 4.414, p < .001, r = .28). This finding is also confirmed by a Kruskal-Wallis test (H(6) = 30.601, p < .001). For post-hoc tests, we used Hochberg's GT2 since Levene's test shows that the assumption of homogeneity of variance applies. Post-hoc tests show that only an offshoring expertise level of seven increases liaison quality values. This effect is significant for offshoring expertise indicator level seven in comparison to levels of one to five. Table 3-24 illustrates these results. The Appendix (pp. 273-274) documents the whole test procedure.

LIAISO5				EXP4			
Hochberg	1	2	3	4	5	6	7
1	-	1.000	1.000	1.000	1.000	.679	.000***
2	1.000	-	1.000	1.000	1.000	.875	.000***
3	1.000	1.000	-	1.000	1.000	.998	.003**
EXP4 4	1.000	1.000	1.000	-	1.000	.980	.002**
5	1.000	1.000	1.000	1.000	-	1.000	.020*
6	.679	.875	.998	.980	1.000	-	.111
7	.000***	.000***	.003**	.002**	.020*	.111	-

* p < .05   ** p < .01   *** p < .001

Table 3-24: Significances of liaison quality mean differences for different offshoring expertise levels

F.3.2.3   Trust in Offshore Service Provider

H5: Trust in Offshore Service Provider (+) → Knowledge Transfer

Figure 3-32 depicts the relationship between perceived trust in OSP (TRUST6, on x-axis) and perceived satisfaction with knowledge transfer (KNOWT8, on y-axis). As stated by hypothesis H5, we expect higher indicator values for knowledge transfer as values of trust increase. The box-plot in Figure 3-32 visually confirms this: median values of knowledge transfer increase for higher levels of trust. Additionally, values scatter less than they did in the previous analyses.

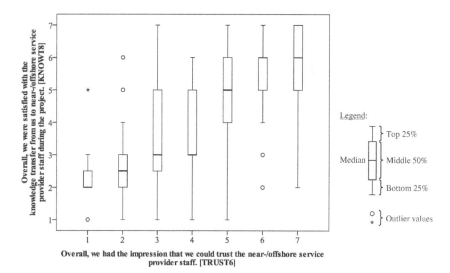

Figure 3-32: Relationship of trust in OSP and knowledge transfer

ANOVA reveals that there is a large significant effect of perceived levels of trust in OSP on perceived levels of knowledge transfer (Welch's F (6, 68.06) = 31.498, p < .001, r = .62). A Kruskal-Wallis test confirms these findings (H(6) = 118.284, p < .001). Again, we used Hochberg's GT2 for post-hoc tests since Levene's test shows that the assumption of homogeneity of variance can be accepted. In contrast to the post-hoc test results of hypotheses H1 to H4, indicator values for knowledge transfer differ for various levels of trust as Table 3-25 shows. The Appendix (pp. 275-276) contains the detailed test results.

KNOWT8 Hochberg		1	2	3	4	5	6	7
						TRUST6		
TRUST6	1	-	1.000	.212	.358	.000***	.000***	.000***
	2	1.000	-	.063	.187	.000***	.000***	.000***
	3	.212	.063	-	1.000	.001***	.000***	.000***
	4	.358	.187	1.000	-	.000***	.000***	.000***
	5	.000***	.000***	.001***	.000***	-	.099	.000***
	6	.000***	.000***	.000***	.000***	.099	-	.429
	7	.000***	.000***	.000***	.000***	.000***	.429	-

* p < .05   ** p < .01   *** p < .001

Table 3-25: Significances of knowledge transfer mean differences for different trust levels

H6: Trust in Offshore Service Provider (+) → Liaison Quality

Figure 3-33 shows the relationship between perceived trust in OSP (TRUST6, on x-axis) and perceived satisfaction with liaison quality (LIAISO5, on y-axis). Based on hypothesis H6 we expect a positive relationship between the two constructs. Figure 3-33 graphically supports this perception: median indicator values of liaison quality increase with increasing levels of trust. However, values scatter widely for trust levels one to five.

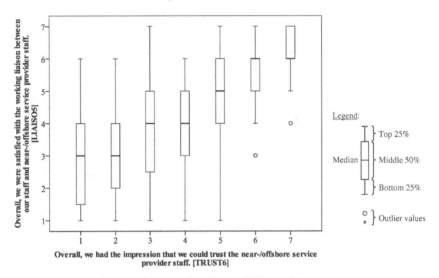

Figure 3-33: Relationship of trust in OSP and liaison quality

ANOVA shows that there is a significant large effect of perceived trust in OSP on levels of liaison quality (Welch's F $(6, 66.40) = 48.025$, $p < .001$, $r = .67$). A Kruskal-Wallis test confirms this result ($H(6) = 140.663$, $p < .001$). In detail, post-hoc tests using the Games-Howell procedure show that mean values for liaison quality differ significantly between various trust levels. Table 3-26 illustrates the significant differences for all trust level values. The Appendix (pp. 277-278) contains the detailed test results.

LIAISO5 Games-Howell				TRUST6			
	1	2	3	4	5	6	7
1	-	1.000	.881	.688	.125	.043[*]	.010[**]
2	1.000	-	.183	.013[*]	.000[***]	.000[***]	.000[***]
TRUST6 3	.881	.183	-	.980	.000[***]	.000[***]	.000[***]
4	.688	.013[*]	.980	-	.002[**]	.000[***]	.000[***]
5	.125	.000[***]	.000[***]	.002[**]	-	.027[*]	.000[***]
6	.043[*]	.000[***]	.000[***]	.000[***]	.027[*]	-	.000[***]
7	.010[**]	.000[***]	.000[***]	.000[***]	.000[***]	.000[***]	-

$* p < .05$ $** p < .01$ $*** p < .001$

Table 3-26: Significances of liaison quality mean differences for different trust levels

H7: Trust in Offshore Service Provider (+) → Offshore Project Success

Figure 3-34 illustrates the relationship between perceived trust in OSP (TRUST6, on x-axis) and perceived offshore project success (SUCCESS5, on y-axis). Following hypothesis H7, we expect a positive relationship between different levels of trust and offshore project success. The box-plot confirms this visually: except for trust level one, median values of offshore project success increase with higher trust levels. However, offshore project success indicator values scatter widely, especially for trust levels of one and five.

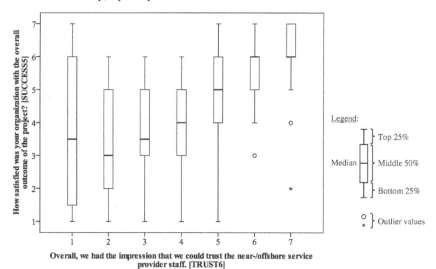

Overall, we had the impression that we could trust the near-/offshore service
provider staff. [TRUST6]

Figure 3-34: Relationship of trust in OSP and offshore project success

ANOVA shows that there is a significant large effect of perceived trust in OSP on levels of offshore project success (Welch's $F(6, 65.75) = 27.830$, $p < .001$, $r = .58$). A Kruskal-Wallis test confirms these findings ($H(6) = 109.809$, $p < .001$). In detail, post-hoc tests using the Games-Howell procedure show that mean values for success differ significantly between trust levels except for trust level one which shows no significant differences to the other trust levels. Table 3-27 illustrates offshore project success mean differences for all trust level values and highlights the significant ones. The Appendix (pp. 279-280) contains further detailed test results.

SUCCESS5 Games-Howell		TRUST6 1	2	3	4	5	6	7
TRUST6	1	-	1.000	1.000	1.000	.892	.486	.183
	2	1.000	-	.945	.992	.007**	.000***	.000***
	3	1.000	.945	-	1.000	.009**	.000***	.000***
	4	1.000	.992	1.000	-	.002**	.000***	.000***
	5	.892	.007**	.009**	.002**	-	.003**	.000***
	6	.486	.000***	.000***	.000***	.003**	-	.004**
	7	.183	.000***	.000***	.000***	.000***	.004**	-

* p < .05 ** p < .01 *** p < .001

Table 3-27: Significances of overall success mean differences for different trust levels

F.3.2.4 Project Suitability

H8: Project Suitability (+) → Offshore Project Success

Figure 3-35 shows the relationship between perceived project suitability for offshoring (SUITA6, on x-axis) and perceived offshore project success (SUCCESS5, on y-axis). Based on hypothesis H8 and similar to the other hypotheses, we expect a positive relationship of the two constructs' indicator values. The box-plot in Figure 3-35 graphically confirms this: median values for offshore project success increase with higher levels of project suitability.

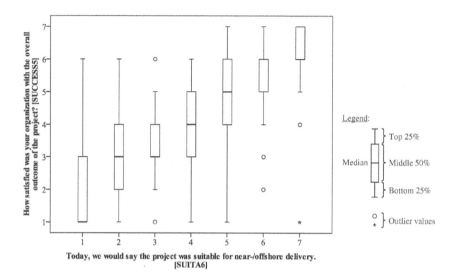

Today, we would say the project was suitable for near-/offshore delivery.
[SUITA6]

Figure 3-35: Relationship of project suitability and offshore project success

ANOVA shows that there is a significant large effect of perceived project suitability on levels of overall success (Welch's F (6, 79.98) = 32.079, p < .001, r = .66). A Kruskal-Wallis test confirms these findings (H(6) = 127.237, p < .001). In detail, post-hoc tests following the Games-Howell procedure show that mean values for overall success differ significantly between many levels of project suitability. Table 3-28 shows the offshore project success mean differences for all levels of project suitability and highlights the significant ones. The Appendix (pp. 281-282) documents the test procedure results in detail.

SUCCESS5 Games-Howell		SUITA6					
	1	2	3	4	5	6	7
1	-	.591	.441	.075	.005**	.001***	.000***
2	.591	-	.999	.266	.000***	.000***	.000***
3	.441	.999	-	.624	.002**	.000***	.000***
4	.075	.266	.624	-	.055	.000***	.000***
5	.005**	.000***	.002**	.055	-	.005**	.000***
6	.001***	.000***	.000***	.000***	.005**	-	.050*
7	.000***	.000***	.000***	.000***	.000***	.050*	-

* p < .05   ** p < .01   *** p < .001

Table 3-28: Significances of overall success mean differences for different levels of project suitability

F.3.2.5   Knowledge Transfer

H9: Knowledge Transfer (+) → Offshore Project Success

Figure 3-36 illustrates the relationship between perceived satisfaction with knowledge transfer (KNOWT8, on x-axis) and perceived offshore project success (SUCCESS5, on y-axis). As stated in hypothesis H9, we anticipate higher indicator values for offshore project success with increasing values of knowledge transfer. The box-plot in Figure 3-36 visually supports this relationship: median values of offshore project success do increase with higher values of knowledge transfer. Additionally, except for knowledge transfer level two, indicator values for offshore project success do not scatter much around their median values.

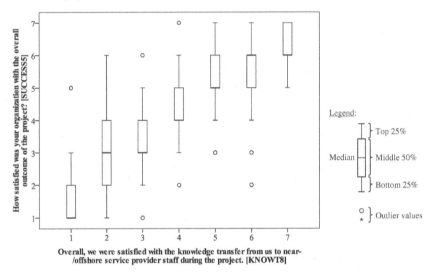

Overall, we were satisfied with the knowledge transfer from us to near-
/offshore service provider staff during the project. [KNOWT8]

Figure 3-36: Relationship of knowledge transfer and offshore project success

ANOVA shows that there is a significant large effect of perceived knowledge transfer on levels of overall success (Welch's F (6, 82.25) = 61.190, p < .001, r = .75). A Kruskal-Wallis test confirms these findings (H(6) = 164.048, p < .001). In detail, post-hoc tests using the Games-Howell procedure show that mean values for overall success differ significantly between almost all levels of knowledge transfer. Table 3-29 shows the mean differences for offshore project success regarding all levels of knowledge transfer. Significant differences are highlighted. The Appendix (pp. 283-284) documents the test procedure in detail.

SUCCES5 Games-Howell	KNOWT8						
	1	2	3	4	5	6	7
1	-	.026*	.006**	.000***	.000***	.000***	.000***
2	.026*	-	.958	.001***	.000***	.000***	.000***
3	.006**	.958	-	.008**	.000***	.000***	.000***
4	.000***	.001***	.008**	-	.032*	.000***	.000***
5	.000***	.000***	.000***	.032*	-	.008**	.000***
6	.000***	.000***	.000***	.000***	.008**	-	.049*
7	.000***	.000***	.000***	.000***	.000***	.049*	-

(Left axis label: KNOWT8)

* p < .05   ** p < .01   *** p < .001

Table 3-29: Significances of overall success mean differences for
different levels of knowledge transfer

F.3.2.6   Liaison Quality

H10: Liaison Quality (+) → Offshore Project Success

Figure 3-37 shows the relationship of perceived satisfaction with liaison quality (LIAISO5, on x-axis) on perceived offshore project success (SUCCESS5, on y-axis). Hypothesis H10 formulates a positive relationship between liaison quality and offshore project success. The box-plot in Figure 3-37 seems to confirm this relationship: indicator median values for offshore project success are higher for increasing values of liaison quality. This perception is strengthened by a low scatter of indicator values around their medians, except for liaison quality levels three and four.

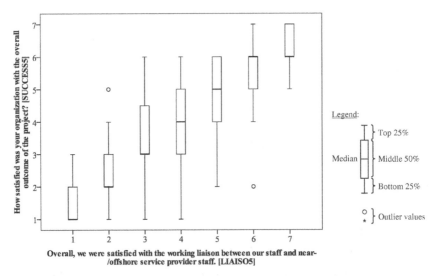

Overall, we were satisfied with the working liaison between our staff and near-
/offshore service provider staff. [LIAISO5]

Figure 3-37: Relationship of liaison quality and offshore project success

ANOVA shows that there is a significant large effect of perceived liaison quality on levels of overall success (Welch's F $(6, 64.82) = 94.623$, $p < .001$, $r = .75$). A Kruskal-Wallis test confirms these findings ($H(6) = 164.902$, $p < .001$). In detail, post-hoc tests according to the Games-Howell procedure show that mean values for overall success differ significantly between almost all levels of liaison quality. Table 3-30 illustrates offshore project success mean differences for all liaison quality values and highlights the significant ones. The Appendix (pp. 285-286) contains the test results.

SUCCES5		LIAISO5					
Games-Howell	1	2	3	4	5	6	7
1	-	.199	.000***	.000***	.000***	.000***	.000***
2	.199	-	.009**	.000***	.000***	.000***	.000***
LIAISO5 3	.000***	.009**	-	.855	.001**	.000***	.000***
4	.000***	.000***	.855	-	.024*	.000***	.000***
5	.000***	.000***	.001**	.024*	-	.000***	.000***
6	.000***	.000***	.000***	.000***	.000***	-	.000***
7	.000***	.000***	.000***	.000***	.000***	.000***	-

* $p < .05$ ** $p < .01$ *** $p < .001$

Table 3-30: Significances of overall success mean differences for different liaison quality levels

F.3.2.7   Summary

Based on the analyses, we can expect that the postulated impact directions from the hypotheses will hold (c.f. Section C.1, p. 154). ANOVA test results showed significant differences and small to large effects. Yet, it is also obvious that effect sizes and number of significant differences for hypotheses H1 to H4 are rather low. Apparently, construct offshoring expertise seems to have a smaller impact than the other constructs of hypotheses H5 to H10. Therefore, we can potentially expect lower, insignificant path coefficients, or both for hypotheses H1 to H4. Table 3-31 provides an overview of the ANOVA and post-hoc test results. Finally, these results need to be treated with care because at this stage we do not know whether the surrogate constructs based on EXP4, TRUST6, SUITA6, KNOWT8, LIAISO6, and SUCCESS5 reflect the latter constructs' values in the PLS analysis well.

Hypotheses	ANOVA		Post-hoc tests
	F-value	Effect size	No. of significant differences
H1: Offshoring expertise (+) → Offshore project success	5.598	medium	5
H2: Offshoring expertise (+) → Project suitability	15.414	medium	6
H3: Offshoring expertise (+) → Knowledge transfer	4.735	small	3
H4: Offshoring expertise (+) → Liaison quality	4.414	small	5
H5: Trust in offshore service provider (+) → Knowledge transfer	31.498	large	13
H6: Trust in offshore service provider (+) → Liaison quality	48.025	large	15
H7: Trust in offshore service provider (+) → Offshore project success	27.830	large	12
H8: Project suitability (+) → Offshore project success	32.079	large	14
H9: Knowledge transfer (+) → Offshore project success	61.190	large	20
H10: Liaison quality (+) → Offshore project success	94.623	large	19

All test results significant at $p < .001$

Table 3-31: Overview of ANOVA test results

F.4 Structural Equation Model Analysis

F.4.1   Quality Criteria

A structural equation model consists of a measurement model and a structural model. The measurement model contains the indicators, or manifest variables, that measure the model's constructs, or latent variables. The structural model consists of the relationships, or paths, between the constructs. The following subsections describe the relevant quality criteria for both model types regarding the PLS approach.

F.4.1.1   Measurement Model

Reflective Constructs

The basic assumption in research models with latent variables is that the indicators "reflect one and only one latent variable. This property of the scale, having each of its measurement items relate to it better than to any others, is known as unidimensionality. [...] Unidimensionality cannot be measured with PLS but is assumed to be there *a priori*. [sic]" (Gefen & Straub, 2005, p. 92). However, with respect to the study, we do not assume unidimensionality implicitly, i.e., untested, since this may lead to undetected errors in the measurement model. We rather test explicitly for unidimensionality before applying any other PLS quality criteria.

Unidimensionality can be assessed using an exploratory factor analysis (EFA) (Gefen & Straub, 2005; Huber et al., 2007). The EFA helps to determine (a) whether the indicators converge into the corresponding constructs, or factors, of the research model, (b) whether each indicator loads with a high coefficient on only one factor, and (c) that this specific factor is the same for all indicators that are supposed to measure it (Gefen & Straub, 2005). Regarding (a), the number of factors is determined by the factors that have an Eigenvalue exceeding 1.0 and should be the same as in the research model. Regarding (b) and (c), indicators should load high on their own factors and load low on other factors. Indicators load highly if their loading coefficient is above .60 and do not load highly if their loading coefficient is below .40 (Gefen & Straub, 2005; Hair, 2006). Indicators with a loading coefficient below .40 should be removed from the research model (Huber et al., 2007; Hulland, 1999). We conduct the EFA using the statistic software package SPSS 16 through a principal components analysis (PCA) with varimax rotation to support interpretation of the results (Huber et al., 2007; SPSS Inc., 2007). Table 3-32 shows the quality criterion, its values, and the corresponding references.

Criterion	Criterion values	References
EFA	Indicator loading > 0.6 on own construct Indicator loading < 0.4 on other constructs	Gefen & Straub, 2005; Hair, 2006; Huber et al., 2007; Hulland, 1999

Table 3-32: Quality criteria: unidimensionality

Having analyzed unidimensionality, it is subsequently necessary to assess factorial validity consisting of convergent validity and discriminant validity. "Convergent validity is shown when each measurement item correlates strongly with its assumed theoretical construct, while discriminant validity is shown when each measurement item correlates weakly with all other constructs except for the one to which it is theoretically associated" (Gefen & Straub, 2005, p. 92).

The degree of convergent validity is determined by a confirmatory factor analysis (CFA) within PLS where the number of factors are specified a priori. Convergent validity is assumed when indicators' loadings on their respective constructs is significant at the 95% level using Bootstrapping (Gefen & Straub, 2005). Indicator loading values should exceed .70 on their constructs, so that more than 50% of an indicator's variance is caused by the construct (Herrmann et al., 2006; Huber et al., 2007; Hulland, 1999). Furthermore, the average variance extracted (AVE), measuring the variance captured by the indicators in relation to the variance caused by the measurement errors of the indicators, should exceed .50 (Fornell & Larcker, 1981). A value of .50 ensures that the captured, i.e., explained, variance is greater than the variance caused by the measurement error (Bagozzi & Yi, 1988; Chin, 1998). We conduct all required tests with the software package SmartPLS (Ringle et al., 2005) using the output of the PLS algorithm and the Bootstrapping procedures. Table 3-33 illustrates the criteria.

Criterion	Criterion values	References
Significance of indicator loadings	Significant, i.e., at 95% level	Gefen & Straub, 2005; Huber et al., 2007
CFA	Indicator loading > .70 on own construct	Huber et al., 2007; Hulland, 1999
AVE	AVE > .50	Bagozzi & Yi, 1988; (Chin, 1998, p. 321); Fornell & Larcker, 1981

Table 3-33: Quality criteria: convergent validity

Discriminant validity is assessed by using the Fornell-Larcker criterion (Fornell & Larcker, 1981) and the cross-loadings between indicators and constructs. The Fornell-Larcker criterion requires that "AVEs of the [constructs] should be greater than the square of the correlations among the [constructs], which indicates that more variance is shared between the [construct] component and its block of indicators than with another component representing a different block of indicators" (Chin, 1998, p. 321). To apply the Fornell-Larcker criterion we use the AVE values as calculated in SmartPLS.

Regarding cross-loadings it is required that indicators load higher with their own constructs than with any other construct. However, literature specifies no distinct loading value as an applicable criterion (Chin, 1998). Again, we use the loadings generated by SmartPLS for analysis purposes. Table 3-34 illustrates the quality criteria regarding discriminant validity.

Criterion	Criterion values	References
Fornell-Larcker	AVE > (correlation of constructs)^2	Chin, 1998; Fornell & Larcker, 1981
Indicator-construct-loadings	Indicators should load higher on their respective constructs than on any other construct (no specified loading level)	Chin, 1998

Table 3-34: Quality criteria: discriminant validity

Construct reliability addresses the internal consistency of a scale, i.e., the adequacy of a latent variable to explain its corresponding block of indicators. There are two measures to assess construct reliability: Cronbach's Alpha and Composite Reliability (CR). Cronbach's Alpha can show values from zero (no internal consistency) to one (complete internal consistency). Nunnally (1967) suggests values exceeding .60 for exploratory and values exceeding .70 for confirmatory research. However, Cronbach's Alpha is criticized because its value increases with augmenting numbers of indicators and for its underlying assumption regarding tau equivalency and equal indicator weightings (Chin, 1998; Hulland, 1999). Therefore, Chin (1998) recommends to use CR as the preferred measure since it overcomes the above-mentioned deficiencies of Cronbach's Alpha. Similar to Cronbach's Alpha, CR values can range from zero to one. Values of at least .60 but preferable exceeding .70 show sufficient levels of construct reliability (Bagozzi & Yi, 1988; Huber et al., 2007; Hulland, 1999). We use values for Cronbach's Alpha and CR as calculated by SmartPLS. Table 3-35 illustrates the respective quality criteria.

Criterion	Criterion values	References
Cronbach's alpha	> .60 for exploratory research > .70 for confirmatory research	Nunnally, 1967
CR	> .70	Chin, 1998; Huber et al., 2007; Hulland, 1999

Table 3-35: Quality criteria: construct reliability

Formative Constructs

Formative constructs are determined by their indicators. Their sets of measurement items should consist of all indicators that have an impact on the construct. Since the indicators cause the construct, by definition interchanging or dropping individual indicators is not permitted. Furthermore, indicators do not have to be correlated at all (c.f. Section D.3, p. 161). Therefore, quality criteria from reflective constructs that build on indicator correlations cannot be applied to formative constructs. (Diamantopoulos & Winklhofer, 2001; Huber et al., 2007)

For quality assessments regarding formative constructs, researchers emphasize the importance of variable construction by thoroughly specifying the constructs as well as their indicators

(Diamantopoulos & Winklhofer, 2001; Rossiter, 2002). "Indicators must cover the entire scope of the latent variable as described under the content specification" (Diamantopoulos & Winklhofer, 2001, p. 271). We fulfilled this requirement by constructing the study's indicators based on an extensive pre-study.

To examine indicators' quality, Huber et al. (2007) suggest examining the regression coefficients between indicators and constructs (Huber et al., 2007). The values of indicators' regression coefficients show the degree of predictive validity, and the corresponding t-values indicate the degree of reliability. However, as stated above, independent from the results of this test, dropping individual indicators would violate the assumption of the underlying formative constructs. In our study, we calculate the regression coefficients and the corresponding t-values using the Bootstrapping procedure of SmartPLS.

Another quality criterion focuses on the aspect of multi-collinearity. Since formative constructs are based on multiple regression, "excessive collinearity among indicators thus makes it difficult to separate the distinct influence of the individual [indicators] on the latent variable" (Diamantopoulos & Winklhofer, 2001, p. 272) and therefore the estimates are getting less reliable. To assess the degree of multi-collinearity we examine the variance inflation factor (VIF) for each indicator. The VIF shows how much of an indicator's variance can be explained by the remaining other indicators from the indicator set. Values exceeding 10 imply a high degree of multi-collinearity (Diamantopoulos & Winklhofer, 2001). To calculate the VIF, we follow the procedure described by Huber et al. (2007). Table 3-36 illustrates the quality criteria applied to the formative construct.

Criterion	Criterion values	References
Indicator weights	Sufficient loading level Significant, i.e., at 95% level	Herrmann et al., 2006; Huber et al., 2007
Multi-collinearity	VIF < 10	Diamantopoulos & Winklhofer, 2001; Huber et al., 2007

Table 3-36: Quality criteria: formative construct

F.4.1.2   Structural Model

The structural model specifies the relationship between the constructs. The first quality assessment therefore focuses on the scores and significances of the path coefficients between the constructs. T-values of path coefficients are calculated using Bootstrapping and should be significant, i.e., at least at the 95% level, to support the postulated hypotheses. Additionally, path coefficients should exceed .10 to account for a certain impact within the model. Furthermore, path coefficients should show the same sign as postulated in the hypotheses. (Chin, 1998; Huber et al., 2007)

The overall coefficient of determination R^2 of the main dependent variable, i.e., the proportion of its variance explained by the other constructs, should be sufficiently high for the model to have a minimum level of explanatory power. To meet this requirement, Huber et al. (2007) demand an R^2 value of at least .30. Other authors interpret R^2 values exceeding .67 as "substantial", values exceeding .33 but lower or equal to .67 as "moderate", and values exceeding .19 but lower or equal to .33 as "weak" (Chin, 1998, p. 323).

The impact of one construct on another can be determined by calculating the effect size f^2 (Chin, 1998). Values for f^2 between .02 and .15, .15 and .35, and exceeding .35 indicate that an independent variable has a small, medium, or large effect on a dependent variable (Cohen, 1988).

Finally, it is recommended to assess the model's predictive validity regarding the dependent reflective constructs. This is done via "a blindfolding procedure that omits a part of the data for a particular block of indicators during parameter estimations and then attempts to estimate the omitted part using the estimated parameters. This procedure is repeated until every data point has been omitted and estimated. As a result of this procedure, a generalized cross-validation measure [...] can be obtained." (Chin, 1998, p. 317). The resulting measure, Stone-Geisser Q^2, indicates how well values are reconstructed by the model. A value for Q^2 exceeding zero indicates that the model has predictive relevance (Chin, 1998; Huber et al., 2007). Table 3-37 illustrates all applied quality criteria on the level of the structural model.

Criterion	Criterion values	References
Path coefficients & significances	Path coefficients > .10 Significant, i.e., at 95% level	Chin, 1998; Huber et al., 2007
R^2	> .19 and <= .33 (weak) > .33 and <= .67 (medium) > .67 (substantial)	Chin, 1998; Huber et al., 2007
Effect size f^2	> .02 and <= .15 (small) > .15 and <= .35 (medium) > .35 (large)	Chin, 1998; Cohen, 1988; Huber et al., 2007
Stone-Geisser Q^2	> 0	Chin, 1998; Huber et al., 2007

Table 3-37: Quality criteria: structural model

F.4.2 Quality Assessment of Measurement Model

F.4.2.1 Reflective Constructs

Unidimensionality

An EFA on the reflective constructs' indicators using PCA with varimax rotation and Kaiser normalization (SPSS Inc., 2007) extracts six factors with Eigenvalues greater than 1.0. Table

3-38 shows the rotated component matrix of the EFA. To increase readability, only loadings exceeding .40 are displayed. The table's top row enumerates the extracted components, i.e., factors. Analyzing the loading pattern, component one seems to represent construct offshore project success, component two represents trust in OSP, component three represents knowledge transfer, component four represents offshoring expertise, component five represents liaison quality, and component six represents – again – knowledge transfer.

	Component					
	1	2	3	4	5	6
EXP1				.825		
EXP2				.868		
EXP3				.830		
EXP4				.884		
TRUST1		.581				
TRUST2		.810				
TRUST3		.675				
TRUST4		.806				
TRUST5		.828				
TRUST6		.777				
KNOWT1			.603			
KNOWT2			.770			
KNOWT3			.829			
KNOWT4			.733			
KNOWT5			.692			
KNOWT6						.690
KNOWT7						.807
KNOWT8	.623					
LIAISO1	.424	.492			.452	
LIAISO2					.726	
LIAISO3					.794	
LIAISO4					.763	
LIAISO5	.570				.485	
SUCCES1	.838					
SUCCES2	.771					
SUCCES3	.822					
SUCCES4	.822					
SUCCES5	.871					

Extraction Method: Principal Component Analysis.
Rotation Method: Varimax with Kaiser Normalization.

Table 3-38: Assessment of unidimensionality with exploratory factor analysis

The results of the factor analysis show that the indicators exhibit a reasonable level of unidimensionality regarding the respective factors they are supposed to measure: most indicators load on one factor and factor loadings are high. However, four specific observations need to be addressed:

(1) TRUST1 loads correctly with the other TRUST-indicators. However, its loading is marginally below the threshold of .60.

(2) KNOWT8 shows a high loading level on the factor representing offshore project success (component one) but not – as intended – on the factor knowledge transfer (represented by components three and six).

(3) Indicators LIAISO1 and LIAISO5 load on more than one factor with loadings exceeding .40 each but below the threshold of .60.

(4) The analysis suggests a two factor solution for knowledge transfer. Apparently, indicators KNOWT1 to KNOWT5 load high on a different aspect of knowledge transfer (represented by component three) than KNOWT6 and KNOWT7 that load on another aspect (represented by component six).

Regarding (1), the descriptive analysis for construct trust in OSP in Section F.2.3.4 (p. 193) already showed that mean scores for indicator TRUST1 differed from the remaining indicators. Following the descriptive analysis's interpretation, we perceive low loading levels of TRUST1 as a result of slightly biased indicator values induced by the way the question was formulated. Considering this and applying the loading criteria threshold of .60 we exclude indicator TRUST1 from further analyses.

Addressing (2), indicator KNOWT8 seems to measure offshore project success rather than knowledge transfer. Although the indicator question explicitly asked for the perceived satisfaction of knowledge transfer, the resulting scores seem to be more closely related to offshore project success instead of knowledge transfer success. Consequently, we drop KNOWT8 as a measurement indicator for knowledge transfer from the analyses.

Observation (3) implies that the question text of indicator LIAISO1 regarding degree of open communication does not only measure liaison quality but addresses aspects of offshore project success, and trust in OSP as well. The other indicator LIAISON5 shows a similar pattern as KNOWT8: it loads higher on offshore project success instead of liaison quality. Considering this and the loading threshold level of .60, we exclude both indicators from further analyses.

Finally, observation (4) represents the most interesting finding: indicators for knowledge transfer load on two separate factors. Apparently, KNOWT1 to KNOWT5 on the one hand and KNOWT6 and KNOWT7 on the other hand measure two different aspects of knowledge transfer. Structurally, KNOWT1 to KNOWT5 were adopted from the study by Lee et al. (2008), whereas KNOWT6 and KNOWT7 are derived from the study by Simonin (1999). The item's wording makes it obvious that KNOWT1 to KNOWT5 focus on the process perspective of knowledge transfer. KNOWT6 and KNOWT7 in contrast are outcome-oriented, i.e., measure the actual achieved knowledge levels of the OSP.

Since construct knowledge transfer represents an important aspect of the research model, we want to retain it in the research model. Keeping this in mind, there are four different options to address the two-factor solution for construct knowledge transfer in the further course of analysis:

(a) Consider both factors assuming a mediating relationship between them.

(b) Consider both factors assuming a moderating relationship between them.

(c) Consider only the factor represented by indicators KNOWT1 to KNOWT5.

(d) Consider only the factor represented by indicators KNOWT6 and KNOWT7.

In the subsequent analyses we will refer to the factor measured by KNOWT1 to KNOWT5 as PROKNW (*knowledge transfer process*) and to the second factor measured by KNOWT6 and KNOWT7 as ACHKNW (*achieved knowledge level*). Furthermore, we assume that the knowledge transfer process must happen before we can assess any achieved knowledge levels in a meaningful way. Thus, we need to incorporate both constructs PROKNW and ACHKNW in the research model.

Regarding option (a), analyses show that there is a significant and large mediating effect: 38% of the total impact of PROKNW on SUCCESS is mediated by ACHKNW ($p < .001$; VAF = .38). Concerning option (b), there is also a moderating effect of ACHKNW on the relationship between PROKNW and SUCCESS ($p < .050$). However, this effect is small ($f^2 = .038$). The Appendix (p. 287) contains a more detailed description of the test results. (Eggert, Fassott, & Helm, 2005)

Option (c) does not make sense with regards to content: PROKNW is only activity related. The theory derived constructs as defined in Section C.4.2 (p. 158), however, focuses on the results of the knowledge transfer process. Directly comparing options (c) and (d) it would therefore be more adequate to focus on option (d), incorporating the outcome-oriented construct ACHKNW despite the fact that it is then only measured by two indicators.

With regard to the further course of our analysis, we will discard options (b) and (c) and further examine options (a) and (d) only regarding the remaining quality criteria. For the final interpretation of results we will compare the models and then choose the model that best fulfills the quality criteria described in Section F.4.1 (p. 221).

Figure 3-38 displays the adapted research model with the one-factor operationalization of knowledge transfer resulting from option (d). The only aspect that changed in comparison to the original research model (c.f. Figure 3-1, p. 154) is the replacement of construct knowledge transfer (KNOWT) by construct achieved knowledge level (ACHKNW).

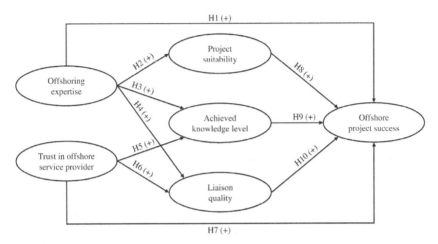

Figure 3-38: Adapted research model with one-factor operationalization of knowledge transfer

Figure 3-39 displays the adapted research model with the two-factor operationalization of knowledge transfer resulting from option (a). Please note the additional hypotheses H9$_a$ and H9$_b$ introduced by alteration of the model.

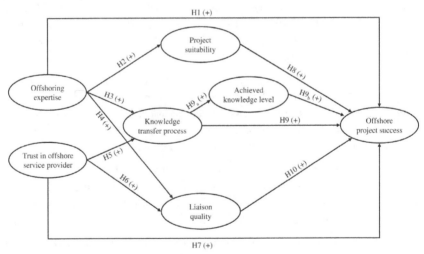

Figure 3-39: Adapted research model with two-factor operationalization of knowledge transfer

Convergent Validity

Table 3-39 shows the assessment results regarding convergent validity for the one-factor model including only construct achieved knowledge level. All quality criteria are fulfilled: indicator loadings exceed .70, are highly significant (p < .001), and AVE scores exceed .50 for all constructs.

Construct	Indicator	Loading > .70	AVE > .50
Offshoring expertise	EXP1	.847 ***	.760
(EXP)	EXP2	.869 ***	
	EXP3	.862 ***	
	EXP4	.907 ***	
Trust in OSP	TRUST2	.844 ***	.745
(TRUST)	TRUST3	.822 ***	
	TRUST4	.860 ***	
	TRUST5	.887 ***	
	TRUST6	.902 ***	
Achieved knowledge level	KNOWT6	.871 ***	.713
(ACHKNW)	KNOWT7	.817 ***	
Liaison quality	LIAISO2	.891 ***	.802
(LIAISO)	LIAISO3	.912 ***	
	LIAISO4	.885 ***	
Offshore project success	SUCCESS1	.844 ***	.791
(SUCCESS)	SUCCESS2	.817 ***	
	SUCCESS3	.911 ***	
	SUCCESS4	.916 ***	
	SUCCESS5	.950 ***	

* p < .050 ** p < .010 *** p < .001

Table 3-39: Assessment of convergent validity for one-factor model

Table 3-40 shows all constructs' indicator loadings, corresponding significances, and construct AVEs as resulting from the PLS analysis for the two-factor model. Except for KNOWT1, all indicators show loadings higher than .70 on their constructs and are highly significant (p < .001). Due to its low loading value, we exclude indicator KNOWT1 from further analysis which then increases PROKNW's AVE score to .676 (not displayed in the table). All AVE scores exceed .50. Therefore, the model containing ACHKNW and PROKNW exhibits a sufficient degree of convergent validity.

Construct	Indicator	Loading > .70	AVE > .50
Offshoring expertise	EXP1	.836 ***	.760
(EXP)	EXP2	.876 ***	
	EXP3	.870 ***	
	EXP4	.904 ***	
Trust in OSP	TRUST2	.848 ***	.745
(TRUST)	TRUST3	.823 ***	
	TRUST4	.859 ***	
	TRUST5	.884 ***	
	TRUST6	.900 ***	
Knowledge transfer process	KNOWT1	.555 ***	.592
(PROKNW)	KNOWT2	.796 ***	
	KNOWT3	.871 ***	
	KNOWT4	.840 ***	
	KNOWT5	.745 ***	
Achieved knowledge level	KNOWT6	.890 ***	.711
(ACHKNW)	KNOWT7	.793 ***	
Liaison quality	LIAISO2	.891 ***	.802
(LIAISO)	LIAISO3	.912 ***	
	LIAISO4	.885 ***	
Offshore project success	SUCCESS1	.843 ***	.791
(SUCCESS)	SUCCESS2	.817 ***	
	SUCCESS3	.911 ***	
	SUCCESS4	.917 ***	
	SUCCESS5	.950 ***	

* $p < .050$ ** $p < .010$ *** $p < .001$

Table 3-40: Assessment of convergent validity for two-factor model

Discriminant Validity

Table 3-41 shows the squared construct correlations for the one-factor model containing only ACHKNW. The matrix's last row contains each construct's AVE. Each construct's AVE exceeds the squared correlations of this construct with any other construct. Thus, the Fornell-Larcker criterion is fulfilled. Additionally, all indicators load higher on their respective constructs than on any other construct (c.f. Appendix, p. 288). Discriminant validity can therefore be assumed.

corr²	EXP	TRUST	ACHKNW	LIAISO	SUCCESS
EXP	1.000				
TRUST	.079	1.000			
ACHKNW	.043	.170	1.000		
LIAISO	.065	.383	.152	1.000	
SUCCESS	.072	.323	.162	.304	1.000
AVE	.760	.745	.713	.802	.791

Table 3-41: Assessment of discriminant validity for one-factor model

Table 3-42 shows the squared construct correlations for the two-factor model. Please note that PROKNW's AVE increased to .676 as a result of removing indicator KNOWT1. The table shows that each construct's AVE (last row) is greater than all squared correlations of this construct with any other construct. Thus, the Fornell-Larcker criterion is also fulfilled. Additionally, all indicators load highest with their own construct than with any other (c.f. Appendix, p. 288). Accordingly, this model exhibits a sufficient level of discriminant validity.

corr²	EXP	TRUST	PROKNW	ACHKNW	LIAISO	SUCCESS
EXP	1.000					
TRUST	.079	1.000				
PROKNW	.055	.188	1.000			
ACHKNW	.043	.172	.178	1.000		
LIAISO	.065	.383	.233	.154	1.000	
SUCCESS	.071	.322	.132	.162	.304	1.000
AVE	.760	.745	.676	.711	.802	.791

Table 3-42: Assessment of discriminant validity for two-factor model

Construct Reliability

Table 3-43 shows that Cronbach's Alpha values are sufficient for all constructs but ACHKNW. However, considering the sensitivity of Cronbach's Alpha towards low indicator numbers – ACHKNW is only measured by two indicators – this score is an unreliable measure and CR should be preferred. CR again shows sufficient scores that exceed .70 for all constructs. Thus we assume sufficient levels of construct reliability.

Construct	CR > .70	Alpha > .70
Offshoring expertise (EXP)	.927	.895
Trust in OSP (TRUST)	.936	.914
Knowledge transfer process (PROKNW)	.893	.839
Achieved knowledge level (ACHKNW)	.831	.600
Liaison quality (LIAISO)	.924	.877
Offshore project success (SUCCESS)	.950	.933

Table 3-43: Assessment of construct reliability

Summary

Apart from minor addressable issues regarding unidimensionality, both models show sufficient degrees of convergent and discriminant validity as well as construct reliability. This could be expected since as a result of the initial EFA we removed some indicators from the measurement model early on.

F.4.2.2   Formative Indicators

To fulfill the content-related quality criteria regarding formative constructs we relied on an extensive pre-study to identify suitable indicators (c.f. Section D.3, p. 161). The quantitative assessment results show that indicator weights and significances are low for SUITA1, SUITA3, and SUITA5. Additionally, only weights for SUITA2 ($p < .05$) and SUITA4 ($p < .001$) are significant. However, multi-collinearity does not represent a problem: all VIF scores are below the threshold level of 10. Table 3-44 illustrates these results.

Construct	Indicator	Weight	VIF
Project suitability	SUITA1	.093	1.295
(SUITA)	SUITA2	.357 [*]	1.287
	SUITA3	.016	1.025
	SUITA4	.885 [***]	1.038
	SUITA5	.081	1.027

[*] p < .050   [**] p < .010   [***] p < .001

Table 3-44: Quality assessment of formative indicators

The results concerning weights and significances require a more detailed discussion. The results for SUITA3 can be easily explained. SUITA3 measures the language spoken on the project. In most of the projects, this was English. Consequently, study participants mostly reported scores of six or seven for this indicator (cf. Figure 3-25, p. 195). This results in the observed insignificant and low weight. Regarding SUITA1 (project volume) and SUITA5 (business specificity) the interpretation is unclear. Despite strong evidence from our pre-study, the impact of these indicators seems to be low and insignificant. However, due to the nature of formative constructs, removing these indicators from the construct is not permitted, since they are an inherent part of the construct's definition and form it.

For better understanding, we conducted an additional analysis using a separate PLS model. Following the approach by Wüllenweber et al. (2008) and Chin (1998), we modeled the relationship between the original formative SUITA measured only by SUITA1 to SUITA5 and a hypothetical reflective SUITA measured by indicator SUITA6. Figure 3-40 illustrates the results of this analysis and shows the path coefficients, corresponding t-values, and the R^2 of the reflectively measured SUITA construct.

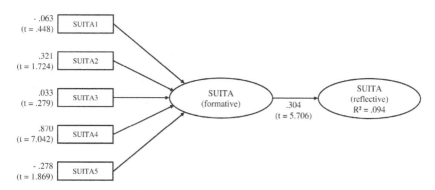

Figure 3-40: Additional assessment of formative measurement model for project suitability

The analysis reveals that the overall R^2 of the reflectively measured SUITA is rather low ($R^2 = .094$). This might be due to a suboptimal measurement of the formative SUITA, the reflective SUITA, or both. The formative implementation obviously shows improvement potential as its weightings show. However, the reflective implementation is also not optimal because it is determined only by SUITA6, i.e., it is "under-measured". More interesting are the signs of the path coefficients in this isolated model as displayed in Figure 3-40. Except for SUITA1 and SUITA2, all path directions are as expected from indicator development. SUITA1 shows a negative sign where we expected a positive relationship. Similarly, SUITA2 has a positive sign where we expected a negative relationship. This finding can be explained by looking again at the process of indicator construction. The pre-study stated that offshoring projects require a certain minimum size and duration. This ensures that additional overhead costs from offshoring can be compensated by the savings arising from the project. Therefore, we anticipated a positive impact of size (SUITA1) and a reversely coded negative impact of duration (SUITA2) on project suitability. However, the pre-study also stated that increasing levels of complexity, for example due to enormous project sizes, negatively impact offshore project success. This seems to apply to the projects in the sample: apparently, minimum sizes and durations were already achieved, so that increasing project volumes and durations negatively impacted offshore project success, thus resulting in the reversed signs of the weights.

Reflecting on these results, we can state that the quality of the formative indicators is lower than the quality for the reflective indicators. This situation emerged although we took the required quality precautions by focusing on content validity using our extensive pre-study. Maybe the most pertinent potential point of critique could be that we should have incorporated more than five indicators from the pre-study. However, as already explained in

Section D.3 (p. 161), this would have negatively impacted the survey regarding length and comprehensibility and was thus not a viable option.

Finally, we need to put this situation in the context of existing research: our study is, to the best of our knowledge, the first paper that operationalizes project suitability for offshoring within an empirical field study. There are no existing measurement instruments to build upon or to perform comparisons with. Thus, we perceive the existing measure at hand, despite some drawbacks regarding quality, as being adequate for analysis because of its content-related foundation, non-existing multi-collinearity, and partially acceptable weights and significances.

F.4.3   Quality Assessment of Structural Model

The one-factor model explains 43% of variance in the main dependent variable offshore project success ($R^2 = .432$). This is a medium level. Levels of R^2 are also medium for construct liaison quality ($R^2 = .391$) but low for the remaining endogenous constructs achieved knowledge level ($R^2 = .180$) and project suitability ($R^2 = .082$). Values for Stone-Geisser Q^2 exceed zero for all endogenous constructs. Thus, the model constructs exhibit a sufficient level of predictive validity. Figure 3-41 shows the result of the PLS calculation for the one-factor model.

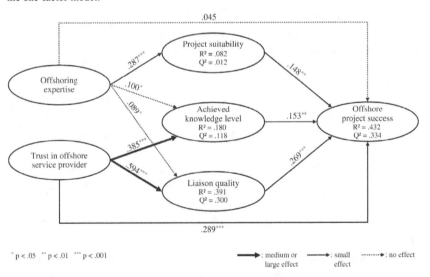

Figure 3-41: PLS results for one-factor model

All path coefficients show positive values, i.e., support the impact directions as postulated in the hypotheses. Offshoring expertise does not have a significant direct impact on offshore project success ($\beta = .045$; $p > .050$). Thus, we cannot find support for hypothesis H1.

However, offshoring expertise does have a positive impact on project suitability ($\beta = .287$; $p < .001$), on achieved knowledge level ($\beta = .100$; $p < .050$), and on liaison quality ($\beta = .089$; $p < .050$) which leads us to accept hypotheses H2, H3, and H4. Although these effects are significant, their sizes are small for hypothesis H2 ($f^2 = .089$) and below the threshold of .02 for small effects regarding hypothesis H3 ($f^2 = .010$) and hypothesis H4 ($f^2 = .012$). The impact of trust in OSP is stronger: trust in OSP has a significant positive effect on achieved knowledge level ($\beta = .385$; $p < .001$), on liaison quality ($\beta = .594$; $p < .001$), and on offshore project success ($\beta = .289$; $p < .001$). Therefore, we can accept hypotheses H5, H6, and H7. The corresponding effect sizes are medium for hypothesis H5 ($f^2 = .166$), large for hypothesis H6 ($f^2 = .533$), and small for hypothesis H7 ($f^2 = .083$). Project suitability also has a significant positive effect on offshore project success ($\beta = .148$; $p < .010$), so we can accept hypothesis H8. This effect is small ($f^2 = .032$). The path coefficient is slightly higher for the significant positive effect of achieved knowledge level on offshore project success ($\beta = .153$; $p < .010$), leading us to accept hypothesis H9, but the effect is also small ($f^2 = .033$). Finally, liaison quality shows a significant positive impact on offshore project success ($\beta = .269$; $p < .001$) with a small effect size ($f^2 = .072$). Therefore, we can accept hypothesis H10. Table 3-45 illustrates the corresponding results of the PLS analysis for the one-factor model, including path coefficients, values for t and f^2, as well as effect sizes.

Regarding total effects, i.e., the sum of a construct's direct and the indirect effects via mediating constructs, offshoring expertise has a significant positive impact on offshore project success ($\beta = .126$; $p < .010$). Similarly, trust in OSP has also a significant positive total impact on offshore project success ($\beta = .507$; $p < .001$).

Hypothesis	Path-β	t-value	f^2	Support	Effect size
H1 Offshoring expertise (+) → Offshore project success	.045	1.282	-.016	no	---
H2 Offshoring expertise (+) → Project suitability	.287 ***	5.281	.089	yes	small
H3 Offshoring expertise (+) → Achieved knowledge level	.100 *	1.928	.010	yes	---
H4 Offshoring expertise (+) → Liaison quality	.089 *	2.160	.012	yes	---
H5 Trust in OSP (+) → Achieved knowledge level	.385 ***	8.229	.166	yes	medium
H6 Trust in OSP (+) → Liaison quality	.594 ***	14.543	.533	yes	large
H7 Trust in OSP (+) → Offshore project success	.289 ***	4.145	.083	yes	small
H8 Project suitability (+) → Offshore project success	.148 **	2.895	.032	yes	small
H9 Achieved knowledge level (+) → Offshore project success	.153 **	2.639	.033	yes	small
H10 Liaison quality (+) → Offshore project success	.269 ***	3.840	.072	yes	small

* $p < .050$ ** $p < .010$ *** $p < .001$ (one-tailed)

Table 3-45: Structural paths and effect sizes for one-factor model

The two-factor model explains 43% of the variance of the main dependent construct offshore project success ($R^2 = .431$). This can be considered as medium (Chin, 1998). R^2 values for the

other endogenous constructs are medium for liaison quality ($R^2 = .391$), weak for knowledge
transfer process ($R^2 = .202$), and non-relevant for project suitability ($R^2 = .083$) as well as
achieved knowledge level ($R^2 = .178$) according to the criteria suggested by Chin (1998).
Values for Stone-Geisser Q^2 exceed zero for all endogenous constructs. Thus, the model
constructs exhibit a sufficient level of predictive validity. Figure 3-42 shows the result of the
PLS calculation.

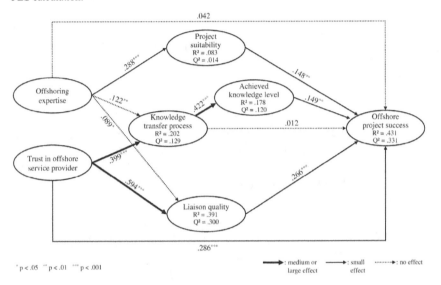

Figure 3-42: PLS results for two-factor model

All path coefficients in the model are positive and therefore confirm the assumed impact
directions as stated in the hypotheses. Looking at the individual constructs, the analysis shows
that offshoring expertise does not have a significant effect on offshore project success
($\beta = .042$; $p > .05$). Thus we cannot find support for hypothesis H1. However, offshoring
expertise does have a significant positive effect on project suitability ($\beta = .288$; $p < .001$), on
the knowledge transfer process ($\beta = .122$; $p < .01$), and on liaison quality ($\beta = .089$; $p < .050$)
which supports hypotheses H2, H3, and H4. The impact is strongest on project suitability with
a small effect size ($f^2 = .090$). The other f^2 values are below the .020 threshold for a small
effect. Trust in OSP is significantly positively associated with the knowledge transfer process
($\beta = .399$, $p < .001$) and liaison quality ($\beta = .594$; $p < .001$). Therefore we find support for
hypotheses H5 and H6. The size of these effects is medium for the impact on the knowledge
transfer process ($f^2 = .184$) and large for liaison quality ($f^2 = .533$). In addition, trust in OSP
does have a significant positive effect on offshore project success ($\beta = .286$; $p < .001$) which

leads us to accept hypothesis H7. However, the size of this direct effect is small. Of the endogenous constructs, project suitability shows a significant positive effect on offshore project success ($\beta = .148$; $p < .010$) and leads us to accept hypothesis H8. The size of this effect is small. Additionally, we find support for the impact of the knowledge transfer process on achieved knowledge level ($\beta = .422$; $p < .001$) and achieved knowledge level on offshore project success ($\beta = .149$; $p < .010$). Thus, we can accept hypotheses H9$_a$ and H9$_b$. Effect sizes are medium for hypothesis H9$_a$ and small for hypothesis H9$_b$. The direct impact of the knowledge transfer process on offshore project success is not significant ($\beta = .012$; $p > .050$). Finally, liaison quality shows a significant positive effect on offshore project success ($\beta = .266$; $p < .001$) with a small effect size. This supports hypothesis H10. Table 3-46 illustrates the corresponding results of the PLS analysis for the two-factor model including path coefficients, values for t and f^2, as well as effect sizes.

Regarding total effects, i.e., the sum of a construct's direct and indirect effects via mediating constructs, offshoring expertise has a significant positive impact on offshore project success ($\beta = .117$; $p < .010$). Similarly, trust in OSP has also a significant positive total impact on offshore project success ($\beta = .474$; $p < .001$).

Hypothesis	Path-β	t-value	f^2	Support	Effect size
H1 Offshoring expertise (+) → Offshore project success	.042	1.228	-.017	no	---
H2 Offshoring expertise (+) → Project suitability	.288 ***	5.306	.090	yes	small
H3 Offshoring expertise (+) → Knowledge transfer process	.122 **	2.576	.017	yes	---
H4 Offshoring expertise (+) → Liaison quality	.089 *	2.180	.012	yes	---
H5 Trust in OSP (+) → Knowledge transfer process	.399 ***	7.521	.184	yes	medium
H6 Trust in OSP (+) → Liaison quality	.594 ***	14.925	.533	yes	large
H7 Trust in OSP (+) → Offshore project success	.286 ***	3.989	.079	yes	small
H8 Project suitability (+) → Offshore project success	.148 **	2.908	.032	yes	small
H9 Knowledge transfer process (+) → Offshore project success	.012	.313	-.001	no	---
H9$_a$ Knowledge transfer process (+) → Achieved knowledge level	.422 ***	8.426	.217	yes	medium
H9$_b$ Achieved knowledge level (+) → Offshore project success	.149 **	2.583	.030	yes	small
H10 Liaison quality (+) → Offshore project success	.266 ***	3.594	.067	yes	small

* p < .050   ** p < .010   *** p < .001   (one-tailed)

Table 3-46: Structural paths and effect sizes for two-factor model

F.4.4   Model Adequacy

The analyzed research models fulfilled the required quality criteria regarding path coefficients, explained variance, effect sizes, and predictive validity. The two models explain 43% of the variance of offshore project success. This value for R^2 can be considered medium. Recently published studies in the field of IS offshoring and outsourcing research exhibited similar levels of R^2 with 44% (Wüllenweber et al., 2008) or 27% and 39% (Lee et al., 2008).

Older studies also showed similar R^2 values ranging from 20% to 54% (c.f. Behrens, 2007 citing Goles, 2003; Kim & Chung, 2003; Poppo & Zenger, 2002).

Comparing the two models with the one-factor and the two-factor operationalization of knowledge transfer, it becomes obvious that they share similar explanatory power regarding offshore project success in terms of R^2. A closer look at the additional construct knowledge transfer process shows that it does have – as causally expected – a considerable impact on achieved knowledge level. However, the direct impact of the knowledge transfer process on offshore project success is not significant and rather small within the full structural model. Thus, the construct knowledge transfer process adds no substantial insight but rather increases complexity of the research model. For these reasons we focus on the model with the one-factor operationalization of knowledge transfer in the further course of analysis. The subsequent subgroup analysis as well as the result interpretation will rely upon the one-factor model.

F.4.5 Subgroup Analysis

The previous analyses regarding offshore project success for different subgroups (c.f. Table 3-19, p. 205) showed that the greatest differences in perceived success could be found between projects that were delivered by an internal or partially owned OSP (Group 1) in contrast to an external service provider (Group 2). Guided by these results, we test the one-factor model in PLS on the two subgroups to find out whether the model fits better with a certain subgroup or not. For these purposes we follow the procedure described by Huber et al. (2007) and run the PLS algorithm with the same model on the data of the two subgroups. Afterwards we compare the resulting path coefficients and t-values and test for significant differences.

Table 3-47 contains the results of the analysis. It shows that the only significant difference between the two subgroups is the impact of offshoring expertise on project suitability as expressed by hypothesis H2. Offshoring expertise has a significantly positive impact on project suitability only for projects delivered by internal or partially owned OSPs ($\beta = .406$; $p < .001$). This difference between the two groups is significant ($p < .01$). Apart from this finding, there are no further additional significant differences between the two groups as can be inferred from the p-values of the test statistics in the last column of Table 3-47.

		Internal/ partially-owned		External SP		Test for differences		
		Path-β	t-Value	Path-β	t-Value	S	t	p
H1	Offshoring expertise (+) → Offshore project success	.156	1.153	.031	.825	.602	1.800	.073
H2	Offshoring expertise (+) → Project suitability	.406 ***	6.575	.133	1.519	.902	2.615	.009
H3	Offshoring expertise (+) → Achieved knowledge level	.117 *	1.752	.041	.713	.784	.843	.400
H4	Offshoring expertise (+) → Liaison quality	.037	.830	.123 *	2.247	.602	1.238	.217
H5	Trust in OSP (+) → Achieved knowledge level	.441 ***	7.074	.335 ***	4.588	.824	1.117	.265
H6	Trust in OSP (+) → Liaison quality	.585 ***	9.357	.646 ***	13.376	.710	.736	.462
H7	Trust in OSP (+) → Offshore project success	.419 *	1.914	.452 ***	5.586	1.119	.261	.794
H8	Project suitability (+) → Offshore project success	.148 *	2.060	.206 **	2.814	.895	.559	.576
H9	Achieved knowledge level (+) → Offshore project success	.211 **	2.600	.110 *	1.696	.933	.937	.349
H10	Liaison quality (+) → Offshore project success	.242 **	2.723	.213 *	2.201	1.138	.221	.825

* p < .050   ** p < .010   *** p < .001   (two-tailed)

Table 3-47: Model differences for projects delivered by an internal or partially owned OSP and projects delivered by an external OSP

G Discussion of Results

G.1 Exogenous Determinants of Offshore Project Success

G.1.1 Offshoring Expertise

The PLS analysis showed support for three of the four hypotheses related to offshoring expertise. Increasing levels of expertise have a significant positive impact on the selection of suitable projects for offshoring (H2), the achieved knowledge level (H3), and levels of liaison quality (H4). Despite their statistical significances, corresponding effect sizes were small for offshoring expertise's impact on project suitability and almost non-existent for its impact on achieved knowledge level and liaison quality. Additionally, we could not find support for a direct positive impact of offshoring expertise on offshore project success as postulated by hypothesis H1. Apparently, offshoring expertise plays only a minor role as a determinant of offshore project success and of the other endogenous constructs incorporated in the research model.

A possible explanation refers to the expertise pattern as represented in the sample. The descriptive analysis showed that expertise levels of organizations and individuals were rather low when the reported projects had been conducted (c.f. Figure 3-17, p. 187, for the finishing dates of the projects; Figure 3-22, p. 192, for self-perceived level of overall expertise; Figure 3-23, p. 193, for the remaining expertise indicator values). Thus, it is possible that the data does not contain sufficient observations of higher levels of expertise to detect corresponding effects on the other constructs. This interpretation also finds support from the surprising negative effect size regarding hypothesis H1 (c.f. Table 3-45, p. 237). Although non-significant, a negative effect size means that offshore project success's R^2 would be marginally higher if we excluded offshoring expertise from the model. Causally this does not make sense. Rather it could be attributed to the biased expertise pattern as explained above.

It might also be that expertise as a form of accumulated knowledge is simply not as important as the other exogenous construct trust in OSP and has therefore comparatively less impact on the endogenous constructs. This interpretation is at first sight supported by study participants' self-perceived importance of constructs for successful execution of offshore projects: participants rank offshore expertise's importance lowest in comparison to the other constructs (c.f. Figure 3-21, p. 191). However, this ranking represents only weak support, because ranking values did not differ much and therefore their discriminatory power is low.

Finally, it could be that the impact of expertise is mediated or moderated by another variable. However, from a content perspective it is not immediately obvious what such a variable and its relation to expertise and the other constructs could be. We can also not rely on existing findings from other studies to reflect this because there is a paucity of research addressing the aspect of expertise in the context of IS offshoring (c.f. Section C.3.1, p. 155).

In summary, we can state a low impact of offshoring expertise within the research model. Presumably, this is due to the overall low level of organizations' and individuals' expertise, as represented in the sample, that prevents the analysis from detecting effects as postulated by the hypotheses.

G.1.2 Trust in Offshore Service Provider

The PLS analysis shows support for all three hypotheses containing the construct trust in OSP. Levels of trust in OSP have a significant positive impact on achieved knowledge level (H5), levels of liaison quality (H6), and offshore project success (H7). In contrast to the findings regarding offshoring expertise's impact, these effects are not only significant but also large for trust's impact on liaison quality, medium for its impact on achieved knowledge level, and small for its direct impact on offshore project success. Obviously, trust in OSP seems to play a major role as a determinant of success and of the other constructs in the research model.

Trust's impact on knowledge transfer is in accordance with what we expected based on previous research. A recent study by Lee et al. (2008), for example, also found support for a positive effect of trust on knowledge sharing ($\beta = .748$; $p < .001$). The results confirm this perception for the offshore-consuming side from a German perspective.

Furthermore, we also expected to find a strong positive influence of trust on liaison quality. Existing research, for example Winkler et al. (2008) in their case study at a German corporation offshoring software development to India, suggested a corresponding effect of trust level on the relationship between offshore consumer and OSP.

However, we were surprised to find a direct – albeit small – significant impact of trust on offshore project success. Although we considered such an effect in the model as expressed by hypothesis H7, we rather assumed the effect of trust as being fully mediated by knowledge transfer and liaison quality (c.f. Section C.3.2, p. 156). We interpret the existence of this effect as a form of reciprocal perception by study participants: maybe trust was fostered during a successful project's execution. The experience of joint progress and initial accomplishments increased participants' levels of trust as the project was successfully carried out. However, this interpretation cannot be related to findings from existing research, since there are no research designs that examine the direct link of trust and success within IS offshoring. In summary, considering its small effect size, we should interpret this finding with the necessary prudence.

G.2 Endogenous Determinants of Offshore Project Success

G.2.1 Project Suitability

Project suitability has a significant positive effect on offshore project success. However, its effect size is small. In comparison to the other endogenous constructs knowledge transfer and liaison quality, project suitability shows the lowest effect on offshore project success.

This finding was unexpected regarding effect size. Although project suitability for offshoring and its impact on offshore project success is less empirically researched, we would have expected a stronger impact based on the results of our qualitative pre-study (Westner & Strahringer, 2008). In the pre-study, experts almost unanimously highlighted the importance of selecting suitable projects for offshoring to be successful. The results from the PLS analysis at least confirm the existence of a positive effect despite its minor size.

One reason for project suitability's low impact could be due to the nature of its measurement indicators. Although we thoroughly developed these indicators, the data analysis retrospectively revealed that measurement quality is medium (c.f. Section F.4.2.2, p. 234). This could have negatively impacted analysis results regarding the detection of project suitability's impact within the research model.

G.2.2 Knowledge Transfer

As expressed by hypothesis H9, knowledge transfer shows a significant positive impact on offshore project success. However, similar to the effect of project suitability on success, the effect size is small.

The low effect size was unexpected. Existing research results suggested a strong impact of knowledge transfer on success. Lee et al. (2008), for example, find that knowledge sharing explains 27% of the variance in success. Considering that the findings of Lee et al. were generated in the area of IS outsourcing, we would have expected an even stronger effect in the field of IS offshoring, since knowledge transfer is especially important in IS offshoring where offshore staff replaces onshore staff (c.f. Section B.1, p. 151).

A potential explanation might be the low number of measurement indicators, since after the model quality assessment, construct achieved knowledge level was measured by only two indicators. However, this argument does not hold because achieved knowledge level nevertheless fulfilled all required quality criteria (c.f. Section F.4.2.1, p. 226) and the two-factor model containing all knowledge-transfer related indicators showed no better R^2 than the one-factor model.

It could also be that knowledge transfer was actually not so important for the reported projects. Maybe there was not much knowledge to transfer within the project context or the degree of explicit knowledge was high thus facilitating the knowledge transfer process. However, the last argument is not supported by the sample data: the descriptive analysis showed that documentation levels were not exceptionally high (c.f. indicator SUITA4 in Figure 3-25, p. 195).

This leaves the question open as to why we detected a weaker effect of knowledge transfer on success than other studies, especially the one by Lee et al. (2008). However, regarding this specific study, we need to consider that the authors applied a reflective measurement to indicators that could have also been accounted for as formative. To draw meaningful comparisons regarding the impact of knowledge transfer on success, it would be interesting to know how study results by Lee et al. changed if a formative measurement was applied.

G.2.3 Liaison Quality

Levels of liaison quality have a significant positive impact on offshore project success as postulated by hypothesis H10. Similar to the impacts of project suitability and knowledge transfer, the effect is slight. However, liaison quality's impact is twice as high in comparison to the other constructs.

We expected these findings based on results from other studies. Research in IS offshoring frequently highlights the importance of mutual collaboration within an offshore project setting (c.f. Section C.4.3, p. 159). The importance of liaison quality for successful offshore project execution was also frequently mentioned by the experts participating in our qualitative pre-study.

Since there is, to the best of our knowledge, no empirical-confirmatory study that examines the effect of liaison quality on offshore project success, we did not have specific expectations regarding effect sizes for the impact of liaison quality and can therefore make no comparative judgment regarding this aspect.

H Conclusions

H.1 Contributions

Our study represents one of the few empirical-confirmatory studies on IS offshoring in general, and for Germany in particular. Thus, the analyses contribute empirically tested results to the existing body of knowledge, especially regarding best practices and determinants of success that had so far been developed using case studies or descriptive research approaches.

The quality of the results is increased by the large size of the analyzed sample. With a sample size of 304 observations, we achieve high degrees of statistical power (c.f. footnote in Section D.4, p. 170) which enabled us to detect effects of small size. This marks a difference from existing research which used smaller samples, for example Lee et al. (2008) with only 165 analyzable observations for their first and 45 for their second model.

Furthermore, the study represents the first attempt to operationalize and then measure constructs offshoring expertise, project suitability, and liaison quality within an empirical research design. Although the operationalization of project suitability is not optimal, it represents a starting point other researchers can build upon.

Regarding content, the analyses confirm findings from previous research studies by other authors and thus strengthens aspects of the existing body of knowledge within IS offshoring. As stated by other researchers, we found support for the positive impact of trust on knowledge transfer and of knowledge transfer on offshore project success.

Finally, the study is the first one to embed offshoring expertise, trust in OSP, project suitability, knowledge transfer, and liaison quality as derived from the implementation process of IS offshoring in an overall model so that these constructs can be analyzed jointly and relative to each other.

H.2 Managerial Implications

The analysis results show that the level of offshoring expertise seems to be less important for offshore project success. Practitioners should rather focus on establishing mutual trust in the OSP and sufficient levels of liaison quality within the project. Both constructs have the greatest direct effect on offshore project success followed by successful knowledge transfer and – of equal importance – the selection of suitable projects. Apparently, the "soft" factors such as trust and liaison quality are of greater importance than "hard" factors such as project suitability or knowledge transfer.

Tangible suggestions for management actions in order to achieve these goals could be to conduct cross-cultural workshops before starting an offshore project, facilitate open and frequent communication, and physically bring domestic and offshore staff together for some time period.

However, practitioners need to consider that we focused on selective determinants of offshore project success. The model explains 43% of the total variance in offshore project success which means that there are still other success determinants. For example, vendor selection, project management, or software engineering may also play a significant role in success and were not examined in the study.

H.3 Limitations

The most pertinent limitation of our study stems from the indicator set to measure project suitability. Although we developed the indicators with the necessary prudence, the resulting measurement quality seemed to be medium. Nevertheless, we found an impact of project suitability, albeit small, as postulated by the hypotheses.

Apart from that, it might be that the sample data does not contain sufficiently different levels of expertise in order to detect expertise's impact as formulated in the hypotheses. This is, however, not a flaw in the research design but rather the result of IS offshoring being a new sourcing option at German companies.

The focus on Germany as a region could limit the generalizability of results to other countries and cultures. Yet, considering that some of the results are similar to studies conducted outside Germany, we do not perceive this limitation as material.

Finally, the applied approach for data collection could be subject to criticism. We did not draw a statistical representative sample because there was no viable option to access the basic population since the unit of analysis was projects.

H.4 Directions for Future Research

Potential directions for future research arise from the previously described limitations of the study. First of all, future research could implement alternative operationalizations or modified indicator sets to measure project suitability.

Regarding the minor importance of offshoring expertise in the research model and the assumed underrepresentation of high levels of expertise in the data, one could repeat the study at a later point of time when organizations and individuals in Germany have presumably accumulated more IS offshoring expertise. Not till then will it be possible to determine the effect of offshoring expertise on success and the other constructs.

Concerning data collection, one could attempt to perform a statistically more representative sampling. However, the general viability of such an endeavor is questionable. An alternative option would be to perform the study at one or two cooperating companies using their project data and thus targeting for statistical representativeness within the context of these companies.

In addition, it would be interesting to incorporate other determinants of success in the research model to test for their direct and relative impacts. Potential construct candidates could be derived from vendor selection, contract design, or the degree of process standardization.

Finally, one could observe and examine one of the latent constructs empirically, for example liaison quality. Applying an alternative research method such as an in-depth case study, researchers could analyze how organizations address aspects of liaison quality and how different levels of liaison quality actually have impact during the course of an offshoring project.

Appendix

Test of Normality

Tests of Normality

	Kolmogorov-Smirnov[a]			Shapiro-Wilk		
	Statistic	df	Sig.	Statistic	df	Sig.
EXP1	.245	304	.000	.859	304	.000
EXP2	.204	304	.000	.875	304	.000
EXP3	.152	304	.000	.919	304	.000
EXP4	.164	304	.000	.920	304	.000
TRUST1	.137	304	.000	.945	304	.000
TRUST2	.180	304	.000	.926	304	.000
TRUST3	.154	304	.000	.942	304	.000
TRUST4	.157	304	.000	.926	304	.000
TRUST5	.161	304	.000	.928	304	.000
TRUST6	.179	304	.000	.929	304	.000
SUITA1	.149	304	.000	.935	304	.000
SUITA2	.161	304	.000	.925	304	.000
SUITA3	.389	304	.000	.586	304	.000
SUITA4	.159	304	.000	.934	304	.000
SUITA5	.243	304	.000	.870	304	.000
SUITA6	.186	304	.000	.905	304	.000
KNOWT1	.194	304	.000	.902	304	.000
KNOWT2	.243	304	.000	.823	304	.000
KNOWT3	.231	304	.000	.833	304	.000
KNOWT4	.185	304	.000	.906	304	.000
KNOWT5	.174	304	.000	.920	304	.000
KNOWT6	.194	304	.000	.903	304	.000
KNOWT7	.156	304	.000	.947	304	.000
KNOWT8	.206	304	.000	.923	304	.000
LIAISO1	.205	304	.000	.908	304	.000
LIAISO2	.216	304	.000	.882	304	.000
LIAISO3	.199	304	.000	.920	304	.000
LIAISO4	.184	304	.000	.921	304	.000
LIAISO5	.203	304	.000	.919	304	.000
SUCCES1	.201	304	.000	.927	304	.000
SUCCES2	.186	304	.000	.905	304	.000
SUCCES3	.185	304	.000	.913	304	.000
SUCCES4	.163	304	.000	.927	304	.000
SUCCES5	.188	304	.000	.907	304	.000

a. Lilliefors Significance Correction

Test for Differences between Early and Late Responders

	Mann-Whitney U	Wilcoxon W	Z	Asymp. Sig. (2-tailed)
EXP1	9193	33064	-.268	.789
EXP2	8985	32856	-.572	.567
EXP3	8569	32440	-1.180	.238
EXP4	8556	32427	-1.200	.230
TRUST1	8247	32118	-1.658	.097
TRUST2	9245	33116	-.191	.849
TRUST3	8491	32362	-1.303	.193
TRUST4	8781	32652	-.874	.382
TRUST5	8523	32394	-1.253	.210
TRUST6	9048	32919	-.481	.630
SUITA1	8801	12542	-.843	.399
SUITA2	8240	32111	-1.669	.095
SUITA3	8736	12477	-1.127	.260
SUITA4	8105	31976	-1.871	.061
SUITA5	9056	12797	-.475	.635
SUITA6	9292	33163	-.122	.903
KNOWT1	8947	32818	-.630	.529
KNOWT2	9000	12741	-.565	.572
KNOWT3	8564	12305	-1.224	.221
KNOWT4	9263	13004	-.165	.869
KNOWT5	8652	12393	-1.066	.286
KNOWT6	9288	13029	-.129	.898
KNOWT7	8843	32714	-.784	.433
KNOWT8	9068	12809	-.452	.651
LIAISO1	8403	32274	-1.444	.149
LIAISO2	8231	32102	-1.719	.086
LIAISO3	8678	32549	-1.034	.301
LIAISO4	8767	32638	-.899	.369
LIAISO5	8976	32847	-.590	.555
SUCCES1	9085	12826	-.427	.669
SUCCES2	8381	12122	-1.468	.142
SUCCES3	8503	12244	-1.290	.197
SUCCES4	8957	12698	-.614	.540
SUCCES5	8627	12368	-1.109	.267

E-Mail Text: First Contact Round

Sehr geehrte/r Frau/Herr [PLATZHALTER],

über Ihr XING "ich biete"-Feld bin ich auf Sie als Near-/Offshoring Experte aufmerksam geworden.

Mein Name ist Markus Westner. Derzeit forsche ich an der TU Dresden und European Business School zusammen mit Frau Prof. Dr. Strahringer im Bereich IT Near-/Offshoring (siehe auch www.it-offshoring.org).

Near-/Offshoring ist auch in Deutschland ein wichtiges Thema in der IT. Jedoch sind nicht alle entsprechenden Vorhaben erfolgreich und erzeugen oft unvorhergesehene Mehraufwände während der Abwicklung. Aus diesem Grund führe ich eine empirische Studie zu Erfolgsfaktoren von IT Near-/Offshoring Projekten in der Anwendungsentwicklung und – wartung in Deutschland durch. Im Rahmen der Studie untersuche ich bestimmte Erfolgsfaktoren und ihren tatsächlichen Beitrag zum Projekterfolg.

Für die Studie würde ich gerne Ihre Expertise mit einbeziehen. Wären Sie bereit, einen kurzen Fragebogen für ein spezifisches Near-/Offshoring Projekt auszufüllen? Die Beantwortung sollte nicht mehr als 15 Minuten Ihrer Zeit in Anspruch nehmen. Den Fragebogen finden Sie unter

http://survey.it-offshoring.org/index.php?lang=en&sid=&token=

Ich würde mich freuen, wenn Sie den Fragebogen innerhalb der nächsten zwei Wochen beantworten würden.

Der Fragebogen fragt nicht nach Unternehmensspezifika. Darüber hinaus werden alle Ihre Angaben selbstverständlich 100% anonym behandelt – ich bin wirklich nur an Ihrer Erfahrung als Experte interessiert. Im Gegenzug erhalten Sie die späteren Ergebnisse des Forschungsvorhabens sowohl im Volltext als auch in Form einer Management-Präsentation.

Für Rückfragen stehe ich Ihnen jederzeit gerne zur Verfügung. Vorab herzlichen Dank für Ihre Unterstützung!

Mit freundlichen Grüßen

Markus Westner

E-Mail Text: Reminder Round

Sehr geehrte/r Herr/Frau [PLATZHALTER],

vor kurzem habe ich Sie zur Teilnahme an meiner Studie zu Erfolgsfaktoren von IT Near-/Offshoring Projekten in der Anwendungsentwicklung und –wartung eingeladen.

Die Studie ist Teil eines Forschungsprojektes an der European Business School und der TU Dresden zur Entwicklung von Ansätzen, mit denen die Erfolgswahrscheinlichkeit von IT Near-/Offshoring Projekten in Deutschland verbessert werden kann.

Die Teilnahme an der Studie ist mit Vorteilen für Sie und Ihr Unternehmen verbunden. Sie werden einen vollständigen Bericht der Forschungsergebnisse sowie eine Executive Summary mit den wichtigsten Management-Implikationen erhalten. Auf diese Weise können Sie die Erfahrungen vieler anderer Unternehmen aus Ihrer und anderen Branchen für sich nutzen: bisher haben schon über 200 Experten auf unser Anschreiben reagiert.

Auch Ihre Unterstützung ist für den Erfolg unserer Studie unverzichtbar! Wenn Sie bisher noch nicht die Zeit gefunden haben, den Fragebogen auszufüllen, so können Sie dies noch in den nächsten Tagen nachholen.

Den Online-Fragebogen finden Sie unter nachfolgender Internet-Adresse. Die meisten bisherigen Teilnehmer haben diesen in weniger als 15 Minuten beantwortet:

http://survey.it-offshoring.org/index.php?lang=en&sid=&token=

In jedem Fall werden wir Ihre Angaben vertraulich behandeln. Jedwede Analyse, Präsentation oder Publikation der Studienergebnisse wird lediglich in anonymisierter und aggregierter Form erfolgen.

Wenn Ihr persönliches Expertiseprofil nicht zu unserem Forschungsvorhaben passt und Sie den Fragebogen deshalb nicht beantworten können bzw. Sie aus anderen Gründen nicht an unserer Studie teilnehmen möchten, geben Sie mir bitte kurz Bescheid. Ich werde Sie dann nicht weiter kontaktieren.

Vielen Dank im Voraus für Ihre Unterstützung!

Mit freundlichen Grüßen

Markus Westner

Survey Instrument

European ≡ Business School
<small>International University Schloss Reichartshausen</small>

Success factors in IS near-/offshoring projects
0% [＿＿＿＿＿] 100%

1. Near-/offshoring expertise

The term **Information Systems (IS) near-/offshoring** describes the transfer of application development or maintenance services to a near-/offshoring service provider (OSP) in a near or far away country. This OSP can be an internal subsidiary, a partially-owned unit, or an external service provider. The services themselves are partially or totally transferred.

---

*When did your organization start to near-/offshore application development or maintenance services?

| ＿＿＿＿＿ years ago

Only numbers may be entered in this field

[?] You may also use decimal numbers (like "3.5 years") in your answer.

---

*How many years of personal experience do you have in IS near-/offshoring?

| ＿＿＿＿＿ years

Only numbers may be entered in this field

[?] You may also use decimal numbers (like "3.5 years") in your answer.

[Exit and clear survey]   Resume later   << Previous   Next >>

European ≡ Business School
International University · Schloss Reichartshausen

2.1 Specific IS near-/offshoring project: Near-/offshore service provider

Now, please think of **one** of the **first finished** **IS near-/offshoring application development or maintenance project** you participated in. Please answer all remaining questions of this questionnaire with respect to **this one specific project.**

---

*From which country were the near-/offshore services delivered from?
Choose one of the following answers

- ⊙ Armenia
- ⊙ Czech Republic
- ⊙ Hungary
- ⊙ India
- ⊙ Latvia
- ⊙ Malaysia
- ⊙ Moldavia

- ⊙ Philippines
- ⊙ Poland
- ⊙ Romania
- ⊙ Russia
- ⊙ Slovakia
- ⊙ Ukraine
- ⊙ Other [_____]

---

*What was the relationship to the near-/offshore service provider?
Choose one of the following answers

- ⊙ The provider was an external company ("near-/offshore outsourcing").
- ⊙ The provider was a partially owned subsidiary ("joint venture with OSP").
- ⊙ The provider was an internal subsidiary of our company ("captive near-/offshoring").

[Exit and clear survey]   Resume later   << Previous | Next >>

European ≣ Business School
International University · Schloss Reichartshausen

2.2 Specific IS near-/offshoring project: Project specifics

Now, please think of **one** of the **first finished IS near-/offshoring application development or maintenance project** you participated in. Please answer all remaining questions of this questionnaire with respect to **this one specific project.**

---

*When was the project finished?

[_____]

Only numbers may be entered in this field

? Please specify the year, i.e. "2007".

---

*What was the duration of the project?

[_____] months

Only numbers may be entered in this field

? The explanatory power of your answers does not depend on numerical accuracy. Please do not hesitate to give estimated numbers in your answer.

---

*What was the project's volume in man months?

Only numbers may be entered in these fields

total (in man months): [_____]

thereof near-/offshore (in %): [_____]

? The explanatory power of your answers does not depend on numerical accuracy. Please do not hesitate to give estimated numbers in your answer.

---

*What was the project's volume in EUR?

Only numbers may be entered in these fields

total (in EUR): [_____]

thereof near-/offshore (in %): [_____]

? The explanatory power of your answers does not depend on numerical accuracy. Please do not hesitate to give estimated numbers in your answer.

---

*What type of project was it?

Only numbers may be entered in these fields
Total of all entries must equal 100

application development (in %):
application maintenance (in %):

| Total: | |
| Remaining: | |

? Please allocate 100 percentage points.

---

*What was the main reason for doing parts or the entire project near-/offshore?
Check any that apply

☐ Cost reduction
☐ Quality increase
☐ Strategic reason
☐ Resource shortage
☐ Productivity increase
☐ Other:

? Multiple selections are possible.

---

*What was your role on the project?
Choose one of the following answers

Please choose one of the following:

○ Managerial role – please specify:
○ Non-managerial role – please specify:

Please enter your comment here:

---

*Where did you primarily reside on the project regarding location?
Choose one of the following answers

○ I resided onshore, i.e. in Germany.
○ I resided near-/offshore.
○ I equally resided on- and near-/offshore.

*Did the client company additionally hire consulting support for conducting the near-/offshore project?
Choose one of the following answers

    ◯ Yes, it hired additional consulting support.
    ◯ No, it did not hire additional consulting support.

*Was the project part of a larger near-/offshoring program of your company?
Choose one of the following answers

    ◯ Yes, it was part of a larger near-/offshoring program at my company.
    ◯ No, it wasn't part of a larger near-/offshoring program at my company.
    ◯ Don't know.

[Exit and clear survey]   Resume later   << Previous   Next >>

European ≡ Business School
International University Schloss Reichartshausen

2.3 Specific IS near-/offshoring project: Client company (i.e. the near-/offshore-consuming company)

Now, please think of **one** of the **first finished** IS near-/offshoring application **development or maintenance project** you participated in. Please answer all remaining questions of this questionnaire with respect to **this one specific project.**

---

*To which industry did your company belong to?
Check any that apply

☐ Banking & Insurance   ☐ Retail & Distribution
☐ Construction   ☐ Telcommunications
☐ Healthcare   ☐ Transportation
☐ Manufacturing   ☐ Utilities
☐ Mining & Extraction   ☐ Other: |
☐ Public Sector

? Multiple selections are possible.

Demographic information of the company at that time (**optional**)

Only numbers may be entered in these fields

Annual revenue: |_____| million EUR approx.

Annual IS budget: |_____| million EUR approx.

? The explanatory power of your answers does not depend on numerical accuracy. Please do not hesitate to give estimated numbers in your answer.

Number of employees of the company at that time (**optional**)
Choose one of the following answers

○ less than 250
○ 251 - 1000
○ 1001 - 5000
○ 5001 - 25000
○ more than 25000
◉ No answer

? The explanatory power of your answers does not depend on numerical accuracy. Please do not hesitate to give estimated numbers in your answer.

Number of internal IS staff of the company at that time. (optional)
Choose one of the following answers

○ less than 50
○ 51 - 250
○ 251 - 1000
○ 1001 - 5000
○ more than 5000
◉ No answer

? The explanatory power of your answers does not depend on numerical accuracy. Please do not hesitate to give estimated numbers in your answer.

[Exit and clear survey]   Resume later   << Previous   Next >>

European ☰ Business School
International University Schloss Reichartshausen

Success factors in IS near-/offshoring projects
0% ▬▬▬▬▭ 100%

3. Project delivery

The following section concentrates on the situation your organisation experienced during the near-/offshore project's delivery. **All questions refer to the IS near-/offshoring application development or maintenance project you described in Section 2.**

---

*At the time the project was started...

	1 - Fully disagree	2	3	4	5	6	7 - Fully agree
...most of our project team members had already gathered work experience in near-/offshore arrangements.	○	○	○	○	○	○	○
...our company had already performed many projects in near-/offshore arrangements.	○	○	○	○	○	○	○
...our company had dedicated processes and organizational structures in place to plan, manage and execute near-/offshore arrangements.	○	○	○	○	○	○	○
overall, our project team considered our level of near-/offshoring expertise as being high.	○	○	○	○	○	○	○

❓Please check the corresponding boxes.

---

*After starting to work with the near-/offshore service provider we realized that its staff...

	1 - Fully disagree	2	3	4	5	6	7 - Fully agree
...makes favorable decisions to us under any circumstances.	○	○	○	○	○	○	○
...is willing to provide assistance to us without exception.	○	○	○	○	○	○	○
...reliably provides pre-specified support.	○	○	○	○	○	○	○
...is honest.	○	○	○	○	○	○	○
...cares about us.	○	○	○	○	○	○	○

❓Please check the corresponding boxes.

---

*Please consider the following statement and indicate your degree of agreement

	1 - Fully disagree	2	3	4	5	6	7 - Fully agree
Overall, we had the impression that we could trust the near-/offshore service provider staff.	○	○	○	○	○	○	○

? Please check the corresponding boxes.

---

*Please consider the following statement and indicate your degree of agreement

	1 - Fully disagree	2	3	4	5	6	7 - Fully agree
The near-/offshore volume in terms of man months was rather large.	○	○	○	○	○	○	○
The near-/offshored project's duration was rather short.	○	○	○	○	○	○	○
The primary operating language of the project was English.	○	○	○	○	○	○	○
Most of the information and knowledge concerning the project was well documented.	○	○	○	○	○	○	○
The project required business-specific know-how of staff members.	○	○	○	○	○	○	○
Today, we would say the project was suitable for near-/offshore delivery.	○	○	○	○	○	○	○

? Please check the corresponding boxes.

---

*During the project, with the near-/offshore service provider staff we shared...

	1 - Fully disagree	2	3	4	5	6	7 - Fully agree
...business proposals and reports.	○	○	○	○	○	○	○
...manuals, models, and methodologies.	○	○	○	○	○	○	○
...know-how from work experience.	○	○	○	○	○	○	○
...each other's know-where and know-whom.	○	○	○	○	○	○	○
...expertise obtained from education and training.	○	○	○	○	○	○	○

? Please check the corresponding boxes.

*During the project, the near-/offshore service provider staff...

	1 - Fully disagree	2	3	4	5	6	7 - Fully agree
...had learned a great deal about the project-related technology/process know-how.	○	○	○	○	○	○	○
...had greatly reduced its know-how-related reliance or dependence upon us since the beginning of the project	○	○	○	○	○	○	○

❓Please check the corresponding boxes.

*Please consider the following statement and indicate your degree of agreement

	1 - Fully disagree	2	3	4	5	6	7 - Fully agree
Overall, we were satisfied with the knowledge transfer from us to near-/offshore service provider staff during the project.	○	○	○	○	○	○	○

❓Pease check the corresponding boxes.

*During the project our staff and near-/offshore service provider staff...

	1 - Fully disagree	2	3	4	5	6	7 - Fully agree
...communicated openly.	○	○	○	○	○	○	○
...developed a mutual understanding of the respective ethnic and corporate cultures.	○	○	○	○	○	○	○
...members each perceived themselves as equal and recognized members of the project team.	○	○	○	○	○	○	○
...formed close individual working connections with each other.	○	○	○	○	○	○	○

❓Please check the corresponding boxes.

*Please consider the following statement and indicate your degree of agreement

	1 - Fully disagree	2	3	4	5	6	7 - Fully agree
Overall, we were satisfied with the working liaison between our staff and near-/offshore service provider staff.	○	○	○	○	○	○	○

❓Please check the corresponding boxes.

*For the successful execution of a near-/offshore project, how important do you consider each of the following?

	1 - Not important	2	3	4	5	6	7 - Very important
Existing near-/offshoring expertise within the client, i.e. offshore-consuming, organization or the project team members' expertise.	○	○	○	○	○	○	○
Trust in the near-/offshore service provider staff.	○	○	○	○	○	○	○
Identification of near-/offshoring-suitable projects.	○	○	○	○	○	○	○
Successful knowledge transfer from own staff to near-/offshore project staff.	○	○	○	○	○	○	○
Good working liaison between own staff and near-/offshore service provider staff.	○	○	○	○	○	○	○

❓Please check the corresponding boxes.

[Exit and clear survey]   Resume later   << Previous   Next >>

European ≡ Business School
International University Schloss Reichartshausen

4. Project outcome

The following section concentrates on the near-/offshore project's outcome your organisation has experienced. **All questions refer to the IS near-/offshoring application development or maintenance project you described in Section 2.**

*How satisfied was your organization with...	1 - Not at all satisfied	2	3	4	5	6	7 - Totally satisfied
...the project performance regarding time schedule.	○	○	○	○	○	○	○
...the project performance regarding budget.	○	○	○	○	○	○	○
...the project performance regarding expected functionality.	○	○	○	○	○	○	○
...the project performance regarding expected quality.	○	○	○	○	○	○	○
...the overall outcome from the project.	○	○	○	○	○	○	○

? Please check the corresponding boxes.

Do you have any further comments on the project you want to share with us? (**optional**)

[Exit and clear survey]   Resume later   << Previous   Next >>

European ☰ Business School
International University. Schloss Reichartshausen

Success factors in IS near-/offshoring projects
0% ▬▬▬▬▬▭ 100%

5. Respondent information

This final section of the questionnaire collects information about your organization and yourself for statistical purposes. Rest assured that your answers will be handled with absolute confidentiality.

---

*Please tell us about yourself

Your current position / job title: [   ]

[?] The information you provide will be used only for statistical purposes.

---

*Please tell us about your personal experience

Only numbers may be entered in these fields

No. of years in current job or similar position: [   ]

No. of years in the field of information systems: [   ]

[?] The information you provide will be used only for statistical purposes.

If you would like to receive a personal copy of the survey results, please provide your name and e-mail address (**optional**)

Name: [   ]

E-Mail: [   ]

[Exit and clear survey]   Resume later   << Previous   Submit

Classification: Near- and Offshore Countries

Nearshore		Offshore	
• *Armenia*	• Poland	• Argentina	• Pakistan
• Belarus	• Portugal	• China	• Philippines
• Bulgaria	• Romania	• Colombia	• Singapore
• Czech Republic	• Russia	• India	• Sri Lanka
• *Egypt*	• Serbia	• Indonesia	• "Several countries"
• France	• Slovakia	• Korea	• Vietnam
• Hungary	• Spain	• Malaysia	
• Ireland	• *Tunesia*	• Mexico	
• Italy	• Turkey		
• Latvia	• Ukraine		
• Lithuania			

Source: own analysis

Pre-Test of Research Model

H1: Offshoring Expertise (+) → Offshore Project Success

Analysis of Variance (ANOVA) Test Results

Test of Homogeneity of Variances

SUCCES5

Levene Statistic	df1	df2	Sig.
3.667	6	297	.002

ANOVA

SUCCES5

	Sum of Squares	df	Mean Square	F	Sig.
Between Groups	70.494	6	11.749	5.055	.000
Within Groups	690.243	297	2.324		
Total	760.737	303			

Robust Tests of Equality of Means

SUCCES5

	Statistic[a]	df1	df2	Sig.
Welch	5.598	6	118.366	.000

a. Asymptotically F distributed.

Kruskal-Wallis Test Results

Ranks

EXP4		N	Mean Rank
SUCCES5	1	41	131.87
	2	60	136.61
	3	60	145.48
	4	43	134.20
	5	31	157.29
	6	43	169.34
	7	26	234.63
	Total	304	

Test Statistics[a,b]

	SUCCES5
Chi-Square	32.395
df	6
Asymp. Sig.	.000

a. Kruskal Wallis Test

b. Grouping Variable: EXP4

Post-Hoc Tests

Multiple Comparisons

SUCCES5
Games-Howell

(I) EXP4	(J) EXP4	Mean Difference (I-J)	Std. Error	Sig.	95% Confidence Interval	
					Lower Bound	Upper Bound
1	2	-.170	.364	.999	-1.27	.93
	3	-.420	.351	.893	-1.49	.64
	4	-.226	.367	.996	-1.34	.89
	5	-.628	.393	.685	-1.82	.57
	6	-.830	.361	.257	-1.92	.26
	7	-1,815*	.397	.000	-3.02	-.61
2	1	.170	.364	.999	-.93	1.27
	3	-.250	.281	.974	-1.09	.59
	4	-.055	.301	1.000	-.96	.85
	5	-.458	.332	.812	-1.47	.55
	6	-.660	.293	.278	-1.54	.22
	7	-1,645*	.337	.000	-2.67	-.62
3	1	.420	.351	.893	-.64	1.49
	2	.250	.281	.974	-.59	1.09
	4	.195	.285	.993	-.66	1.05
	5	-.208	.317	.995	-1.17	.76
	6	-.410	.276	.753	-1.24	.42
	7	-1,395*	.322	.001	-2.38	-.41
4	1	.226	.367	.996	-.89	1.34
	2	.055	.301	1.000	-.85	.96
	3	-.195	.285	.993	-1.05	.66
	5	-.402	.336	.892	-1.42	.62
	6	-.605	.297	.399	-1.50	.29
	7	-1,589*	.340	.000	-2.63	-.55
5	1	.628	.393	.685	-.57	1.82
	2	.458	.332	.812	-.55	1.47
	3	.208	.317	.995	-.76	1.17
	4	.402	.336	.892	-.62	1.42
	6	-.203	.328	.996	-1.20	.80
	7	-1,187*	.368	.032	-2.31	-.06
6	1	.830	.361	.257	-.26	1.92
	2	.660	.293	.278	-.22	1.54
	3	.410	.276	.753	-.42	1.24
	4	.605	.297	.399	-.29	1.50
	5	.203	.328	.996	-.80	1.20
	7	-.985	.333	.065	-2.00	.03
7	1	1,815*	.397	.000	.61	3.02
	2	1,645*	.337	.000	.62	2.67
	3	1,395*	.322	.001	.41	2.38
	4	1,589*	.340	.000	.55	2.63
	5	1,187*	.368	.032	.06	2.31
	6	.985	.333	.065	-.03	2.00

*. The mean difference is significant at the 0.05 level.

H2: Offshoring Expertise (+) → Project Suitability

ANOVA Test Results

Test of Homogeneity of Variances

SUITA6

Levene Statistic	df1	df2	Sig.
4.654	6	297	.000

ANOVA

SUITA6

	Sum of Squares	df	Mean Square	F	Sig.
Between Groups	104.434	6	17.406	6.640	.000
Within Groups	778.500	297	2.621		
Total	882.934	303			

Robust Tests of Equality of Means

SUITA6

	Statistic[a]	df1	df2	Sig.
Welch	15.414	6	122.206	.000

a. Asymptotically F distributed.

Kruskal-Wallis Test Results

Ranks

	EXP4	N	Rank
SUITA6	1	41	125.66
	2	60	130.31
	3	60	140.78
	4	43	151.02
	5	31	152.05
	6	43	173.13
	7	26	241.94
	Total	304	

Test Statistics[a,b]

	SUITA6
Chi-Square	39.477
df	6
Asymp. Sig.	.000

a. Kruskal Wallis Test

b. Grouping Variable: EXP4

Post-Hoc Tests

Multiple Comparisons

SUITA6
Games-Howell

(I) EXP4	(J) EXP4	Mean Difference (I-J)	Std. Error	Sig.	95% Confidence Interval	
					Lower Bound	Upper Bound
1	2	-.213	.389	.998	-1.39	.96
	3	-.496	.375	.839	-1.63	.64
	4	-.597	.417	.784	-1.86	.67
	5	-.700	.423	.648	-1.99	.58
	6	-1.062	.387	.102	-2.24	.11
	7	-2,252*	.357	.000	-3.34	-1.16
2	1	.213	.389	.998	-.96	1.39
	3	-.283	.295	.961	-1.17	.60
	4	-.384	.347	.924	-1.43	.66
	5	-.488	.354	.812	-1.56	.59
	6	-.849	.310	.099	-1.78	.08
	7	-2,040*	.272	.000	-2.86	-1.22
3	1	.496	.375	.839	-.64	1.63
	2	.283	.295	.961	-.60	1.17
	4	-.101	.332	1.000	-1.10	.90
	5	-.204	.339	.997	-1.24	.83
	6	-.566	.293	.464	-1.45	.32
	7	-1,756*	.252	.000	-2.52	-1.00
4	1	.597	.417	.784	-.67	1.86
	2	.384	.347	.924	-.66	1.43
	3	.101	.332	1.000	-.90	1.10
	5	-.104	.386	1.000	-1.27	1.07
	6	-.465	.345	.828	-1.51	.58
	7	-1,656*	.311	.000	-2.60	-.71
5	1	.700	.423	.648	-.58	1.99
	2	.488	.354	.812	-.59	1.56
	3	.204	.339	.997	-.83	1.24
	4	.104	.386	1.000	-1.07	1.27
	6	-.362	.353	.946	-1.44	.71
	7	-1,552*	.319	.000	-2.54	-.57
6	1	1.062	.387	.102	-.11	2.24
	2	.849	.310	.099	-.08	1.78
	3	.566	.293	.464	-.32	1.45
	4	.465	.345	.828	-.58	1.51
	5	.362	.353	.946	-.71	1.44
	7	-1,191*	.269	.001	-2.01	-.37
7	1	2,252*	.357	.000	1.16	3.34
	2	2,040*	.272	.000	1.22	2.86
	3	1,756*	.252	.000	1.00	2.52
	4	1,656*	.311	.000	.71	2.60
	5	1,552*	.319	.000	.57	2.54
	6	1,191*	.269	.001	.37	2.01

*. The mean difference is significant at the 0.05 level.

H3: Offshoring Expertise (+) → Knowledge Transfer
ANOVA Test Results

Test of Homogeneity of Variances

KNOWT8

Levene Statistic	df1	df2	Sig.
2.015	6	297	.064

ANOVA

KNOWT8

	Sum of Squares	df	Mean Square	F	Sig.
Between Groups	72.143	6	12.024	4.672	.000
Within Groups	764.406	297	2.574		
Total	836.549	303			

Robust Tests of Equality of Means

KNOWT8

	Statistic[a]	df1	df2	Sig.
Welch	4.735	6	118.288	.000

a. Asymptotically F distributed.

Kruskal-Wallis Test Results

Ranks

	EXP4	N	Mean Rank
KNOWT8	1	41	124.18
	2	60	127.14
	3	60	156.54
	4	43	156.19
	5	31	162.21
	6	43	155.94
	7	26	222.98
	Total	304	

Test Statistics[a,b]

	KNOWT8
Chi-Square	27.643
df	6
Asymp. Sig.	.000

a. Kruskal Wallis Test
b. Grouping Variable: EXP4

Post-Hoc Tests

Multiple Comparisons

KNOWT8
Hochberg

(I) EXP4	(J) EXP4	Mean Difference (I-J)	Std. Error	Sig.	95% Confidence Interval Lower Bound	Upper Bound
1	2	-.178	.325	1.000	-1.17	.81
	3	-.695	.325	.503	-1.69	.30
	4	-.753	.350	.492	-1.82	.32
	5	-.840	.382	.450	-2.01	.33
	6	-.707	.350	.609	-1.78	.36
	7	-1,887*	.402	.000	-3.12	-.66
2	1	.178	.325	1.000	-.81	1.17
	3	-.517	.293	.815	-1.41	.38
	4	-.575	.321	.794	-1.55	.40
	5	-.662	.355	.739	-1.75	.42
	6	-.528	.321	.886	-1.51	.45
	7	-1,709*	.377	.000	-2.86	-.56
3	1	.695	.325	.503	-.30	1.69
	2	.517	.293	.815	-.38	1.41
	4	-.058	.321	1.000	-1.04	.92
	5	-.145	.355	1.000	-1.23	.94
	6	-.012	.321	1.000	-.99	.97
	7	-1,192*	.377	.035	-2.34	-.04
4	1	.753	.350	.492	-.32	1.82
	2	.575	.321	.794	-.40	1.55
	3	.058	.321	1.000	-.92	1.04
	5	-.087	.378	1.000	-1.24	1.07
	6	.047	.346	1.000	-1.01	1.10
	7	-1.134	.399	.094	-2.35	.08
5	1	.840	.382	.450	-.33	2.01
	2	.662	.355	.739	-.42	1.75
	3	.145	.355	1.000	-.94	1.23
	4	.087	.378	1.000	-1.07	1.24
	6	.134	.378	1.000	-1.02	1.29
	7	-1.047	.427	.264	-2.35	.26
6	1	.707	.350	.609	-.36	1.78
	2	.528	.321	.886	-.45	1.51
	3	.012	.321	1.000	-.97	.99
	4	-.047	.346	1.000	-1.10	1.01
	5	-.134	.378	1.000	-1.29	1.02
	7	-1.181	.399	.067	-2.40	.04
7	1	1,887*	.402	.000	.66	3.12
	2	1,709*	.377	.000	.56	2.86
	3	1,192*	.377	.035	.04	2.34
	4	1.134	.399	.094	-.08	2.35
	5	1.047	.427	.264	-.26	2.35
	6	1.181	.399	.067	-.04	2.40

*. The mean difference is significant at the 0.05 level.

H4: Offshoring Expertise (+) → Liaison Quality

ANOVA Test Results

Test of Homogeneity of Variances

LIAISO5

Levene Statistic	df1	df2	Sig.
1.725	6	297	.115

ANOVA

LIAISO5

	Sum of Squares	df	Mean Square	F	Sig.
Between Groups	57.698	6	9.616	4.277	.000
Within Groups	667.799	297	2.248		
Total	725.497	303			

Robust Tests of Equality of Means

LIAISO5

	Statistic[a]	df1	df2	Sig.
Welch	4.414	6	117.228	.000

a. Asymptotically F distributed.

Kruskal-Wallis Test Results

Ranks

	EXP4	N	Mean Rank
LIAISO5	1	41	135.74
	2	60	134.08
	3	60	145.49
	4	43	139.92
	5	31	150.90
	6	43	168.28
	7	26	234.23
	Total	304	

Test Statistics[a,b]

	LIAISO5
Chi-Square	30.601
df	6
Asymp. Sig.	.000

a. Kruskal Wallis Test
b. Grouping Variable: EXP4

Post-Hoc Tests

Multiple Comparisons

LIAISO5
Hochberg

(I) EXP4	(J) EXP4	Mean Difference (I-J)	Std. Error	Sig.	95% Confidence Interval Lower Bound	95% Confidence Interval Upper Bound
1	2	-.134	.304	1.000	-1.06	.79
	3	-.301	.304	1.000	-1.23	.63
	4	-.192	.327	1.000	-1.19	.81
	5	-.344	.357	1.000	-1.43	.75
	6	-.634	.327	.679	-1.63	.37
	7	-1,673*	.376	.000	-2.82	-.52
2	1	.134	.304	1.000	-.79	1.06
	3	-.167	.274	1.000	-1.00	.67
	4	-.058	.300	1.000	-.97	.86
	5	-.210	.332	1.000	-1.22	.80
	6	-.500	.300	.875	-1.42	.42
	7	-1,538*	.352	.000	-2.61	-.46
3	1	.301	.304	1.000	-.63	1.23
	2	.167	.274	1.000	-.67	1.00
	4	.109	.300	1.000	-.81	1.02
	5	-.043	.332	1.000	-1.06	.97
	6	-.333	.300	.998	-1.25	.58
	7	-1,372*	.352	.003	-2.45	-.30
4	1	.192	.327	1.000	-.81	1.19
	2	.058	.300	1.000	-.86	.97
	3	-.109	.300	1.000	-1.02	.81
	5	-.152	.353	1.000	-1.23	.93
	6	-.442	.323	.980	-1.43	.55
	7	-1,480*	.373	.002	-2.62	-.34
5	1	.344	.357	1.000	-.75	1.43
	2	.210	.332	1.000	-.80	1.22
	3	.043	.332	1.000	-.97	1.06
	4	.152	.353	1.000	-.93	1.23
	6	-.290	.353	1.000	-1.37	.79
	7	-1,329*	.399	.020	-2.55	-.11
6	1	.634	.327	.679	-.37	1.63
	2	.500	.300	.875	-.42	1.42
	3	.333	.300	.998	-.58	1.25
	4	.442	.323	.980	-.55	1.43
	5	.290	.353	1.000	-.79	1.37
	7	-1.038	.373	.111	-2.18	.10
7	1	1,673*	.376	.000	.52	2.82
	2	1,538*	.352	.000	.46	2.61
	3	1,372*	.352	.003	.30	2.45
	4	1,480*	.373	.002	.34	2.62
	5	1,329*	.399	.020	.11	2.55
	6	1.038	.373	.111	-.10	2.18

*. The mean difference is significant at the 0.05 level.

H5: Trust in Offshore Service Provider (+) → Knowledge Transfer

ANOVA Test Results

Test of Homogeneity of Variances

KNOWT8

Levene Statistic	df1	df2	Sig.
1.374	6	297	.225

ANOVA

KNOWT8

	Sum of Squares	df	Mean Square	F	Sig.
Between Groups	325.534	6	54.256	31.533	.000
Within Groups	511.015	297	1.721		
Total	836.549	303			

Robust Tests of Equality of Means

KNOWT8

	Statistic[a]	df1	df2	Sig.
Welch	31.498	6	68.062	.000

a. Asymptotically F distributed.

Kruskal-Wallis Test Results

Ranks

	TRUST6	N	Mean Rank
KNOWT8	1	8	51.94
	2	30	68.65
	3	44	110.49
	4	42	104.71
	5	75	163.97
	6	66	200.84
	7	39	232.62
	Total	304	

Test Statistics[a,b]

	KNOWT8
Chi-Square	118.284
df	6
Asymp. Sig.	.000

a. Kruskal Wallis Test

b. Grouping Variable: TRUST6

Post-Hoc Tests

Multiple Comparisons

KNOWT8
Hochberg

(I) TRUST6	(J) TRUST6	Mean Difference (I-J)	Std. Error	Sig.	95% Confidence Interval Lower Bound	95% Confidence Interval Upper Bound
1	2	-.358	.522	1.000	-1.95	1.24
	3	-1.284	.504	.212	-2.82	.26
	4	-1.173	.506	.358	-2.72	.37
	5	-2,332*	.488	.000	-3.82	-.84
	6	-2,958*	.491	.000	-4.46	-1.46
	7	-3,548*	.509	.000	-5.10	-1.99
2	1	.358	.522	1.000	-1.24	1.95
	3	-.926	.311	.063	-1.87	.02
	4	-.814	.314	.187	-1.77	.14
	5	-1,973*	.283	.000	-2.84	-1.11
	6	-2,600*	.289	.000	-3.48	-1.72
	7	-3,190*	.319	.000	-4.16	-2.22
3	1	1.284	.504	.212	-.26	2.82
	2	.926	.311	.063	-.02	1.87
	4	.111	.283	1.000	-.75	.98
	5	-1,048*	.249	.001	-1.81	-.29
	6	-1,674*	.255	.000	-2.45	-.89
	7	-2,264*	.288	.000	-3.15	-1.38
4	1	1.173	.506	.358	-.37	2.72
	2	.814	.314	.187	-.14	1.77
	3	-.111	.283	1.000	-.98	.75
	5	-1,159*	.253	.000	-1.93	-.39
	6	-1,786*	.259	.000	-2.58	-.99
	7	-2,375*	.292	.000	-3.27	-1.48
5	1	2,332*	.488	.000	.84	3.82
	2	1,973*	.283	.000	1.11	2.84
	3	1,048*	.249	.001	.29	1.81
	4	1,159*	.253	.000	.39	1.93
	6	-.627	.221	.099	-1.30	.05
	7	-1,216*	.259	.000	-2.01	-.43
6	1	2,958*	.491	.000	1.46	4.46
	2	2,600*	.289	.000	1.72	3.48
	3	1,674*	.255	.000	.89	2.45
	4	1,786*	.259	.000	.99	2.58
	5	.627	.221	.099	-.05	1.30
	7	-.590	.265	.429	-1.40	.22
7	1	3,548*	.509	.000	1.99	5.10
	2	3,190*	.319	.000	2.22	4.16
	3	2,264*	.288	.000	1.38	3.15
	4	2,375*	.292	.000	1.48	3.27
	5	1,216*	.259	.000	.43	2.01
	6	.590	.265	.429	-.22	1.40

*. The mean difference is significant at the 0.05 level.

H6: Trust in Offshore Service Provider (+) → Liaison Quality

ANOVA Test Results

Test of Homogeneity of Variances

LIAISO5

Levene Statistic	df1	df2	Sig.
4.368	6	297	.000

ANOVA

LIAISO5

	Sum of Squares	df	Mean Square	F	Sig.
Between Groups	329.958	6	54.993	41.293	.000
Within Groups	395.539	297	1.332		
Total	725.497	303			

Robust Tests of Equality of Means

LIAISO5

	Statistic[a]	df1	df2	Sig.
Welch	48.025	6	66.396	.000

a. Asymptotically F distributed.

Kruskal-Wallis Test Results

Ranks

	TRUST6	N	Mean Rank
LIAISO5	1	8	71.19
	2	30	61.03
	3	44	99.39
	4	42	107.69
	5	75	162.96
	6	66	197.05
	7	39	252.22
	Total	304	

Test Statistics[a,b]

	LIAISO5
Chi-Square	140.663
df	6
Asymp. Sig.	.000

a. Kruskal Wallis Test
b. Grouping Variable: TRUST6

Post-Hoc Tests

Multiple Comparisons

LIAISO5
Games-Howell

(I) TRUST6	(J) TRUST6	Mean Difference (I-J)	Std. Error	Sig.	95% Confidence Interval Lower Bound	95% Confidence Interval Upper Bound
1	2	.000	.666	1.000	-2.48	2.48
	3	-.795	.667	.881	-3.27	1.68
	4	-1.048	.656	.688	-3.52	1.43
	5	-2.013	.641	.125	-4.49	.46
	6	-2,561*	.636	.043	-5.04	-.08
	7	-3,385*	.637	.010	-5.86	-.91
2	1	.000	.666	1.000	-2.48	2.48
	3	-.795	.321	.183	-1.77	.18
	4	-1,048*	.296	.013	-1.95	-.15
	5	-2,013*	.261	.000	-2.81	-1.21
	6	-2,561*	.250	.000	-3.33	-1.79
	7	-3,385*	.252	.000	-4.16	-2.61
3	1	.795	.667	.881	-1.68	3.27
	2	.795	.321	.183	-.18	1.77
	4	-.252	.299	.980	-1.16	.65
	5	-1,218*	.264	.000	-2.02	-.42
	6	-1,765*	.253	.000	-2.54	-.99
	7	-2,589*	.256	.000	-3.37	-1.81
4	1	1.048	.656	.688	-1.43	3.52
	2	1,048*	.296	.013	.15	1.95
	3	.252	.299	.980	-.65	1.16
	5	-,966*	.234	.002	-1.67	-.26
	6	-1,513*	.221	.000	-2.18	-.84
	7	-2,337*	.224	.000	-3.02	-1.66
5	1	2.013	.641	.125	-.46	4.49
	2	2,013*	.261	.000	1.21	2.81
	3	1,218*	.264	.000	.42	2.02
	4	,966*	.234	.002	.26	1.67
	6	-,547*	.171	.027	-1.06	-.04
	7	-1,371*	.175	.000	-1.90	-.85
6	1	2,561*	.636	.043	.08	5.04
	2	2,561*	.250	.000	1.79	3.33
	3	1,765*	.253	.000	.99	2.54
	4	1,513*	.221	.000	.84	2.18
	5	,547*	.171	.027	.04	1.06
	7	-,824*	.157	.000	-1.30	-.35
7	1	3,385*	.637	.010	.91	5.86
	2	3,385*	.252	.000	2.61	4.16
	3	2,589*	.256	.000	1.81	3.37
	4	2,337*	.224	.000	1.66	3.02
	5	1,371*	.175	.000	.85	1.90
	6	,824*	.157	.000	.35	1.30

*. The mean difference is significant at the 0.05 level.

H7: Trust in Offshore Service Provider (+) → Offshore Project Success

ANOVA Test Results

Test of Homogeneity of Variances

SUCCES5

Levene Statistic	df1	df2	Sig.
8.328	6	297	.000

ANOVA

SUCCES5

	Sum of Squares	df	Mean Square	F	Sig.
Between Groups	258.877	6	43.146	25.534	.000
Within Groups	501.860	297	1.690		
Total	760.737	303			

Robust Tests of Equality of Means

SUCCES5

	Statistic[a]	df1	df2	Sig.
Welch	27.830	6	65.748	.000

a. Asymptotically F distributed.

Kruskal-Wallis Test Results

Ranks

	TRUST6	N	Mean Rank
SUCCES5	1	8	120.44
	2	30	92.48
	3	44	104.95
	4	42	97.40
	5	75	152.19
	6	66	195.33
	7	39	246.33
	Total	304	

Test Statistics[a,b]

	SUCCES5
Chi-Square	109.809
df	6
Asymp. Sig.	.000

a. Kruskal Wallis Test

b. Grouping Variable: TRUST6

Post-Hoc Tests

Multiple Comparisons

SUCCES5
Games-Howell

(I) TRUST6	(J) TRUST6	Mean Difference (I-J)	Std. Error	Sig.	95% Confidence Interval Lower Bound	Upper Bound
1	2	.350	.898	1.000	-2.97	3.67
	3	-.045	.867	1.000	-3.36	3.27
	4	.083	.868	1.000	-3.23	3.40
	5	-.983	.852	.892	-4.30	2.34
	6	-1.689	.848	.486	-5.01	1.63
	7	-2.429	.853	.183	-5.75	.89
2	1	-.350	.898	1.000	-3.67	2.97
	3	-.395	.384	.945	-1.57	.78
	4	-.267	.384	.992	-1.44	.91
	5	-1,333*	.348	.007	-2.41	-.26
	6	-2,039*	.337	.000	-3.09	-.99
	7	-2,779*	.351	.000	-3.87	-1.69
3	1	.045	.867	1.000	-3.27	3.36
	2	.395	.384	.945	-.78	1.57
	4	.129	.307	1.000	-.80	1.06
	5	-,938*	.260	.009	-1.73	-.15
	6	-1,644*	.245	.000	-2.39	-.90
	7	-2,384*	.264	.000	-3.19	-1.58
4	1	-.083	.868	1.000	-3.40	3.23
	2	.267	.384	.992	-.91	1.44
	3	-.129	.307	1.000	-1.06	.80
	5	-1,067*	.261	.002	-1.86	-.28
	6	-1,773*	.246	.000	-2.52	-1.02
	7	-2,513*	.265	.000	-3.32	-1.71
5	1	.983	.852	.892	-2.34	4.30
	2	1,333*	.348	.007	.26	2.41
	3	,938*	.260	.009	.15	1.73
	4	1,067*	.261	.002	.28	1.86
	6	-,706*	.184	.003	-1.26	-.16
	7	-1,446*	.208	.000	-2.07	-.82
6	1	1.689	.848	.486	-1.63	5.01
	2	2,039*	.337	.000	.99	3.09
	3	1,644*	.245	.000	.90	2.39
	4	1,773*	.246	.000	1.02	2.52
	5	,706*	.184	.003	.16	1.26
	7	-,740*	.189	.004	-1.31	-.17
7	1	2.429	.853	.183	-.89	5.75
	2	2,779*	.351	.000	1.69	3.87
	3	2,384*	.264	.000	1.58	3.19
	4	2,513*	.265	.000	1.71	3.32
	5	1,446*	.208	.000	.82	2.07
	6	,740*	.189	.004	.17	1.31

*. The mean difference is significant at the 0.05 level.

H8: Project Suitability (+) → Offshore Project Success

ANOVA Test Results

Test of Homogeneity of Variances

SUCCES5

Levene Statistic	df1	df2	Sig.
3.067	6	297	.006

ANOVA

SUCCES5

	Sum of Squares	df	Mean Square	F	Sig.
Between Groups	326.393	6	54.399	37.197	.000
Within Groups	434.344	297	1.462		
Total	760.737	303			

Robust Tests of Equality of Means

SUCCES5

	Statistic[a]	df1	df2	Sig.
Welch	32.079	6	79.984	.000

a. Asymptotically F distributed.

Kruskal-Wallis Test Results

Ranks

	SUITA6	N	Mean Rank
SUCCES5	1	13	52.96
	2	32	77.08
	3	21	80.50
	4	43	111.59
	5	68	150.57
	6	79	193.66
	7	48	232.88
	Total	304	

Test Statistics[a,b]

	SUCCES5
Chi-Square	127.237
df	6
Asymp. Sig.	.000

a. Kruskal Wallis Test

b. Grouping Variable: SUITA6

Post-Hoc Tests

Multiple Comparisons

SUCCES5
Games-Howell

(I) SUITA6	(J) SUITA6	Mean Difference (I-J)	Std. Error	Sig.	95% Confidence Interval	
					Lower Bound	Upper Bound
1	2	-.988	.562	.591	-2.85	.87
	3	-1.150	.572	.441	-3.04	.73
	4	-1.723	.551	.075	-3.56	.12
	5	-2,490*	.528	.005	-4.29	-.69
	6	-3,174*	.521	.001	-4.97	-1.38
	7	-3,748*	.531	.000	-5.56	-1.94
2	1	.988	.562	.591	-.87	2.85
	3	-.162	.356	.999	-1.26	.94
	4	-.735	.321	.266	-1.71	.24
	5	-1,502*	.280	.000	-2.36	-.64
	6	-2,186*	.266	.000	-3.01	-1.37
	7	-2,760*	.285	.000	-3.63	-1.89
3	1	1.150	.572	.441	-.73	3.04
	2	.162	.356	.999	-.94	1.26
	4	-.573	.338	.624	-1.62	.47
	5	-1,340*	.299	.002	-2.28	-.40
	6	-2,024*	.286	.000	-2.93	-1.12
	7	-2,598*	.304	.000	-3.55	-1.65
4	1	1.723	.551	.075	-.12	3.56
	2	.735	.321	.266	-.24	1.71
	3	.573	.338	.624	-.47	1.62
	5	-.767	.257	.055	-1.54	.01
	6	-1,452*	.241	.000	-2.19	-.72
	7	-2,026*	.262	.000	-2.82	-1.23
5	1	2,490*	.528	.005	.69	4.29
	2	1,502*	.280	.000	.64	2.36
	3	1,340*	.299	.002	.40	2.28
	4	.767	.257	.055	-.01	1.54
	6	-,684*	.183	.005	-1.23	-.14
	7	-1,259*	.210	.000	-1.89	-.63
6	1	3,174*	.521	.001	1.38	4.97
	2	2,186*	.266	.000	1.37	3.01
	3	2,024*	.286	.000	1.12	2.93
	4	1,452*	.241	.000	.72	2.19
	5	,684*	.183	.005	.14	1.23
	7	-,574*	.191	.050	-1.15	.00
7	1	3,748*	.531	.000	1.94	5.56
	2	2,760*	.285	.000	1.89	3.63
	3	2,598*	.304	.000	1.65	3.55
	4	2,026*	.262	.000	1.23	2.82
	5	1,259*	.210	.000	.63	1.89
	6	,574*	.191	.050	.00	1.15

*. The mean difference is significant at the 0.05 level.

Appendix

283

H9: Knowledge Transfer (+) → Offshore Project Success

ANOVA Test Results

Test of Homogeneity of Variances

SUCCES5

Levene Statistic	df1	df2	Sig.
3.354	6	297	.003

ANOVA

SUCCES5

	Sum of Squares	df	Mean Square	F	Sig.
Between Groups	426.847	6	71.141	63.281	.000
Within Groups	333.890	297	1.124		
Total	760.737	303			

Robust Tests of Equality of Means

SUCCES5

	Statistic[a]	df1	df2	Sig.
Welch	61.190	6	82.254	.000

a. Asymptotically F distributed.

Kruskal-Wallis Test Results

Ranks

	KNOWT8	N	Mean Rank
SUCCES5	1	12	26.92
	2	40	73.38
	3	45	83.21
	4	33	131.09
	5	82	175.76
	6	66	215.00
	7	26	247.29
	Total	304	

Test Statistics[a,b]

	SUCCES5
Chi-Square	164.048
df	6
Asymp. Sig.	.000

a. Kruskal Wallis Test
b. Grouping Variable: KNOWT8

Post-Hoc Tests

Multiple Comparisons

SUCCES5
Games-Howell

(I) KNOWT 8	(J) KNOWT 8	Mean Difference (I-J)	Std. Error	Sig.	95% Confidence Interval Lower Bound	95% Confidence Interval Upper Bound
1	2	-1,483*	.411	.026	-2.83	-.13
	3	-1,756*	.401	.006	-3.09	-.43
	4	-2,758*	.408	.000	-4.10	-1.41
	5	-3,492*	.371	.000	-4.77	-2.21
	6	-4,045*	.372	.000	-5.33	-2.76
	7	-4,564*	.378	.000	-5.85	-3.27
2	1	1,483*	.411	.026	.13	2.83
	3	-.272	.279	.958	-1.12	.57
	4	-1,274*	.288	.001	-2.15	-.40
	5	-2,009*	.233	.000	-2.72	-1.30
	6	-2,562*	.236	.000	-3.28	-1.84
	7	-3,081*	.244	.000	-3.82	-2.34
3	1	1,756*	.401	.006	.43	3.09
	2	.272	.279	.958	-.57	1.12
	4	-1,002*	.273	.008	-1.83	-.17
	5	-1,736*	.215	.000	-2.39	-1.09
	6	-2,290*	.218	.000	-2.95	-1.63
	7	-2,809*	.226	.000	-3.50	-2.12
4	1	2,758*	.408	.000	1.41	4.10
	2	1,274*	.288	.001	.40	2.15
	3	1,002*	.273	.008	.17	1.83
	5	-,734*	.226	.032	-1.43	-.04
	6	-1,288*	.229	.000	-1.99	-.59
	7	-1,807*	.237	.000	-2.53	-1.08
5	1	3,492*	.371	.000	2.21	4.77
	2	2,009*	.233	.000	1.30	2.72
	3	1,736*	.215	.000	1.09	2.39
	4	,734*	.226	.032	.04	1.43
	6	-,554*	.154	.008	-1.01	-.09
	7	-1,072*	.166	.000	-1.58	-.57
6	1	4,045*	.372	.000	2.76	5.33
	2	2,562*	.236	.000	1.84	3.28
	3	2,290*	.218	.000	1.63	2.95
	4	1,288*	.229	.000	.59	1.99
	5	,554*	.154	.008	.09	1.01
	7	-,519*	.170	.049	-1.04	.00
7	1	4,564*	.378	.000	3.27	5.85
	2	3,081*	.244	.000	2.34	3.82
	3	2,809*	.226	.000	2.12	3.50
	4	1,807*	.237	.000	1.08	2.53
	5	1,072*	.166	.000	.57	1.58
	6	,519*	.170	.049	.00	1.04

*. The mean difference is significant at the 0.05 level.

H10: Liaison Quality (+) → Offshore Project Success

ANOVA Test Results

Test of Homogeneity of Variances

SUCCES5

Levene Statistic	df1	df2	Sig.
4.799	6	297	.000

ANOVA

SUCCES5

	Sum of Squares	df	Mean Square	F	Sig.
Between Groups	430.921	6	71.820	64.674	.000
Within Groups	329.815	297	1.110		
Total	760.737	303			

Robust Tests of Equality of Means

SUCCES5

	Statistic[a]	df1	df2	Sig.
Welch	94.623	6	64.822	.000

a. Asymptotically F distributed.

Kruskal-Wallis Test Results

Ranks

	LIAISO5	N	Mean Rank
SUCCES5	1	8	18.06
	2	25	44.34
	3	36	94.92
	4	41	110.34
	5	83	151.31
	6	79	207.90
	7	32	255.73
	Total	304	

Test Statistics[a,b]

	SUCCES5
Chi-Square	164.902
df	6
Asymp. Sig.	.000

a. Kruskal Wallis Test
b. Grouping Variable: LIAISO5

Post-Hoc Tests

Multiple Comparisons

SUCCES5
Games-Howell

(I) LIAISO5	(J) LIAISO5	Mean Difference (I-J)	Std. Error	Sig.	95% Confidence Interval Lower Bound	95% Confidence Interval Upper Bound
1	2	-.900	.353	.199	-2.06	.26
	3	-2,111*	.355	.000	-3.27	-.95
	4	-2,500*	.329	.000	-3.61	-1.39
	5	-3,247*	.293	.000	-4.31	-2.19
	6	-4,133*	.284	.000	-5.19	-3.08
	7	-4,844*	.284	.000	-5.90	-3.79
2	1	.900	.353	.199	-.26	2.06
	3	-1,211*	.328	.009	-2.21	-.21
	4	-1,600*	.300	.000	-2.52	-.68
	5	-2,347*	.260	.000	-3.16	-1.54
	6	-3,233*	.251	.000	-4.02	-2.45
	7	-3,944*	.250	.000	-4.73	-3.16
3	1	2,111*	.355	.000	.95	3.27
	2	1,211*	.328	.009	.21	2.21
	4	-.389	.302	.855	-1.30	.53
	5	-1,136*	.262	.001	-1.94	-.33
	6	-2,022*	.253	.000	-2.80	-1.24
	7	-2,733*	.252	.000	-3.51	-1.95
4	1	2,500*	.329	.000	1.39	3.61
	2	1,600*	.300	.000	.68	2.52
	3	.389	.302	.855	-.53	1.30
	5	-,747*	.226	.024	-1.43	-.06
	6	-1,633*	.215	.000	-2.29	-.98
	7	-2,344*	.214	.000	-3.00	-1.69
5	1	3,247*	.293	.000	2.19	4.31
	2	2,347*	.260	.000	1.54	3.16
	3	1,136*	.262	.001	.33	1.94
	4	,747*	.226	.024	.06	1.43
	6	-,886*	.154	.000	-1.35	-.42
	7	-1,597*	.154	.000	-2.06	-1.13
6	1	4,133*	.284	.000	3.08	5.19
	2	3,233*	.251	.000	2.45	4.02
	3	2,022*	.253	.000	1.24	2.80
	4	1,633*	.215	.000	.98	2.29
	5	,886*	.154	.000	.42	1.35
	7	-,711*	.137	.000	-1.12	-.30
7	1	4,844*	.284	.000	3.79	5.90
	2	3,944*	.250	.000	3.16	4.73
	3	2,733*	.252	.000	1.95	3.51
	4	2,344*	.214	.000	1.69	3.00
	5	1,597*	.154	.000	1.13	2.06
	6	,711*	.137	.000	.30	1.12

*. The mean difference is significant at the 0.05 level.

Analyses of Mediating and Moderating Effects between Constructs PROKNW and ACHKNW

For the analyses of mediating and moderating effects between two constructs we follow the procedures as described by Eggert et al. (2005).

Analysis of Mediating Effect

The analysis reveals significant positive effects of PROKNW on ACHKNW ($\beta_a = .433$, $p < .001$) and on SUCCESS ($\beta_c = .221$, $p < .001$). Additionally, ACHKNW shows a significant positive effect on SUCCESS ($\beta_b = .310$, $p < .001$). This means that ACHKNW has a partially mediating effect on SUCCESS. This mediating effect is confirmed by the z-statistic ($z = 4.337$, $p < .001$). The VAF is of medium to large size with 38% of the total impact of PROKNW on SUCCESS mediated by ACHKNW. The following figure illustrates the R^2 values, path coefficients, corresponding t-values, and standard errors for the sub-model with the mediating effect.

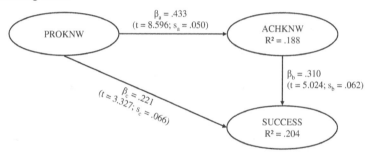

Analysis of Moderating Effect

The analysis reveals a significant moderating effect ($p < .05$) of ACHKNW on the relationship between PROKNW and SUCCESS. However, the effect size is small ($f^2 = .038$). The moderator variable does not significantly correlate with PROKNW or ACHKNW. The following figure illustrates the test results.

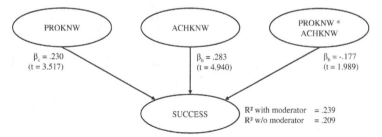

Cross-Loadings of Constructs

One-Factor Model

	EXP	TRUST	ACHKNW	LIAISO	SUCCESS
EXP1	**.847**	.275	.185	.219	.261
EXP2	**.869**	.217	.146	.210	.194
EXP3	**.862**	.248	.194	.240	.203
EXP4	**.907**	.236	.195	.220	.274
TRUST2	.248	**.844**	.291	.500	.410
TRUST3	.283	**.822**	.383	.556	.534
TRUST4	.209	**.860**	.332	.509	.446
TRUST5	.199	**.887**	.381	.523	.469
TRUST6	.267	**.902**	.382	.574	.570
KNOWT6	.176	.404	**.871**	.375	.348
KNOWT7	.176	.285	**.817**	.277	.333
LIAISO2	.288	.571	.340	**.891**	.507
LIAISO3	.218	.557	.343	**.912**	.486
LIAISO4	.173	.533	.366	**.885**	.488
SUCCESS1	.214	.423	.259	.419	**.844**
SUCCESS2	.206	.447	.312	.457	**.817**
SUCCESS3	.257	.529	.378	.509	**.911**
SUCCESS4	.267	.551	.396	.537	**.916**
SUCCESS5	.243	.558	.424	.518	**.950**

Two-Factor Model

	EXP	TRUST	PROKNW	ACHKNW	LIAISO	SUCCESS
EXP1	**.837**	.276	.131	.185	.219	.261
EXP2	**.876**	.218	.228	.146	.210	.194
EXP3	**.869**	.249	.258	.194	.240	.203
EXP4	**.904**	.236	.188	.193	.220	.274
TRUST2	.248	**.848**	.385	.294	.500	.411
TRUST3	.281	**.823**	.422	.385	.556	.534
TRUST4	.208	**.859**	.340	.335	.509	.447
TRUST5	.197	**.884**	.356	.385	.523	.469
TRUST6	.267	**.900**	.362	.384	.574	.570
KNOWT2	.255	.327	**.793**	.323	.343	.265
KNOWT3	.187	.381	**.881**	.347	.415	.286
KNOWT4	.198	.412	**.850**	.389	.474	.325
KNOWT5	.124	.295	**.758**	.322	.342	.321
KNOWT6	.176	.404	.432	**.888**	.375	.349
KNOWT7	.175	.284	.260	**.796**	.277	.333
LIAISO2	.288	.572	.447	.342	**.891**	.507
LIAISO3	.219	.557	.402	.344	**.912**	.486
LIAISO4	.172	.533	.448	.370	**.885**	.488
SUCCESS1	.214	.422	.245	.256	.419	**.843**
SUCCESS2	.204	.446	.289	.311	.457	**.817**
SUCCESS3	.254	.529	.346	.378	.509	**.911**
SUCCESS4	.265	.550	.372	.397	.537	**.917**
SUCCESS5	.240	.557	.347	.425	.518	**.950**

References

Apte, U. M. (1992). Global outsourcing of information systems and processing services. *The Information Society, 7*, 287–303.

Apte, U. M., Sobol, M. G., Hanaoka, S., Shimada, T., Saarinen, T., & Salmela, T., et al. (1997). IS outsourcing practices in the USA, Japan, and Finland: A comparative study. *Journal of Information Technology, 12*(4), 289–304.

Armstrong, J. S., & Overton, T. S. (1977). Estimating nonresponse bias in mail surveys. *Journal of Marketing Research, 14*(3), 396–402.

Aron, R., & Singh, J. V. (2005). Getting offshoring right. *Harvard Business Review, 83*(12), 135–143.

Backhaus, K., Erichson, B., Plinke, W., & Weiber, R. (2006). *Multivariate Analysemethoden: Eine anwendungsorientierte Einführung:* Springer Berlin.

Bagozzi, R. P., & Yi, Y. (1988). On the evaluation of structural equation models. *Journal of the Academy of Marketing Science, 16*(1), 74–95.

Balaji, S., & Ahuja, M. K. (2005). Critical team-level success factors of offshore outsourced projects: A knowledge integration perspective. In R. Sprague Jr. (Ed.), *Proceedings of the 38th Annual Hawaii International Conference on System Sciences* (pp. 52–59). Los Alamitos, CA: IEEE CS Press.

Behrens, S. (2007). *Information systems outsourcing: Five essays on governance and success.* Aachen: Shaker.

Bitkom (2005). *Leitfaden Offshoring.* Retrieved March 07, 2007, from http://www.bitkom.org/files/documents/BITKOM_Leitfaden_Offshoring_31.01.2005.pdf.

Boes, A., Schwemmle, M., & Becker, E. (2004). *Herausforderung Offshoring: Internationalisierung und Auslagerung von IT-Dienstleistungen.* Düsseldorf: Hans-Böckler-Stiftung.

Boudreau, M.-C., Gefen, D., & Straub, D. W. (2001). Validation in information systems research: A state-of-the-art assessment. *MIS Quarterly, 25*(1), 1–16.

Bright, B. (2008). *Outsourcing looks closer to home.* Retrieved August 29, 2008, from The Wall Street Journal: http://online.wsj.com/article/SB118159871575631717.html.

Bugajska, M. (2007). Piloting knowledge transfer in IT/IS outsourcing relationship towards sustainable knowledge transfer process: Learnings from swiss financial institution. In *Proceedings of the 13th Americas Conference on Information Systems* (pp. 2–18).

Carmel, E., & Agarwal, R. (2001). Tactical approaches for alleviating distance in global software development. *IEEE Software, 18*(2), 22–29.

Carmel, E., & Agarwal, R. (2002). The maturation of offshore sourcing of information technology work. *MIS Quarterly Executive, 1*(2), 65–78.

Carmel, E., & Beulen, E. (2005). Managing the offshore transition. In E. Carmel & P. Tjia (Eds.), *Offshore outsourcing of information technology work, Offshore outsourcing of information technology work* (pp. 130–148). Cambridge, UK.

Carmel, E., & Nicholson, B. (2005). Small firms and offshore software outsourcing: High transaction costs and their mitigation. *Journal of Global Information Management, 13*(3), 33–54.

Chin, W. W. (1998). The partial least squares approach to structural equation modeling. In G. A. Marcoulides (Ed.), *Modern methods for business research* (pp. 295–336). Mahwah, NJ: Lawrence Erlbaum Associates.

Chua, A. L., & Pan, S. L. (2008). Knowledge transfer and organizational learning in IS offshore sourcing. *Omega, 36*(2), 267–281.

Chua, A.-L., & Pan, S. (2006). Knowledge transfer in offshore insourcing. In W. Haseman, D. W. Straub, & S. Klein (Eds.), *Proceedings of the 27th International Conference on Information Systems* (pp. 1039–1054). Milwaukee, WI.

Churchill, G. A. (1999). *Marketing research: Methodological foundations* (7th ed.). Fort Worth, TX: The Dryden Press.

Cohen, J. (1988). *Statistical power analysis for the behavioural sciences* (2nd edition). New York: Academic Press.

Computerwoche (2008). *Offshoring: Die großen Konzerne tun es.* Retrieved September 26, 2008, from http://www.computerwoche.de/heftarchiv/2008/39/1224623/.

Creswell, J. W. (1994). *Research design: Qualitative and quantitative approaches.* Thousand Oaks, CA: Sage.

Dahlberg, T., & Nyrhinen, M. (2006). A new instrument to measure the success of IT outsourcing. In *Proceedings of the 39th Annual Hawaii International Conference on System Sciences* (pp. 1–10). Hawaii.

Davenport, T. S., & Prusak, L. (1998). *Working knowledge: How organizations manage what they know.* Boston, MA: Harvard Business School Press.

Day, G. S., & Montgomery, D. B. (1983). Diagnosing the experience curve. *Journal of Marketing, 47*(2), 44.

Dhar, S., & Balakrishnan, B. (2006). Risks, benefits, and challenges in global IT outsourcing: Perspectives and practices. *Journal of Global Information Management, 14*(3), 39–69.

Diamantopoulos, A., Riefler, P., & Roth, K. P. (2008). Advancing formative measurement models. *Journal of Business Research, 61*(12), 1203–1218.

Diamantopoulos, A., & Winklhofer, H. M. (2001). Index construction with formative indicators: An alternative to scale development. *Journal of Marketing Research, 38*(2), 269–277.

Dibbern, J., Goles, T., Hirschheim, R., & Jayatilaka, B. (2004). Information systems outsourcing: A survey and analysis of the literature. *The Data Base for Advances in Information Systems, 35*(4), 6–102.

Dibbern, J., Winkler, J., & Heinzl, A. (2006). *Offshoring of application services in the banking industry: A transaction cost analysis,* from Universität Mannheim: http://wifo1.bwl.uni-mannheim.de/fileadmin/files/publications/Working_Paper_16-2006.pdf.

Dillman, D. A. (1978). *Mail and telephone surveys: The total design method.* New York: Wiley.

Eberl, M. (2006). Formative und reflektive Konstrukte und die Wahl des Strukturgleichungsverfahrens. *Betriebswirtschaft, 66*(6), 651–668.

Eggert, A., Fassott, G., & Helm, S. (2005). Identifizierung und Quantifizierung mediierender und moderierender Effekte in komplexen Kausalstrukturen. In F. Bliemel, A. Eggert, G. Fassott, & J. Henseler (Eds.), *Handbuch PLS-Pfadmodellierung. Methode, Anwendung, Praxisbeispiele* (pp. 101–116). Stuttgart: Schäffer-Poeschel.

Emerson, R. (1972). Exchange theory, part I: A psychological basis for social exchange and exchange theory, Part II: Exchange relations and network structures. In J. Berger, M. Zelditch & B. Anderson (Eds.), *Sociological theories in progress, Sociological theories in progress* . New York: Houghton Mifflin.

Erber, G., & Sayed-Ahmed, A. (2005). Offshore outsourcing: A global shift in the present IT industry. *Intereconomics, 40*(2), 100–112.

Erdfelder, E. F. F. &. B. A. (1996). GPOWER: A general power analysis program. *Behavior Research Methods, Instruments, & Computers,* (28), 1–11.

Erickson, J. M., & Ranganathan, C. (2006). Project management capabilities: Key to application development offshore outsourcing. In *Proceedings of the 39th Annual Hawaii International Conference on System Sciences* (pp. 199–208). Hawaii.

Field, A. (2005). *Discovering statistics using SPSS* (2nd edition). London: Sage.

Fish, K. E., & Seydel, J. (2006). Where IT outsourcing is and where it is going: A study across functions and department sizes. *Journal of Computer Information Systems, 46*(3), 96–103.

Fisher, J., Hirschheim, R., & Jacobs, R. (2008). Understanding the outsourcing learning curve: A longitudinal analysis of a large Australian company. *Information Systems Frontiers, 10*(2), 165–178.

Fornell, C., & Larcker, D. F. (1981). Evaluating structural equation models with unobservable variables and measurement error. *Journal of Marketing Research, 18*(1), 39–50.

Fowler, F. J. (1988). *Survey research methods.* Newbury Park, CA: Sage.

Ganesh, J., & Moitra, D. (2004). An empirical examination of the determinants of successful transition management in offshore business process outsourcing. In *Proceedings of the 10th Americas Conference on Information Systems* (pp. 3493–3500). New York.

Gefen, D., & Straub, D. (2005). A practical guide to factorial validity using PLS-Graph: Tutorial and annotated example. *Communications of AIS, 2005*(16), 91–109.

Gefen, D., Straub, D. W., & Boudreau, M.-C. (2000). Structural equation modeling and regression: Guidelines for research practice. *Communications of the AIS, 4*(7), 1–77.

Ghemawat, P. (1985). Building strategy on the experience curve. *Harvard Business Review, 63*(2), 143–149.

Goles, T. (2003). Vendor capabilities and outsourcing success: A resource-based view. *Wirtschaftsinformatik, 45*(2), 199–206.

Goodhue, D., Lewis, W., & Thompson, R. (2006). PLS, small sample size, and statistical power in MIS research. In *Proceedings of the 39th Annual Hawaii International Conference on System Sciences* (pp. 1–10). Hawaii.

Gopal, A., Sivaramakrishnan, K., Krishnan, M., & Mukhopadhyay, T. (2003). Contracts in offshore software development: An empirical analysis. *Management Science, 49*(12), 1671–1683.

Grover, V., Cheon, M., & Teng, J. (1996). The effect of service quality and partnership on the outsourcing of information systems functions. *Journal of Management Information Systems, 12*(4), 89–117.

Hair, J. F. (2006). *Multivariate data analysis* (6. ed.). Upper Saddle River, NJ: Pearson/Prentice Hall.

Heeks, R., Krishna, S., Nicholsen, B., & Sahay, S. (2001). Synching or sinking: Global software outsourcing relationships. *IEEE Software, 18*(2), 54–60.

Herbsleb, J. D., & Mockus, A. (2003). An empirical study of speed and communication in globally distributed software development. *IEEE Transactions on Software Engineering, 29*(6), 481–494.

Herrmann, A., Huber, F., & Kressmann, F. (2006). Varianz- und kovarianzbasierte Strukturgleichungsmodelle: Ein Leitfaden zu deren Spezifikation, Schätzung und Beurteilung. *zfbf, 58*, 34–66.

Hirschheim, R., Loebbecke, C., Newman, M., & Valor, J. (2005). Offshoring and its implications for the information systems discipline. In D. Avison, D. Galletta, & J. I. DeGross (Eds.), *Proceedings of the 26th International Conference on Information Systems* (pp. 1003–1018). Las Vegas, NV.

Holmström Olsson, H., Conchúir, E. Ó., Ågerfalk, P. J., & Fitzgerald, B. (2008). Two-stage offshoring: An investigation of the irish bridge. *MIS Quarterly, 32*(2), 257–279.

Homburg, C., & Giering, A. (1996). Konzeptualisierung und Operationalisierung komplexer Konstrukte: Ein Leitfaden für die Marketingforschung. *Marketing - Zeitschrift für Forschung und Praxis, 18*(1), 5–24.

Huber, F., Herrmann, A., Meyer, F., Vogel, J., & Vollhardt (2007). *Kausalmodellierung mit Partial Least Squares: Eine anwendungsorientierte Einführung.* Wiesbaden: Gabler.

Hulland, J. (1999). Use of partial least squares (PLS) in strategic management research: A review of four recent studies. *Strategic Management Journal, 20*(2), 195–204.

Jahns, C., Hartmann, E., & Bals, L. (2006/7). Offshoring: Dimensions and diffusion of a new business concept. *Journal of Purchasing and Supply Management, 12*(4), 218–231.

Jarvis, C. B., Mackenzie, S. B., Podsakoff, P. M., Mick, D. G., & Bearden, W. O. (2003). A critical review of construct indicators and measurement model misspecification in marketing and consumer research. *Journal of Consumer Research, 30*(2), 199–218.

Jennex, M. E., & Adelakun, O. (2003). Success factors for offshore system development. *Journal of Information Technology Cases and Applications, 5*(3), 12–31.

Kaiser, K. M., & Hawk, S. (2004). Evolution of offshore software development: From outsourcing to cosourcing. *MIS Quarterly Executive, 3*(2), 69–81.

Kim, S., & Chung, Y. (2003). Critical success factors for IT outsourcing implementation from an interorganizational relationship perspective. *Journal of Computer Information Systems, 43*(4), 81–90.

King, W. R. (2008). The post-offshoring IS organization. *Information Resources Management Journal, 21*(1), 77–88.

King, W. R., & He, J. (2005). External validity in IS survey research. *Communications of AIS, 2005*(16), 880–894.

King, W. R., & Torkzadeh, G. (2008). Information systems offshoring: Research status and issues. *MIS Quarterly, 32*(2), 205–225.

Klepper, R. (1995). The management of partnering development in I/S outsourcing. *Journal of Information Technology, 10,* 249–258.

Knapp, K., Sharma, S., & King, K. (2007). Macro-economic and social impacts of offshore outsourcing of information technology: Practitioner and academic perspectives. *International Journal of E-Business Research, 3*(4), 112–132.

Kobitzsch, W., Rombach, D., & Feldmann, R. L. (2001). Outsourcing in India. *IEEE Software, 18*(2), 78–86.

Koh, C., Soon Ang, & Straub, D. W. (2004). IT outsourcing success: A psychological contract perspective. *Information Systems Research, 15*(4), 356–373.

Kruskal, W. H., & Wallis, W. A. (1952). Use of ranks in one-criterion variance analysis. *Journal of the American Statistical Association, 47*(260), 583–621.

Kumar, K., & Willcocks, L. (1996). Offshore outsourcing: A country too far? In J. D. Coelho, J. Tawfik, W. König, H. Krcmar, R. O'Callaghan, & M. Sääksjarvi (Eds.), *Proceedings of the 4th European Conference on Information Systems* (pp. 1309–1325). Lisbon, Portugal.

Kumar, N., & Palvia, P. (2002). A framework for global IT outsourcing management: Key influence factors and strategies. *Journal of Information Technology Cases and Applications, 4*(1), 56–75.

Kumar, N., Stern, L. W., & Anderson, J. C. (1993). Conducting interorganizational research using key informants. *Academy of Management Journal, 36*(6), 1633–1651.

Lacity, M. C., & Willcocks, L. (1998). An empirical investigation of information technology sourcing practices: Lessons from experience. *MIS Quarterly, 22*(3), 363–408.

Lee, J.-N., Huynh, M. Q., & Hirschheim, R. (2008). An integrative model of trust on IT outsourcing: Examining a bilateral perspective. *Information Systems Frontiers, 10*(2), 145–163.

Lee, J.-N., & Kim, Y.-G. (1999). Effect of partnership quality on IS outsourcing success: Conceptual framework and empirical validation. *Journal of Management Information Systems, 15*(4), 29–61.

Lee, J.-N., Miranda, S. M., & Kim, Y.-M. (2004). IT outsourcing strategies: Universalistic, contingency, and configurational explanations of success. *Information Systems Research, 15*(2), 110–131.

Levina, N., & Vaast, E. (2008). Innovating or doing as told?: Status differences and overlapping boundaries in offshore collaboration. *MIS Quarterly, 32*(2), 307–332.

Mann, H. B., & Whitney, D. R. (1947). On a test of whether one of two random variables is stochastically larger than the other. *Annals of Mathematical Statistics, 18*, 50–60.

Marcoulides, G. A., & Saunders, C. (2006). PLS: A silver bullet? *MIS Quarterly, 30*(2), iii–ix.

Mertens, P. (2005). *Die (Aus-)Wanderung der Softwareproduktion: Eine Zwischenbilanz.* Erlangen: Univ. Erlangen-Nürnberg Inst. für Informatik.

Metters, R., & Verma, R. (2008). History of offshoring knowledge services. *Journal of Operations Management, 26*(2), 141–147.

Mirani, R. (2006). Client-vendor relationships in offshore applications development: An evolutionary framework. *Information Resources Management Journal, 19*(4), 72–86.

Moczadlo, R. (2002). *Chancen und Risiken des Offshore-Development: Empirische Analyse der Erfahrungen deutscher Unternehmen.* Retrieved November 07, 2006, from http://www.competence-site.de/offshore.nsf/8FB68EAB823EF285C1256D72005BBCD1/$File/studie _offshore_prof_moczadlo.pdf.

Murray, M. J., & Crandall, R. E. (2006). IT offshore outsourcing requires a project management approach. *SAM Advanced Management Journal, 71*(1), 4–12.

Nicholson, B., & Sahay, S. (2004). Embedded knowledge and offshore software development. *Information & Organization, 14*(4), 329–365.

Nicklisch, G., Borchers, J., Krick, R., & Rucks, R. (2008). *IT-Near- und -Offshoring in der Praxis: Erfahrungen und Lösungen.* Heidelberg: dpunkt.

Niederman, F., Kundu, S. K., & Salas, S. (2006). IT software development offshoring: A multi-level theoretical framework and research agenda. *Journal of Global Information Management, 14*(2), 52–74.

Nunnally, J. C. (1967). *Psychometric theory.* New York: McGraw-Hill.

Orlikowski, W. J. (2002). Knowing in practice: Enacting a collective capability in distributed organizing. *Organization Science, 13*(3), 249–273.

Oshri, I., Kotlarsky, J., & Willcocks, L. (2007). Managing dispersed expertise in IT offshore outsourcing: Lessons from Tata Consultancy Services. *MIS Quarterly Executive, 6*(2), 53–65.

Park, J.-Y., & Im, K. (2007). The role of IT human capability in knowledge transfer process under IT outsourcing situations. In *Proceedings of the 13th Americas Conference on Information Systems.*

Phillips, L. W. (1981). Assessing measurement error in key informant reports: A methodological note on organizational analysis in marketing. *Journal of Marketing Research, 18*(4), 395–415.

Poornima, S. C. (2008). Preferences as a strategic approach to tackle attrition: IT and ITES industry perspective. *ICFAI Journal of Management Research, 7*(3), 25–34.

Poppo, L., & Zenger, T. (2002). Do formal contracts and relational governance function as substitutes or complements? *Strategic Management Journal, 23*(8), 707–725.

Prehl, S. (2008). *Deutschen Managern fehlt die Erfahrung.* Retrieved September 26, 2008, from Computerwoche: http://www.computerwoche.de/heftarchiv/2008/39/1224626/.

Prikladnicki, R., Audy, J. L., & Evaristo, R. (2004). An empirical study on global software development: Offshore insourcing of IT projects. In D. Damian, F. Lanubile, E. Hargreaves, & J. Chisan (Eds.), *Proceedings of the 3rd International Workshop on Global Software Development* (pp. 53–58). IEEE CS Press.

Rajkumar, T., & Mani, R. (2001). Offshore software development: The view from Indian suppliers. *Information Systems Management, 18*(2), 63–73.

Ranganathan, C., & Balaji, S. (2007). Critical capabilities for offshore outsourcing of information systems. *MIS Quarterly Executive, 6*(3), 147–164.

294   References

Rao, M. T., Poole, W., Raven, P. V., & Lockwood, D. L. (2006). Trends, implications, and responses to global IT sourcing: A field study. *Journal of Global Information Technology Management, 9*(3), 5–23.

Ringle, C. M., Wende, S., & Will, A. (2005). *SmartPLS: 2.0 (beta)*. Hamburg, Germany, from University of Hamburg: http://www.smartpls.de.

Rogelberg, S. G., & Stanton, J. M. (2007). Introduction: Understanding and dealing with organizational survey nonresponse. *Organizational Research Methods, 10*(2), 195–209.

Rossiter, J. R. (2002). The C-OAR-SE procedure for scale development in marketing. *International Journal of Research in Marketing, 19*(4), 305–335.

Rottman, J. W. (2008). Successful knowledge transfer within offshore supplier networks: A case study exploring social capital in strategic alliances. *Journal of Information Technology, 23*(1), 31–43.

Rottman, J. W., & Lacity, M. C. (2008). A US Client's learning from outsourcing IT work offshore. *Information Systems Frontiers, 10*(2), 259–275.

Rottman, J. W., & Lacity, M. C. (2006). Proven practices for effectively offshoring IT work. *Sloan Management Review, 47*(3), 56–63.

Schaaf, J., & Weber, J. (2005). *Offshoring report 2005: Ready for take-off*. Retrieved November 06, 2006, from: http://www.dbresearch.de/PROD/DBR_INTERNET_DE-PROD/PROD0000000000188986.pdf.

Schaffer, E. M. (2006). A decision table: offshore or not? *Interactions, 13*(2), 32–33.

Schuhmann, S. (2000). *Repräsentative Umfrage: Praxisorientierte Einführung in empirische Methoden und statistische Analyseverfahren* (3rd ed.). München: Oldenbourg.

Siegel, S., & Castellan, N. J. (1988). *Nonparametric statistics for the behavioral sciences* (2nd edition). New York: McGraw-Hill.

Simonin, B. L. (1999). Ambiguity and the process of knowledge transfer in strategic alliances. *Strategic Management Journal, 20*(7), 595–623.

Smith, D. (2006). Offshoring: Political myths and economic reality. *World Economy, 29*(3), 249–256.

SPSS Inc. (2007). *SPSS 16.0 base user's guide*. Upper Saddle River, NJ: Prentice Hall.

Srivastava, S. C., Teo, T. S. H., & Mohapatra, P. S. (2008). Business-related determinants of offshoring intensity. *Information Resources Management Journal, 21*(1), 44–58.

Stratman, J. K. (2008). Facilitating offshoring with enterprise technologies: Reducing operational friction in the governance and production of services. *Journal of Operations Management, 26*(2), 275–287.

Stringfellow, A., Teagarden, M. B., & Nie, W. (2008). Invisible costs in offshoring services work. *Journal of Operations Management, 26*(2), 164–179.

Tomarken, A. J., & Serlin, R. C. (1986). Comparison of ANOVA alternatives under variance heterogeneity and specific noncentrality structures. *Psychological Bulletin, 99*, 90–99.

van der Stede, W. A., Young, S. M., & Chen, C. X. (2005). Assessing the quality of evidence in empirical management accounting research: The case of survey studies. *Accounting, Organizations & Society, 30*(7/8), 655–684.

Voigt, B., Novak, J., & Schwabe, G. (2007). How to manage knowledge transfer in IT - Outsourcing relationships: Towards a reference model. In *Proceedings of the 13th Americas Conference on Information Systems* (pp. 1–10).

Wang, E. T. G. (2002). Transaction attributes and software outsourcing success: An empirical investigation of transaction cost theory. *Information Systems Journal, 12*(2), 153–181.

Wang, P., Tong, T. W., & Koh, C. P. (2004). An integrated model of knowledge transfer: From MNC parent to China subsidiary. *Journal of World Business, 39*(2), 168–182.

Welch, B. L. (1951). On the comparison of several mean values: An alternative approach. *Biometrika,* *38*(3/4), 330–336.

Westner, M. (2007). *Information systems offshoring: A review of the literature* (Dresdner Beiträge zur Wirtschaftsinformatik No. 51/07). Dresden.

Westner, M. (2009). Antecedents of success in IS offshoring projects: Proposal for an empirical research study. In *Proceedings of the 17th European Conference on Information Systems (in press)* (pp. n/a). Verona.

Westner, M., & Strahringer, S. (2008). Evaluation criteria for selecting offshoring candidates: An analysis of practices in German businesses. *Journal of Information Technology Management,* *19*(4), 16–34.

Wiener, M. (2006). *Critical success factors of offshore software development projects: The perspective of German-speaking companies.* Wiesbaden: Dt. Univ.-Verl.

Wilkinson, L. (1999). Statistical methods in psychology journals. *American Psychologist, 54*(8), 594–604.

William, A., Mayadas, F., & Vardi, M. Y. (2006). *Globalization and offshoring of software: A report of the ACM job migration task force.* Retrieved December 12, 2006, from Association for Computing Machinery: http://www.acm.org/globalizationreport.

Winkler, J. K., Dibbern, J., & Heinzl, A. (2008). The impact of cultural differences in offshore outsourcing: Case study results from German–Indian application development projects. *Information Systems Frontiers, 10*(2), 243–258.

Wüllenweber, K., Beimborn, D., Weitzel, T., & König, W. (2008). The impact of process standardization on business process outsourcing success. *Information Systems Frontiers, 10*(2), 211–224.

Xu, P., & Yao, Y. (2006). Knowledge transfer in system development offshore outsourcing projects. In I. Garcia & R. Trejo (Eds.), *Proceedings of the 12th Americas Conference on Information Systems* (pp. 3125–3130).

Young-Ybarra, C., & Wiersema, M. (1999). Strategic flexibility in information technology alliances: The influence of transaction cost economics and social exchange theory. *Organization Science, 10*(4), 439–459.

Zaheer, A., McEvily, B., & Perrone, V. (1998). Does trust matter?: Exploring the effects of interorganizational and interpersonal trust on performance. *Organization Science, 9*(2), 141–159.

ZEW (2007). *IKT-Umfrage 2007: Internetwirtschaft weiter auf dem Vormarsch,* from Zentrum für Europäische Wirtschaftsforschung GmbH: ftp://ftp.zew.de/pub/zew-docs/div/IKTRep/IKT_Report _2007.pdf.

GABLER RESEARCH

„EBS Forschung", Schriftenreihe der EUROPEAN BUSINESS SCHOOL
International University · Schloss Reichartshausen
Herausgeber: Univ.-Prof. Dr. Ansgar Richter
zuletzt erschienen:

Band 69:
Christian Funke
Selected Essays in Empirical Asset Pricing
2008. XVIII, 108 S., Br. € 39,90
ISBN 978-3-8349-1142-1

Band 70:
Armin Müller
Anlageberatung bei Retailbanken
Einfluss auf das Anlageverhalten und die Performance von Kundendepots
2008. XXI, 241 S., 39 Abb., 54 Tab. Br. € 49,90
ISBN 978-3-8349-0917-6

Band 71:
Jan-Peer Laabs
**The Long-Term Success of Mergers and Acquisitions
in the International Automotive Supply Industry**
2009. XX, 198 S., 6 Abb., 50 Tab., Br. € 49,90
ISBN 978-3-8349-1693-8

Band 72:
Gaston Michel
Real Estate Risk in Equity Returns
Empirical Evidence from U.S. Stock Markets
2009. XX, 167 S., 9 Abb., 34 Tab., Br. € 39,90
ISBN 978-3-8349-1769-0

Band 73:
Markus Westner
IT Offshoring
Essays on Project Suitability and Success
2010. X, 295 S., 61 Abb., 71 Tab., Br. € 49,90
ISBN 978-3-8349-2046-1

Änderungen vorbehalten. Stand: September 2009.
Erhältlich im Buchhandel oder beim Verlag.
Gabler Verlag . Abraham-Lincoln-Str. 46 . 65189 Wiesbaden . www.gabler.de

GABLER